Francis Bacon Revisited

Twayne's English Authors Series

Arthur F. Kinney, Editor

University of Massachusetts, Amherst

TEAS 523

Francis Bacon, Viscount St. Albans. Portrait by an unknown artist. *Courtesy of the National Portrait Gallery, London.*

Francis Bacon Revisited

W. A. Sessions

Georgia State University

Twayne Publishers
An Imprint of Simon & Schuster Macmillan
New York

Prentice Hall International
London • Mexico City • New Delhi • Singapore • Sydney • Toronto

Twayne's English Authors Series No. 523

Francis Bacon Revisited
W. A. Sessions

Twayne Publishers
An Imprint of Simon & Schuster Macmillan
1633 Broadway
New York, New York   10019

Library of Congress Cataloging-in-Publication Data

Sessions, W. A.
    Francis Bacon revisited / W. A. Sessions.
        p. cm. — (Twayne's English authors series ; no. 523)
    Includes bibliographical references and index.
    ISBN 0-8057-7833-0 (cloth)
    1. Bacon, Francis, 1561–1626—Criticism and interpretation.
I. Title.   II. Series: Twayne's English authors series ; TEAS 523.
PR2208.S47 1996
824'.3—dc20   96-12873
                                                                    CIP

The paper used in this publication meets the minimum requirements of American National Standard for Information Sciences—Permanence of Paper for Printed Library Materials. ANSI Z39.48-1984. ∞ ™

10 9 8 7 6 5 4 3 2 1

Printed in the United States of America

For my father-in-law Andreas Deliyannis and my brother-in-law Dr. Angelos Deliyannis, who represent that European curiosity of mind to which Francis Bacon gave originating form.

Contents

Editor's Note

W. A. Sessions's new study of Francis Bacon seeks the unity of Bacon's extraordinary life and all his written works, from counsel to Essex, Elizabeth I, and James I, through the various editions of his aphoristic *Essays*, to the great exploratory works of philosophy and science in both English and Latin. What emerges in this landmark study is an accessible portrait of a man who, through a largely solitary life of good and bad fortune, persistently pursued a life of *philanthropia*—of learning and public service as equal acts of social charity. "I have taken all knowledge to be my province," he wrote a potential patron in 1592, early in his career, and he never wavered in his attempt to link knowledge—which he saw as an ongoing process of labor and invention—with the interplay and tension in his work between an unavoidable subjectivity and the objective social realms of history that together permitted the only usable stage for *philanthropia*. Much of Bacon's writing was performative, seeking through rhetoric and disguise to confront the discontinuity of human history with a deeper understanding of the possibilities of time. In the two major themes of his writing—the world as it is and the world as it might be—he traced philosophy, science, and invention, culminating in his own utopian work, the *New Atlantis*, which is designed to convert the reader to a brave new world of technology. Bacon's probing and magisterial style, drawing on antique wisdom, myth, humanist thought, and scientific treatises, was not only the first to define the process of induction as a way of understanding nature but managed also to adumbrate modern linguistics, sociology, historiography, and cultural anthropology in ways that have long established him as one of the great thinkers as well as one of the great prose stylists of the Western world. In this welcome study, Sessions makes passionately clear why this is so.

Arthur F. Kinney

Preface

When I was first asked to write a volume on Bacon for Twayne English Authors Revisited, I could only think of the last line of George Herbert's magnificent Latin ode to Bacon—still the single best piece of Bacon criticism. In this twenty-seven-line tribute to the 1620 publication of Bacon's masterwork, the *Magna Instauratio*, Herbert surveys all the vast range of Bacon's career in a brilliant imitation of Bacon's aphoristic style, calling him "Dux Notionum; veritatis Pontifex; / Inductionis Dominus, & Verulamij" (Commander of concepts; pontifex of truth; / Lord of induction and Verulam). The young poet to whom Bacon would dedicate his own *Certaine Psalms* also shows unusual knowledge of Bacon's texts ("Child of time from the mother truth"). Herbert is finally unable to finish, however, and must turn to future audiences to complete the narrative: "O I'm truly exhausted! Help, Posterity!"

Herbert's strategy would be, I decided early on, my own in writing this new volume on Bacon. The task was too immense without writing a work that would directly aim to involve as many audiences as possible. So, for this volume that would replace an earlier Twayne monograph on Bacon, I determined to survey Bacon's work within an encompassing rubric and then make it as accessible as possible for a modern audience. The new readers of Bacon would then complete the analyses in my book, reading original sources and more complex recent scholarship of this "unique master of things" and experience and not just "arts," as Herbert notes, this "Noah's dove who, having determined / no place and peace in ancient arts, / stood firm returning to self and to the mother-ark."[1] Remarkably, in the ode, Herbert understood immediately (as did Ben Jonson in his ode three years later) the lasting nature of Bacon's audience. Francis Bacon, Baron Verulam, Viscount St. Albans (1561–1626) would mark his time and the centuries that followed as have few other figures in European culture. As Herbert's ode predicted, Bacon would influence the very means by which European and then world culture would come to think of themselves, either directly or indirectly, through the processes of thinking and learning he set in motion.

Yet, if the breadth of this influence both then and now easily identifies itself for audiences, the source does not. Was Francis Bacon fundamentally a scientist or philosopher or literary strategist, inventing new forms? Or was he simply a superlawyer and judge, using rhetoric for his own purposes? Faced with a plentitude of texts and talents, most general readers have been content to read a little and ignore the rest, lacking any unified approach to their reading. The purpose of this study must, so I concluded, be to provide a compendious book that will invite the reader to form answers to these questions, however tentative, and then read more. The task ahead would have to aim at providing an intelligent general audience with a short book that will open a door toward a comprehensive, not partial, understanding of Bacon. In this sense, it would suggest that the modern reader of Francis Bacon does not have to agree with James I, who on reading the *Instauratio Magna*, remarked that the book was like the peace of God: "It passeth all understanding."

Rather, the method itself of this brief text should lead the reader toward immediate understanding of the directness and simplicity, the broader outlines, of what Bacon intended in his canon. There is no mystery here, and recognizing these contours will be quite enough for any initial acts of reading Bacon's texts. From this recognition, the reader may expand reflection on these texts and evolve greater comprehension through the discovery of other more complex studies of Bacon (and ours is an unusually active period of Bacon scholarship and criticism). One major objective of this book, then, is to invite the reader toward the complexity lying beyond the scope of this book and into the liberating habits of reading and perception Bacon's canon can provide.

Such a method as I have chosen should guide the reader to Bacon's texts themselves. In this method, text and context provide a kind of dialectic through which the reader can locate the meaning of a work. For this reason, I have developed my analysis as a kind of Horatian *multum in parvo*, a specific analysis that reveals larger contexts of language and thought. If this method of analysis at times appears reductive, it will be seen to be grounded, I hope, in the awareness that Baconian texts never stand alone. Bacon's literary and philosophical strategies are always plural, social, looking toward the context of authorizing political and historical frames and their discourse. In this sense, his texts are always moving to the next stage, where these frames may have altered dramatically. The plan of the book points to this sense of movement by revealing (however succinctly) the context that defines each work and its place in a progression of texts.

One consequence of such contextualization is that I have stressed, as a subtext, the life of Francis Bacon. I have emphasized Bacon's subjectivity as it expresses itself at every juncture of his canon. The term *subjectivity* may be new or "late," as Bacon says of Michel Montaigne's "essay" in his 1612 dedication to Prince Henry, "but the thing is ancient." In fact, Bacon's extraordinary self-consciousness, especially in originating texts, arises from a subjectivity particularly evident, on the one hand, in the self-fashioning of the Renaissance and, on the other, in the Reformation, where the term takes on cosmic dimensions, especially in Luther's violent dichotomy and his early influence on texts like Queen Catherine Parr's widely read *Lamentacion of a Sinner* (in whose court Bacon's mother served). The term has even deeper roots in the old subject-object dichotomy developed in the West from both classical and Biblical cultures, vividly expressed in a proverb of Solomon (4:23) that Bacon used as a motif throughout his texts: "Keep thy heart with all diligence, for thereout come the actions of thy life." This aphorism from King Solomon not only defines the meaning of subjectivity in Bacon but shows how it functions for him in shaping reality itself. Indeed, this term always entails, certainly as Bacon is using it, a living dialectic between an ever-reflecting self and the active making of reality. All subjective probability (or reason or rightness) or subjectivism as a determinant of reality is, in Bacon, found only in this tension between self and the making of reality by the self, a making that involves an invention or objective "thing," to use Bacon's recurrent term for the Latin *res*.

In fact, Bacon's making of his own objective texts—the subject of this book—can be seen in the two aspects of Bacon's work into which this study divides itself: (1) Bacon's response in his texts to the world as he actually lived its history and (2) his making and representation of probable structures within that history. Subjectivity that originates text here operates in a dialectical relationship. Because Bacon's texts are complementary and the actual and the probable always one (as his actual history and time were filled with structures of probability), so any such dichotomy must begin and end with the mixture of particulars of time and of probability to be found in each text. At the same time, as the reader will soon discover, certain texts fit Bacon's perspectives on the world as it is while others represent Bacon's perspectives on a world that might be. In fact, for the historical and ever audience-oriented structures in which Bacon grounded all his work, the double analysis works, as I show in specific exercises, to reveal the direction of Bacon's whole canon. In this sense, with a special irony, prophetic discourse such as Bacon's can be best revealed through generic *explication de texte*. This method of discourse had been used, in fact, by the earliest Biblical scholars and especially by the early English reformer William Tyndale, whose pioneering texts had such totalizing effect on Bacon's world and its language of conversion.

This analytical method provides, then, true to Baconian epistemology, a good experimental instrument with which to enter Bacon's texts. Precisely because he was revolutionary not only as he conceptualized his time but as he chose linguistic forms to articulate these conceptualizations, his texts thus analyzed will uncover the Baconian principle of composition worthy of Chekhov or Henry James: the specific part reveals the whole; the detail makes any larger direction possible. Thus, with the awareness of precisely how a Baconian text functions, the reader can find in this new comprehensive approach to the life and work of Francis Bacon a deeper consciousness of his texts. Texts can be viewed both as contemplative inscriptions in themselves and as instruments for the remaking of history, in short, the two steps outlined by Bacon himself in his renewal of history.

In this way, the book offers the beginning reader a step forward. What follows this initial encounter should be greater reading and greater perception of these texts that helped to change the history not only of European and American cultures but of the entire modern world. In this sense, the reader should develop, through deeper reading and perception, the evolving understanding Bacon sought for all his audiences as they make their own choices in time and history. Bacon's texts offer a level of freedom James I may not have understood but that a modern reader just might.

Acknowledgments

In writing a composite text like this study, an author accumulates a number of debts. I need first to thank Arthur F. Kinney, the editor of this series, not only for the opportunity to write this volume but for almost two decades of support and interest in my work. If my work has value, it is to him the value belongs because he has generally provided opportunities I could not imagine. I owe Dr. Graham Rees special thanks for help with this volume. In his reading and his strictures, he has revealed once more his extraordinary sensitivity to the Bacon texts, especially those in Latin. Of course, neither he nor Professor Kinney are responsible for the limitations of this book. They have both provided directions like those at Hercules' famous crossroad (a favorite Baconian motif). The failures are mine alone.

I am grateful for the continuing support of my department chairs, Professor Virginia Spencer Carr and Professor Robert Sattelmeyer. Their achievements have set a model for my own. I also am grateful to the Dean of the School of Arts and Sciences at Georgia State University, Professor Ahmed Abdelal, whose intellectual vision has provided an incentive to excellence few modern state universities can be said to offer. I also acknowledge two Georgia State University Research Grants as well as travel grants from the National Endowment for the Humanities for the development of this book. I want to thank my colleagues Patricia Graves, Robert Arrington, Marion Leathers Kuntz, and Raymond Carter Sutherland for their collegiality and interest in my work. Also I thank Michael Franklin, my graduate assistants Barbara Melville, Larry Paul, Eric Merrifield, and Evangeline Bennett for work on this project. Finally I want to extend thanks to my aunt, Bee Sessions, for her special interest over the years; to Evelyn Snider, in whose high school classes in literature and history I learned that an act or text or monument did indeed have meaning beyond itself; and to Turner Cassity and Sally Fitzgerald for conversations on art and the making of texts. My deepest debt is to my wife, Zenobia Urania Sessions, whose beauty acts every day as the "plus ultra" beyond my Gates of Hercules.

Chronology

1593   Leads unsuccessful opposition in the House of Commons to Queen Elizabeth I's Triple Subsidy Bill, an act that determined his political career for the rest of Elizabeth's reign.

1594   With Essex's support seeks Attorney-Generalship over rival Sir Edward Coke; Queen supports Coke and will not give him the Solicitor-Generalship in the next year. Writes "Speeches of the Counsellors" for *Gesta Grayorum*, the Twelfth Night revels at Gray's Inn.

1595   Given Twickenham Park by Essex in compensation for his failures at court and for Bacon's help to him. Made "Queen's Counsel, Extraordinary" by Elizabeth I, position of much lesser status.

1596–1597   Writes his *Maximes of the Law*; publishes first edition of his *Essays*, with dedication to his brother Anthony; loses the hand of Lady Hatton, rich young widow, in marriage to Coke; finances worsen.

1601   Essex rebellion suppressed; Bacon named by Queen as special advocate to secure Essex's conviction; Essex executed February 25 at age 33; brother Anthony dies May 31. Inherits the family estate of Gorhambury, just outside Saint Albans and at the old Roman city Verulamium, in Hertfordshire, where his mother still lived. Especially active in Parliament and writes *A Declaration of the Practices and Treasons Attempted and Committed by Robert, late Earle of Essex.*

1603   Elizabeth I dies; James VI of Scotland becomes James I of England; Bacon tries to gain favor of the new king but, on July 23, is knighted in a group of 300 people. Publishes *Discourse Touching the Happy Union of England and Scotland* that supports James I's plans for unity; writes early works *Temporis Partus Masculus (The Masculine Birth of Time)* and *Valerius Terminus of the Interpretation of Nature.*

1604   Granted office of King's Counsel by James I; writes most of the *Advancement of Learning.*

1605   Publishes *Advancement of Learning* in same month as Gunpowder Plot is discovered.

1606   Marries Alice Barnham, daughter of London alderman and an heiress; he is 45 and she is 14. Finances improve.

1607   After years of waiting and struggle, appointed Solicitor-General.

1608–1609   Time for active writing, including a memorial on Queen Elizabeth, his notebook *Commentarius Solutus*, a *Discourse on the Plantation of Ireland*, numerous sketches for the later works and shorter key texts like *Cogitata et Visa* and the *Redargutio Philosophiarum*. Made Treasurer of Gray's Inn. Publishes *De Sapientia Veterum (Of the Wisdom of the Ancients)*.

1610   Mother dies. Makes vigorous defense of the King's prerogative in Parliament as he will until his downfall.

1612   His cousin (and enemy) Robert Cecil, the Earl of Salisbury, the son of Lord Burghley, dies. Publishes second edition of *Essays*, dedicated first to Henry Prince of Wales, who dies in October, and then to his brother-in-law Sir John Constable.

1613   Appointed Attorney-General.

1616   Prosecutes the Earl of Somerset, the King's former favorite, for the murder of Sir Thomas Overbury; the next month, with influence of new favorite George Villiers, Earl of Buckingham, named Privy Councillor to the King.

1617   On death of the Lord Chancellor Ellesmere, Bacon appointed Lord Keeper of the Seal. Is caught in dispute with Buckingham (and entrapment by Coke) that is almost fatal for his career.

1618   On January 4 appointed Lord Chancellor. On July 12 elevated to peerage as Baron Verulam of Verulam. Leaves House of Commons for House of Lords; chosen by King to serve on commission and try Sir Walter Ralegh; delivers death sentence to Ralegh; also involved in prosecution of Suffolk and Yelverton.

1620   On October 12, at height of political career, publishes his *Instauratio Magna* with the *Novum Organum*.

1621   On January 22, celebrates 60th birthday at York House, where he was born, now his place of residence; praised in ode by Ben Jonson. On January 27, elevated to Viscount St. Albans, the social zenith of his life. On March 14 first charges of bribery against him raised in Parliament, where there was bitter resentment of King's favorite Buckingham. On March 20 received copy of charges. On March 27 makes formal submission to the Lords without answering charges, confessing on March 30 to "a great deal of corruption and neglect." On May 1, stripped of Great Seal, and on May 3, sentence passed with heavy fine, imprisonment in the Tower, ban on holding public office, on serving in Parliament, and on coming to court; after few days of imprisonment, released, and fine assigned by King to friends who would not collect, but the ban from coming within 12 miles of court holds; begins his last five years of intense intellectual activity.

1622   Publishes *History of Henry VII*, finished without access to archives or libraries; publishes *Historia Naturalis et Experimentalis* and *Historia Ventorum*.

1623   Publishes *Historia Vitae et Mortis* and expands version of the *Advancement of Learning*, the *De Augmentis Scientiarum*.

1625   Publishes complete edition of *Essays*; then his *Apophthegms*; then his *Translation of Certaine Psalms into English Verse*; writes his compilation of natural history, *Sylva Sylvarum*, and his utopian *New Atlantis* that will appear after death in 1626. Death of James I; accession of Charles I. Bacon presses for pardon and entry into House of Lords but is denied.

1626   In April, tries experiment in snow with refrigeration of chicken, becomes ill. On April 9 dies of pneumonia at the Highgate villa of the Earl of Arundel. Burial probably at St. Michael's Church at Gorhambury, but exact place unknown.

Chapter One

The Life of Sir Francis Bacon, Baron Verulam, Viscount St. Albans

"I have taken all knowledge to be my province," Francis Bacon at thirty-three wrote his uncle Lord Burghley in 1592, and then added: *"philanthropia* is so fixed in my mind as it cannot be removed."[1] These two poles of universal knowledge and social charity (expressed in Bacon's neologism *philanthropia*) signify the basis for both Francis Bacon's life and career. If knowledge always means to Bacon a making, a self-induced process of labor and invention,[2] then the goal of such self-expression as that of knowing and making could only be outward—in service to history, the kingdom of time in which the Renaissance Bacon lived. In fact, this interplay or tension between an intense subjectivity and the objective social realms of history are spelled out clearly in Bacon's letter: *philanthropia* is "so fixed" in his consciousness of self that he declares with passion "it cannot be removed." The two poles are further united in the act and language of the 1592 letter seeking preferment and higher service to the state from Bacon's uncle, the most powerful person in the kingdom after Elizabeth I.

If the letter reveals an overwhelming certainty of self and vocation, it was hardly less the case twenty-eight years later. At the start of his 1620 text describing the Great Instauration or Renewal he wanted to bring to England and Europe, Bacon, now Lord High Chancellor of the entire realm, takes on the third-person voice, as had Julius Caesar in his *Gallic Wars*. In first lines specially printed on the page, Bacon proclaims: "Francis of Verulam / Reasoned Thus with Himself / And Judged It To be for the Interest of the Present and Future / Generations that They Should be Made Acquainted / With His Thoughts" (4:7). Once more, a text unites total self-centering and an audience needing the result of labor emanating from that self. In the years between (as well as in the remaining years of Bacon's life) such self-centering, if not solipsism, would underpin most of Bacon's major texts, either explicitly or implicitly marking them. From this perspective, the great systems of objective method he designed for science and philosophy and all the texts of literature, history, and law, including the *Essays*, proceed from a life and subjectivity that carried a peculiar self-election. As William Rawley, Bacon's chaplain and secretary in his last years, was careful to note in his short biography, "for though he was a great reader of books, yet he had not his knowledge from books, but from some ground and notions from within himself; which, notwithstanding, he vented with great caution and circumspection" (1:11).

As Rawley suggests, intuition, "notions," even self-election were not enough. Caution would dictate the most conscious of methodologies and styles for his texts; textualization of the world around him would require scrupulous placement and even disguise. Bacon's radical difference of self that he himself had early recognized could only lead to cunning and constant manipulation of text after text in the theater of power in which he existed. The 1592 letter illustrates one of these strategies. Writing to his powerful uncle, Bacon uses calculated motifs that could make their points by indirection better than direction. Indeed, as Bacon would demonstrate throughout his works, a series of leit-motifs or determined ramifications of text would argue better than syllogisms. By rhetorical arrangement, they offer a better entrance into the reader's mind.

Thus Bacon's 1592 letter reveals not only his self-centering but a fundamental characteristic of his style, a particularizing that reveals the whole—in this case, a rhetorical series of clear leit-motifs that would expand as commonplaces or topoi throughout his works. He uses the aging motif ("I wax now somewhat ancient; one and thirty years is a great deal of sand in the hour-glass"); the ambition/humility motif ("I have vast contemplative ends, as I have moderate civil ends"—this a ploy to his uncle so that he would not fear Bacon as competition for his own son, Robert Cecil, the future Lord Salisbury); the errors of "frivolous disputations" and "blind experiments," to be later metonymized in his famous insect imagery; the first mention of a Pre-Socratic, Anaxagoras, "who reduced himself with contemplation unto voluntary poverty" (in this reference, Bacon introduces to Europe the radical value of these earliest Greek philosophers who would continue to influence Western thought until Heidegger); the conceptualizing of corporate or scientific enterprise as adumbrated in Bacon's utopia the *New Atlantis*; and finally his invention and transformation of language, the mannered discourse Bacon reinvents with a particular strategy: "This which I have writ unto your Lordship is rather thoughts than words, being set down without all art, disguising, or reservation" (8:108–9). In this last emphasis on literary style, Bacon is as cunning as ever in delineating his difference. He had learned that no text of his could ever be quite so spontaneous as he describes the writing of his letter to his uncle. Rawley remarks on such self-consciousness of Bacon, the text-maker. He had seen many versions of a single text ("I myself have seen at the least twelve copies of the *Instauration*, revised year by year one after another") and been aware of the constant drive in them toward "a masculine and clear expression that Bacon saw as the best objectifying form of his profound subjectivity" (1:11). As Bacon himself noted on taking his seat in the Chancery as Lord Keeper of the Great Seal, "And this I shall do, my Lords, *in verbis masculis*; no flourishing or painted words, but such words as are fit to go before deeds" (18:183).

In fact, this letter by Bacon to his powerful uncle gives evidence of yet another of Bacon's techniques of caution and linguistic manipulation. Bacon takes an old word and reshapes its meaning for his own elected purposes. The first instance in English of the modern meaning of the word *philanthropia* or philanthropy occurs here: originally, the Greek word means little more than a benevolence or present and, in post-classical Latin, a gift. Bacon reinvests the term with its modern sense of gifts and service to society as a whole. With Bacon, the word and the concept change dramatically, and in Bacon the greater objectivity of the act of philanthropy has its meaning precisely, as here, in proportion to the giver's sense or "notions" of his or her own election. Later in mid-career (1603), Bacon would begin a proem to what he calls "The Interpretation of Nature" with the same intense solipsism and self-election that motivates the new *philanthropia*: "Believing that I was born for the service of mankind, and regarding the care of the commonwealth as a kind of common property which like the air and water belongs to everybody, I set myself to consider in what way mankind might be best served, and what service I was myself fitted by nature to perform." Performance and the staging of oneself could only come, as the Proem further states, from the difference of self he recognized: "For myself, I found that I was fitted for nothing so well as for the study of Truth." After a litany of congratulatory self-appraisals that objectify, ironically, a new scientist or Bacon's new social hero, the forty-two-year-old lawyer ends with the humility topos of ancient oratory Bacon knew well. He is "a man that neither affects what is new nor admires what is old, and that hates every kind of imposture." Then follows once more Bacon's

bold egoism: "So I thought my nature had a kind of familiarity and relationship with Truth" and "if I came to hold office in the state, I might
get something done too for the good of men's souls" (10:84–5).

First Years

What signifies Bacon's career and texts, then, is this continual interplay
and tension between an intense subjectivity—an almost missionary
search for what he names "Truth"—and the ambiguous time and history
the son of a former Lord Keeper must enter and reshape, if not reform.
Such a dialectic between an extraordinary self and an extraordinary history may offer, therefore, some explanation for a life so dramatic that, if
Bacon did not write Shakespeare's texts, Shakespeare might have written
the text of Bacon's life. High drama began at the moment of his birth, on
January 22, 1561, at York House in London: as with Mary Queen of
Scots, Bacon's beginning foreshadowed his end. If parents imprint their
children's end, Bacon's did so in a special way. His father, Sir Nicholas
Bacon, was the Lord Keeper of the great Seal of the realm, "a lord of
known prudence, sufficiency, moderation, and integrity," comments
Rawley (1:3), and Bacon was the last of his eight children, six children by
a first wife and two sons by Bacon's mother, Lady Anne Bacon. Sir
Nicholas had risen from minor gentry in Suffolk through a Cambridge
education and study of law at Gray's Inn, one of the Inns of Court where
young men studied and practiced law. He had survived the reigns of
Henry VIII, Edward VI, and, despite his strong Protestant beliefs, Mary
I, to become, shortly after the accession of Elizabeth I, Lord Keeper of the
Seal. This speed was due, no doubt, to Sir William Cecil, later Lord
Burghley, his brother-in-law. Both men had married daughters of Sir
Anthony Cooke, a humanist Protestant intellectual who was tutor to
Edward VI, a Marian exile, and then an opponent of the Elizabethan religious settlement (that is, the English monarch as head or supreme governor of the Church of England) because this arrangement did not fit his
own Calvinist model of the Christian state. From his father, therefore,
Bacon knew as a child his career lay in politics, service to the state, and
the life of court and parliament, not in the contemplative existence of
clergy or university life. He had learned from his father (as from his
humanist "fathers" like Cicero) that public good was the highest of all
goods, as demonstrated in his essay "Of the Wisdom for a Man's Self,"
and most dramatically stated in his 1605 *Advancement of Learning*: "men
must know, that in this theatre of man's life it is reserved only for God

and Angels to be lookers on" (3:421). Long before Elizabeth called the little boy growing up in this elaborate political world her "young Lord Keeper" (1:4), Bacon knew from his father where the "theatre" of his own life would be.

If his father helped to determine the objective social drive in Bacon's life, his mother, Lady Anne, helped to breed in him an intense subjectivity. Bacon's special sense of language came to him literally in the womb, for his mother's sense of election had found its voice at the Tudor court of the 1540s not only in Protestant theories of self and language (such as espoused in the religious texts of Queen Catherine Parr, for example) but in her father's strict training of her in the classics. Lady Anne and her sisters represented the powerful current of feminine intellectual achievement in sixteenth-century England, not matched until the nineteenth century. Begun by Queen Catherine of Aragon and her court and culminating in Elizabeth I, it was centered on training in classical languages. A true daughter to her fiery father, Lady Anne—"a choice lady," in Rawley's phrase—combined her scrupulous power of classical languages with Protestant zeal, a sense of both reform and humanism, that became transfigured in her younger son. "Exquisitely skilled" (1:3) in both Greek and Latin, as her generally fierce letters to her sons reveal from their use of the ancient languages, Bacon's mother exhibited the linguistic power taught her by her father (as Sir Thomas More had taught his daughter Margaret) as well as his religious fervor. The two are seen most powerfully in her famous translation into English of the Anglican Bishop John Jewel's *Apologia Ecclesiae Anglicanae*. Because of Lady Bacon's translation, this vastly influential work, a polemic against the Roman Catholic Church with its counter-argument of the greater primitive church now being renewed in England, would be a cornerstone of developing English Protestantism. In fact, its translation is so elegant and forceful that, if judging by a single work, Bacon's mother could be accounted, according to C. S. Lewis, the greatest translator of sixteenth-century England.[3]

Bacon's brother Anthony was born in 1558 after the deaths of two daughters, and he would die soon after his friend the Earl of Essex's downfall in 1601, most of his adult life spent as an invalid. His life would be shadowy, much of it expended in France as a secret agent for English interests and then in England, after 1593, for Essex's interests in France and Scotland. In France, the brother had famous intellectual acquaintances, including Montaigne, and to his brother, Francis Bacon would dedicate his first collection of essays in 1597, the form modeled

on Montaigne's. Early on, the brothers were close; each was acknowledged in his time as a homosexual and each shared the same political
interests and generally the same circle of friends. Because both were
younger sons, with little prospects of inheritance, both entered law and
therefore government service. They were admitted together on June 27,
1576, to Gray's Inn, their father's alma mater. In fact, already at the age
of twelve the young Francis had matriculated at Trinity College, Cambridge University, where he had remained before entering Gray's Inn at
fifteen. Shortly after entry to Gray's Inn, however, Bacon was summoned
to the entourage of Sir Amias Paulet, the English ambassador in France,
probably at his father's request. There, during his formative adolescent
years (15–18), Bacon lived in Paris, then a center of violent religious and
political controversy as well as the intellectual capital of Europe. When
Bacon later dramatized one of his philosophical texts, *Redargutio
Philosophiarum*, the scene of the older man with revolutionary concepts
lecturing students (and radically sitting on their level) is set in Paris.

It was also in Paris that the first major blow of Francis Bacon's life
occurred. He learned that his father had died, having contracted pneumonia after being shaved one late winter day, in front of an open window at York House in London. The youngest son, for whom the father
had only just begun making provisions of a special kind, was left penni-
less. Consequently, Bacon returned from France to Gray's Inn to begin
the study of law in earnest. Bacon remained there, off and on, for the
rest of his life, returning in the exile of his last five years. His potential
talent was immense. In the same year, Nicholas Hilliard painted the 18-
year-old's portrait, adding at the bottom *"Si tabula daretur digna, animum
mallem"* (if one could but paint his mind) (8:7). Although Bacon wrote
steadily to his uncle Burghley for the next fifteen years, he was refused
any preferment. Bacon thus began his political career independently in
1581 by securing a seat in the House of Commons in Parliament (from
Cornwall). He remained in Commons for thirty-seven years until he was
made Baron Verulam and entered the House of Lords. At Gray's Inn,
therefore, Bacon established the legal career that formed the spine of his
livelihood and dominated his life schedule.

As a result, by the time of the accession of James I in 1603, Bacon
had shown exceptional legal prowess, and by 1620 he would become
one of England's most famous lawyers and judges and would remain so
within the history of jurisprudence in the English-speaking world. By
1582, he was admitted as utter [outer] barrister at Gray's Inn; in 1586,
he was declared bencher and then, in 1587, gave his first reading "On

Advowsons," becoming a double reader in 1600. He was also selected for the elite committee that tested existing statutes by English common law, a task he would later perform in his own texts. During these same years, while still in his twenties, Bacon wrote two significant political pieces that show a remarkable maturity for such a young intellectual as well as a cool tolerance far in advance of his time in history. The first, the "Letter of Advice to Queen Elizabeth," advises milder treatment of the Puritans and (radically) of the Catholics as well, replacing the Oath of Supremacy with one requiring all English citizens to take up arms against any foreign enemy, including the Roman Pontiff. The second, *An Advertisement Touching the Controversies of the Church of England*, analyzes the bitter antagonism of the Puritans to what Bacon considered the rigid religious conformity required by the state; it calls for reform in order to bring peace to the realm.

By 1591, at age thirty, Bacon had entered into one of the crucial relationships of his life, his friendship with the handsome Robert Dudley, Earl of Essex, at twenty-three considered the heir to the courtly roles of both Sir Philip Sidney (whose widow he had married) and the Earl of Leicester, Essex's step-father. The aged Elizabeth's fascination with the young Essex is well known, but both Bacon and especially his older brother were also attracted to him. By 1592 Francis was writing speeches for a masque that Essex was giving for the Queen, a set of discourses for *A Conference of Pleasure*, one of which Bacon would turn into *Certain Observations Made Upon a Libel*. With a certain confidence, then, the Bacon of the law courts could think of entering government service with the larger ends of *philanthropia* as he represented these to his uncle in his letter of 1592.

The Last Years of Elizabeth I

In 1593 Bacon made a mistake that almost cost him his political career. All the wisdom evinced in his letter of the year before proved fruitless when he led an unsuccessful opposition in the House of Commons to the Queen's Triple Subsidy Bill, a hefty increase in taxes requested by the royal presence but unprecedented and unjust, so Bacon thought, in terms of the needs of the state. It would set a bad precedent, he believed. At least, as Bacon later rationalized his action, he thought this, and at the time "spake simply and only to satisfy my conscience" (8:234), his deepest self. It would be a "conscience" he would never try "to satisfy" again in this way. The Queen never forgave

Bacon for his brilliant opposition. To the end of her life she never offered him patronage, in spite of the entreaties of both Essex and even Burghley, except to make him in 1595 "Queen's Counsel, Extraordinary," hardly an advancement. It was a terrible blow, especially to a young man with the grand ambitions expressed in his letter to Burghley. This rejection and that by his uncle Burghley, the Lord Treasurer, and Burghley's son, Sir Robert Cecil, in practice Principal Secretary to the Privy Council, destroyed any hopes for him in the patronage system dominated by the Cecils and derived from the Queen.

This political disaster may explain Bacon's turn in the 1590s to the war-party of the Essex faction, for which his brother Anthony had acted as spy abroad and in London. Bacon and Essex were complementary in their needs; the younger man had the best connections as the most dashing figure at court, with a sense of heroic military action. He lacked the precise sagacity of the law courts or the interests of the university and scholarly world that Bacon represented. In turn Essex offered Bacon an opportunity. Through this handsome and powerful younger man, Bacon could follow a new role for himself as adviser. He could also use the new political and intellectual strategy he had devised since his debacle in Parliament. Having alienated Queen Elizabeth, Bacon turned to a different kind of strategy that would hereafter affect all his representational strategies, as Levy notes: "The language of truth and of conscience, having failed him, he determined the reverse, the language of seeming" or probability.[4] It is a question if Bacon actually developed such an absolute program of representation after the trauma of 1593 or if he instead used the new strategies to enhance the situation of Essex at court or elsewhere. But at some early point Bacon did develop, in fact, a two-fold strategy. He would define it, at least in one text, as "magistral" and "initiative," the latter directed "ad filios" (to the sons), as Bacon wrote in his notebook of 1608 (11:64). He looked, at least from the time of Essex on, toward differing representations: one, for a world as it actually is, however contingent and latent with need for reform; and two, for a world as it might be, the probable actualized in Bacon's world as he was living it and representing it. Arthur B. Ferguson has suggested such a dichotomy for understanding Bacon's conception of history, but it can be extended further.[5] Although Bacon's work is much too incremental and too mixed with the crossing of texts to admit a precise divide, still after 1593 Bacon had every reason to make such a demarcation in his representations if he wanted to find the right audiences for his ideas.

Essex thus served Bacon at this turning-point of his career as a means to develop new strategies of power. If in these years Bacon lost out rather continually to Sir Edward Coke, his legal and jurist rival (as earlier he had lost the hand of the rich and young widow Lady Hatton to Coke), the increasingly impoverished Bacon would be given such compensations by Essex as Twickenham Park near Richmond Palace. In turn Bacon wrote texts for Essex and letters of advice. In 1594 Bacon wrote "Speeches of the Counsellors" for a masque that he helped to produce at Gray's Inn, the *Gesta Grayorum*. In it, to Essex and others, Bacon would announce his full and early statement of his goals of *philanthropia*; the goals would be acted out in a masque for all London to hear in reverence to this "Prince of Purpoole" who could have "the visible memory of himself in the magnificence of goodly and royal buildings and foundations, and the new institutions of orders, ordinances, and societies" (8:336). His mother writing to her son Anthony remarks on Bacon's theater production: "I trust they will not mum nor mask nor sinfully revel at Gray's Inn" and adds her advice that may refer to Essex, "Who were sometime counted first, God grant they wane not daily and deserve to be named last" (8:326). As always, she is concerned about the salvation of her sons: "I trust you, with your servants, use prayer twice in a day, having been where reformation is. . . . Your brother is too negligent herein, but do you well and zealously; it will be looked for of the best learned sort, and that is best" (8:113).

Bacon would send a more direct text in 1596 after Essex's enormous success in his raids on Cadiz. On October 4, shortly after these raids gave Essex national popularity, Bacon warns the twenty-eight-year-old Essex to avoid such acclaim and turn to acts of devotion, even flattery, toward the Queen. Two years later, having published his *Essays* with surprising success, Bacon advises the restless Essex to look to Ireland as an arena for his best talents. In the next year, Essex attempted an invasion of Ireland that began grandly but became more and more disastrous, finally ending in Tyrone's counterattack (in the course of which Spenser's castle was burned). In Essex's disgrace, Bacon tried to mitigate the Queen's wrath but also, as one of her learned counsel, he was forced to accuse his patron before the Privy Council in June 1600.

When, after his abortive rebellion in the winter of the next year, Essex was arrested, Bacon took, at the Queen's specific request, a strong part in the trial of his patron and friend and of those of his supporters, like Henry Wriothesley, the Earl of Southampton, the friend of Donne and Shakespeare. Bacon helped to secure the conviction of Essex and even drafted for the Queen the harsh *Declaration of the Practices and Trea-sons Attempted and Committed by Robert, late Earle of Essex*. After the young courtier and former admirer of Bacon was beheaded on February 25, Bacon gained a sinister reputation, exemplified by a contemporary's (possibly John Donne's) cryptic epigram about Mr. Swineskin. The proof of this bad feeling came about in 1604 when, after the accession of James I, who had admired Essex, Bacon published his own apology for the event. No condemnation had been quite so powerful, however, as Essex's own outcry during the trial: "I call Mr. Bacon against Mr. Bacon."[6]

Three months after Essex's execution, Bacon's brother Anthony died leaving no records of his death or burial. Bacon now inherited the family estate of Gorhambury, just outside Saint Albans and just beyond the old Roman city and theater at Verulamium in Hertfordshire. Here his mother was still living (and would live, virtually mad, for another nine years). On March 24, 1603, Elizabeth I died. By May, James VI of Scotland, son of the beheaded Mary Queen of Scots, was crowned King James I of England. The moment for Bacon's own accession to power had come.

"A Winding Stair"

"It is a strange desire," writes Bacon in his 1625 essay "Of Great Place," "to seek power and to lose liberty: or to seek power over others and to lose power over a man's self." The path of such "desire" is "a winding stair." Bacon sees in his own time, as he had read in the Greek and Roman texts he quotes, the ambiguities and terrible ironies of power: "The rising unto place is laborious and by pains men come to greater pains; and it is sometimes base; and by indignities men come to digni-ties" (6:401;398–9). The "indignities" had begun early for the impover-ished Bacon, and they continued. After vainly trying to make contact with the new King for several months, Bacon had to settle for a dignity of the lowest order: he was knighted on July 23, 1603, in a group of three hundred. He then published his thoughtful *Discourse Touching the Happy Union of England and Scotland*, hoping for the attention of the King, but to no avail, except that by 1604, James granted him the office of King's Counsel, one among several, and hardly a significant position for a leading lawyer of the kingdom.

During this period when further political activity was not being encouraged, Bacon completed his first major work, the 1605 *Advance-*

ment of Learning. He also began to write a series of key manuscripts that would adumbrate the major texts that would appear in his *Instauratio Magna*. Of these fragments, *Temporis Partus Masculus* (Masculine Birth of Time) and *Valerius Terminus of the Interpretation of Nature* originated key motifs. The *Advancement* appeared in the same month that the Gunpowder Plot was discovered and so became lost in the turmoil that followed, but its power as a text, blending with the popularity of the *Essays* he had published first in 1597, soon gave Bacon greater recognition, and, in 1607, after years of waiting and struggle, Bacon was appointed Solicitor-General.

But now Bacon needed new financial resources as well as greater social approval. In 1606, he married Alice Barnham, a daughter of a former Alderman of London and an heiress. Bacon was forty-five, and she fourteen; from the start the union had the signs of a marriage of convenience, with a question as to whether it was ever consummated. Although John Aubrey would note over fifty years later that Bacon was a pederast (Aubrey keeps the word in Greek and adds "His Ganimeds and Favourites tooke Bribes"), the question of Bacon's sexuality was never crucial in any social definition of himself or his creative tasks. Nor was it to Aubrey: immediately after commenting on Bacon's sexuality, even the gossipy Aubrey turns to the more important fact of Bacon's character and success as jurist: "his Lordship always gave Judgement *secundum aequum et bonum* [according as was just and good]." What counted most for Bacon was the immediate reforming task at hand, and for that, he would sacrifice a great deal. Rawley records a curious fact that every morning, in a bowl of "thin warm broth," Bacon took "three grains" of nitre or saltpeter. Rawley offers no comment but Bacon may have believed the folk tradition that the "broth" could curb the male erection or any desire that would wreck his vocation and confuse his sense of election (1:17). Bacon's marriage lasted until his death; as letters and documents have shown, his consort clearly enjoyed her high rank and the enormous power of her position. In December just before his death, however, Bacon changed his will essentially disinheriting his wife. By then her liaison with her Gentleman-Usher Sir John Underhill must have become known, and eleven days after Bacon's death, his widow married Underhill, whom, according to Aubrey, "she made deafe and blinde with too much of Venus."[7]

In those first years of his marriage to a wife the age of a daughter, Bacon had another respite from his career, at least long enough to write some crucial fragments, such as *Cogitata et Visa* (Things Thought and

Observed) and *Redargutio Philosophiarum* (The Rejection of Philosophies), that acted as rehearsals for his grander statements later on. He wrote his tribute to Elizabeth I in Latin for a European audience as well as his university; he also wrote a political tract that showed his power as foreign policy adviser, *Discourse on the Plantation of Ireland*, a New Year's Day gift to James I; and in that new year of 1609, Bacon published one of his most significant works, the Latin *De Sapientia Veterum* (Of the Wisdom of the Ancients). By 1612, when Bacon published his second edition of the *Essays*, he had entered into greater political power. He wrote a series of papers—one on the jurisdiction of the Council of Wales in which he advocates the rights of the royal prerogative over the general rights of those below it, and another advocating relaxations of the restrictions on religious nonconformity. Since 1610, Bacon had become more and more an ardent defender of the King's prerogative, the powerful right of the monarch to supervene over the rights of Parliament. His cousin, Robert Cecil, the Earl of Salisbury, had finally died and Bacon could now be considered on his own merits. By 1613 he was appointed Attorney-General. The ties between monarch and Bacon drew closer. In 1616 Bacon prosecuted the King's former favorite, the handsome Earl of Somerset, whom Bacon had earlier befriended, for the murder of Sir Thomas Overbury. Within a month of this trial, with the help of Bacon's new friend, George Villiers, the Earl of Buckingham, the King's new favorite, Bacon was at last named Privy Councillor to the King. In the next year, 1617, on the death of the Lord Chancellor Ellesmere, Bacon was appointed Lord Keeper of the Seal.

By 1618 Bacon had become essential to the political functioning of an increasingly unpopular King, and so on January 4, he was appointed Lord Chancellor of a realm out of which, at the same time, dissidents (later called Pilgrims in America) would flee. To this realm Bacon brought the King's order, serving on the commission to try Sir Walter Ralegh, delivering the death sentence to him, and then prosecuting the Earl of Suffolk and the statesman Yelverton. In reward, honors now flowed from James I. As Bacon himself recalled, James I *"was that master to him, that had raised and advanced him nine times; thrice in dignity, and six times in office"* (1:7). One of these dignities came on July 12, 1618, when Bacon was elevated to the peerage as Baron Verulam of Verulam, leaving forever the House of Commons for the House of Lords. During this period, as Aubrey notes, "he was Lord Protector during King James's Progresse into Scotland," the King's first since he had left his native country fifteen years before. Now Bacon "gave Audiences in great state to Ambassadors in the Banquetting-house at Whitehall." Opening Parliament, he rode in his carriage like the King himself, with over 100 horsemen before him and more than 200 soldiers and guards behind.

Two years later, on October 12, 1620, at the height of his political career, Bacon published his *Instauratio Magna* and with it, in the *Novum Organum*, his master text, the description of his New Logic. This was the centerpiece of *his* reformation of time and history. Within three months, Bacon celebrated his sixtieth birthday at York House, where he had been born, now his residence on the Thames. At York House Bacon had been living like a prince, with an aviary that alone cost £300 and a dining table "strewed with Sweet Herbes and Flowers, which he sayd did refresh his spirits and memorie." Whenever he worked or "meditated," whether at York House in London or at Gorhambury, he wanted music played "in the next roome" for an almost Proustian effect. Furthermore, in residence, he demanded that no servant wear any leather boots except Spanish, for the smell of other leathers offended him. Such servants wore livery that carried the crest of the Bacons (a boar), and, says Aubrey, "his Watermen were more imployed by Gentlemen than any other, even the King's."[8] Indeed, when the King sent a deer to him, Bacon tipped the keeper fifty pounds. Three of his servants even kept their own coaches and some, racehorses. Not surprisingly, his servants began to steal from him, taking such items as a cabinet of jewels sent by the East India Merchants. In such a setting, Ben Jonson composed his birthday ode to Bacon and may have read it to him at the celebration on January 22, 1621.

Jonson praised Bacon on his sixtieth birthday for the Lord Chancellor's power of building social harmony and projecting his own special destiny that Jonson calls him the "Genius" of the "antient" London residence and then turns to Bacon's power of harmonizing the world around him: "How comes it all things so about thee smile?" In the middle of conviviality, "the fire, the wine, the men," Bacon stands "as if some Mysterie thou did'st!"[9] In the next decade, with Bacon dead and nothing to gain, Jonson praised him again, paraphrasing Seneca (a compliment in itself). The former Lord Chancellor was a civilizer whose success rested precisely on his power of language: "There hapn'd, in my time, one noble *Speaker*, who was full of gravity in his speaking. His language, (where hee could spare, or passe by a jest) was nobly *censorious*" and there was no person who "spake more neatly, more presly, more weightily, or suffer'd lesse emptinesse, lesse idlenesse, in what hee utter'd." In fact, with every part of his speech consisting "of his owne grace: His hearers could not cough, or looke aside from him, without losse. Hee commanded where hee spoke; and had his Judges angry, and pleased at his devotion," and "the feare of every man that heard him, was, lest hee should make an end." A marginal note beside this passage from *Discoveries* confirms this praise. Bacon "perform'd that in our tongue, whch may be compar'd, or preferr'd, either to insolent *Greece*, or haughty *Rome*" and "hee may be nam'd, and stands as the *marke*, and *akmè* of our language," seeming "to mee ever, by his worke, one of the greatest men, and most worthy of admiration, that had been in many Ages."[10] Oddly, Jonson here echoes motifs from his ode to Shakespeare.

In all this splendor and "admiration," Bacon remained surprisingly efficient. However loosely he controlled his household (bribes often occurred without his knowledge, especially as his wealth increased daily), he kept a firm control over his responsibilities for James I. Thus, Bacon as Lord Chancellor ran interference for the role of the prerogative in an increasingly demanding and defiant Parliament. In fact, soon deprived of Parliamentary grants, the King and his court had to rely on unpopular expedients, not the least of which was the sale of monopolies. Bacon also became James I's point-man against judges like Coke who upheld the rights of Commons and other representative bodies. He soon became essential to the functioning of a King who had already set the terms for the English Revolution. As a further reward, on January 27, 1621, Bacon was elevated to Viscount St. Albans, entering the higher aristocracy. This was the social zenith of his life, as the recent appearance of the *Instauratio Magna* celebrated the height of his intellectual career. For once there were no ambiguities. As in a Greek tragedy, it was the high point with all its attendant hubris or, in the medieval wheel of fortune, the apex. The timing could not have been more exact nor the event more theatrical for the moment of his fall.

Bacon's Fall and the *Quinquennium*

On March 14, barely six weeks after his sixtieth birthday, the first charges of bribery against Bacon began to surface in the newly assembled House of Commons. In three days the charges moved to the House of Lords. Bacon had already warned the King about the dangers of royal monopolies and the anger building in the nation; he had suggested measures designed to ameliorate them, canceling the more obnoxious. It was clear that this Parliament James I had been forced to call now meeting for the first time since 1614 wanted victims. Although Buckingham was the real target, Parliament could not approach so exalted a level. The charges against Bacon began to spread like wildfire. Soon Bacon became too ill to leave York House or to respond to accusations against him. By March 20 Bacon received the charges from the chamber where he had served for thirty-seven years. He was accused of accepting bribes in chancery suits where he had acted as the highest judge. The exact truth of this charge cannot be determined without understanding Stuart legal perspectives and accepted traditions, but, as Judge John Noonan has demonstrated, such transactions did occur. Whatever Bacon's culpability, the renowned Victorian historian James Gardiner (as did Spedding) exonerated him (14:251). A comprehensive modern study has investigated the whole case in detail and shown Bacon's relative innocence.[11] In any case, Bacon saw immediately the forces lining up to trap and destroy him. For their side, the Commons knew he could never turn on the King or on Buckingham.

By March 27, 1621, Bacon came to a decision. He made formal submission to Lords without answering specific charges and, in confessing on March 30, admitted only to "a great deal of corruption and neglect." This confession was a masterpiece of evasion and manipulation, as John C. Briggs has detailed.[12] On April 16, Bacon spoke to the King and, setting up three kinds of possible bribery in a judge, he acknowledged that he had possibly allowed the second to happen, which is "a neglect in the Judge to inform himself whether the cause to be fully at an end or no, what time he receives the gift; but takes it upon the credit of the party, that all is done; or otherwise omits to enquire" (14:238). With various discourses, from a newly written prayer to a newly formed last will and testament to letters strewed with Biblical allusions, Bacon set the stage for his innocence. Yet on May 1 the Lord Chancellor was stripped of the Great Seal. The whole Stuart state had been threatened. In fact, with his prescience about history, Bacon may have seen his destruction—at least its terms—as a major warning about impending revolution and even civil war. Bacon had surrendered rather than let his Stuart world totally collapse in 1621 as it would in two decades.

Two days later, on May 3, Bacon received his sentence, the heavy fine of £40,000, imprisonment in the Tower, a ban on holding office or sitting in Parliament, and a ban on attending court. The sentence obliterated Bacon's role as a force in the world around him. King James and Buckingham recognized the sacrifice: Bacon was released from the Tower within a few days; his immense fine was assigned by the King to

friends who would never collect. That was all they could do without
jeopardizing their own increasingly fragile positions—a fragility now set
in place for the next King, the young Charles. Bacon did not come to
court until the next year, when, after bitter dispute, he finally agreed to
sell York House to Buckingham or his representative. He never again
served in Parliament or held any position of power in English society.
His time of active *philanthropia* was over. Bacon had been caught in the
paradoxes he himself had described in his *Essays* and his *History of Henry
VII*. His subjective description of his condemnation may be, because of
its ambiguity, the most accurate: "I was the justest judge that was in
England these fifty years. But it was the justest censure in parliament
that was these two hundred years" (14:560).

Ironically, in the five years that followed, the last of his life, Bacon
had the most intense intellectual activity of his life. Rawley singles out
this period especially, noting no fewer than twenty-two works produced,
most of them original texts or translations into Latin that required
recomposition in part or whole. Bacon's great Victorian editor James
Spedding calls this period Bacon's *quinquennium*, and Bacon himself uses
the term in a letter to James I in the summer following his downfall. In
this request to return to court and service to the state, Bacon compares
himself to Seneca and (oddly) James to Nero: "*utar*, saith Seneca to his
Master, *magnis exemplis; nec meae fortunae, sed tuae* [use great examples,
and not my fortune but yours]." Seneca had been banished "for divers
corruptions; yet was afterwards restored, and an instrument of that
memorable *Quinquennium Neronis*" (14:297). In the case of Bacon's life,
the "memorable" five years refer more to Bacon's final productions.

Already in the fall of 1621 Bacon was handing the King a copy of his
new history of the reign of Henry VII for his comments and, in the next
year, this text, one of Bacon's most important, was published. Bacon
also published in 1622 his *Historia Naturalis et Experimentalis Ad Conden-
dam Philosophiam* that contains the first of his series of natural histories,
his *Historia Ventorum* (History of the Winds). In 1623 he published the
Historia Vitae et Mortis (History of Life and Death) as well as a major
work, his longest and most complex text, that is, the expanded Latin
version of the *Advancement of Learning: De Augmentis Scientiarum*. From
1624 on, Bacon wrote other natural histories, compiling his loose collection of natural and social phenomena called *Sylva Sylvarum* and compos-
ing his unfinished utopia the *New Atlantis*, published with the *Sylva* in
the year of his death. In 1625 Bacon published the complete and final
edition of his *Essays*. He also published his *Apophthegms* and his *Transla-*

tion of Certaine Psalms into English Verse, dedicated to his young friend, the poet George Herbert, soon to be ordained an Anglican priest. In 1626 James I died, and his son Charles I ascended the throne. Bacon asked once more to return to Parliament but was denied. Only his texts could direct the way for that new world Bacon recognized had already arrived.

Bacon's death represents, as related by Bacon's one-time secretary Thomas Hobbes to Aubrey, a metonymy for his whole life. On April 6, 1626, Bacon was driving in his coach with the King's physician when he suddenly decided to try an experiment in refrigeration. Traveling toward Highgate, on the outskirts of London, where "snow lay on the ground . . . it came into my Lord's thoughts, why flesh might not be preserved in snow, as in Salt." Getting out of the coach, Bacon went "into a poore woman's house at the bottom of Highgate hill" where he bought a hen, had the woman eviscerate it, and then stuffed it with snow, "and my Lord did help to doe it himselfe." But "the snow so chilled him that he immediately fell so extremely ill" that he could not return to Gray's Inn at Holborn, where he had come to live, estranged from his wife and his estate at Gorhambury. He went instead to the nearby villa of the Earl of Arundel, and there he was fatally placed into the best bed of the house that, although "warmed with a Panne," had not been slept in for a year and was quite damp. He soon developed pneumonia, and on Easter Sunday 1626, three days later, Bacon "dyed of Suffocation."[13]

Bacon thus died in (and for) an act of experimentation, and Bertolt Brecht's powerful narrative based on this episode of Bacon's death is called, in fact, "Das Experiment." Death had come at the point Bacon always sought: the moment where subjective fascination with the objective world of nature made contact with that world in experimentation and trial. In that trial, always a matter of labor, Bacon could textualize nature with its own particular history and, in the process, make his own representation of it. In ways Rawley could never have realized, Bacon did become, in fact, at least for the next three centuries, "the glory of his age and nation, the adorner and ornament of learning" (1:3). Bacon's early and continual solipsism and self-election had been correct. But, as always, history had its own contingencies. In a final irony, after an elaborate funeral and burial at St. Michael's Church near Gorhambury where a baroque memorial statue designates the spot, Bacon's body can no longer be found. All that remains are his texts.

PART ONE
Bacon's World as It Is

Chapter Two

The *Essays:* Reading Them as "Dispersed Meditacions"

Francis Bacon published his first book of essays in 1597. He dedicated them to his brother Anthony, who had been a correspondent in France with Michel Montaigne, the originator of the form. The ten essays were groups of sentences, most set off by paragraph signs (as in the Bible verses of that day) to emphasize their aphoristic base. From the beginning, as revealed by these special signs, the structure of Bacon's *Essays* existed in a kind of tension between an aphoristic base and the steady progression and evolution of individual sentences into the whole of the essay and then these essays into the whole of the book. In fact, precisely this dialectic[1] between the single assertive aphorism—what one may call the central self of the essay—and the progression in the book as a whole defines the act of reading of these texts. This progression of essays may be modern in its syncopation, resembling a series of "sound-bytes." Yet the linguistic and stylistic dynamic in each essay—sudden conclusion after brief assertion—was profound and could not be missed by readers from any tradition. From the first in 1597, as the continuous popularity of the *Essays* has proved, audiences found the immense life generated by this rhythmic formal interplay of ideas adaptable to their own lives. For them too, self and time, individuality and history, have held, whether in 1597 or 1997, unresolved tensions both as syncopated *and* continuous as in the *Essays*.

From the beginning, these essays revealed, even in the deliberately truncated versions of 1597, the threefold interpretation that four centuries since have given them: they have performed, in Michael Kiernan's terms, "as commonplace books writ large, as contributions to psychology and political science (part of Bacon's Great Instauration), and as a mirror for the Renaissance ruling class."[2] Although they served as much more than this when English-speaking and European cultures attempted to colonize the globe, these three rather simple lines indicate the scope of the texts, subsuming even the later essays, whose power "inheres," at least for Stanley Fish, "in the accommodation within them of disparate and contradictory visions."[3]

To add to the innovation of the first edition for the late 1590s audience (including readers like Shakespeare, Jonson, and Donne), Bacon appended two other kinds of short prose discourse—the Latin *Meditationes Sacrae* and the English *Coulers of good and evil* (with titles for each unit of prose in Latin). These additional pieces reflect Bacon's awareness that he was in a tradition, however radically he would modify it, of the "mirror" or "institute," as Levy has called it, whether "descriptive," like More's *Utopia*, or "prescriptive," like Sir Thomas Elyot's *The Boke named the Governour*. The whole volume would appear then to want to achieve that special shaping of self that in the nineteenth century Jacob Burckhardt identified as a sign of the Renaissance.[4] The printer's title as advertised at the end of January 1596 (1597 in the new calendar) reflects this synthesis of short prose pieces designed to shape subjectivity toward action in the objective world: *Essayes. Religious Meditations. Places of perswasion and disswasion. Seene and allowed. At London, Printed for Humfrey Hooper, and are to be sold at the blacke Beare in Chauncery Lane. 1597.*

The dedicatory letter to Bacon's invalid brother also carries this same sense of personal activity and historical context: "Louing and beloued Brother," Bacon writes, "I doe now like some that haue an Orcharde il neighbored, that gather their fruit before it is ripe, to preuent stealing." If Bacon is also making a rhetorical sleight-of-hand here by first making the standard Renaissance apology for publishing one's work, he also turns himself into judge and then defender of his own work. In that process, he announces with considerable cunning the real purpose of his text. In a corrupt and mixed world, the "medicinable" aspects of his therapeutic texts will remain: Bacon as "Inquisitor" or official censor has found "nothing in them contrarie or infectious to the state of Religion, or manners, but rather (as I suppose) medicinable" (6:523). Health of mind does not belong only to formal religion. The concept is not only innovative but revolutionary.

The volume was immediately popular and reprinted in 1598, 1604, and 1606. During these years, Bacon revised the essays, making few deletions but considerably reshifting motifs, syntax, and imagery, and then adding new material. In late autumn 1612 Bacon published the essays again, dropping the religious meditations and the *Colors of Good and Evil*. This new text, an elegant slim volume, appeared in two printed versions. A political tragedy for England marks the difference. Bacon had dedicated the original edition "To the most high & excellent

Prince / Henry, Prince of Wales, D of Cornwall / and Earle of Chester."
Unfortunately, although Bacon's new volume of *Essays* had been entered
in the Stationers' Register almost a month before, the young Prince and
heir to James I died suddenly on November 6, 1612. Bacon had not
only lost a patron, but, as Roy Strong and Christopher Hill have shown,[5]
the kingdom had lost a new Renaissance prince, the only Stuart who
might have prevented the English Revolution.

Bacon's dedication to the young Prince of Wales is therefore poignant
in its hopes.[6] In the formal terms required in such a letter to a member
of the royal family, Bacon focuses his own identity. Because in "princely
affaiers" and in Bacon's "continuall Services" what is most lacking is
"leasure" both for writing and reading, he has chosen to write "certain
breif notes, sett downe rather significantlye, then curiously, wch I have
called *Essaies.*" Remembering Montaigne, Bacon notes: "The word is
late, but the thing is auncient." Indeed, from ancient Rome, the civilization that was the cultural model for Renaissance England, had come an
archetype in Seneca's Epistles to Lucilius, which, Bacon continues, "yf
youe marke them well, are but *Essaies*" or "dispersed Meditacions"
(11:340). If the term appears oxymoronic to readers who see the process
of meditation as sustained and stretching beyond time, the term cap-
tures Bacon's formal dialectic. The central aphoristic base, the concentrated frame for the self's meditation, plays against the growth, even
free-fall evolution, of the text itself into the larger progression of the
essays and book. Neither term—"Meditacions" of self or "dispersed"
structures of time and history surrounding that self—could be lost or
discounted in the process of reading.

In this dedication Bacon builds one more perspective for his reader:
the form though modern is really ancient. This reversal of time Bacon
would use over and over, not least in his 1609 *De Sapientiâ Veterum* and
his utopic *New Atlantis*: that is, in the most contemporary projections of
the future can be found the primitive, or in the ancient past can be
found the future. Thus, in 1612 the therapeutic or "medicinable" aim of
his prose discourse not only had classical and Roman warrant but was
suited, as a dispersed or scattered meditation, for the modern European
without leisure. If such "medicinable" prose was designed for what
Bacon in his 1623 Latin translation of the *Advancement of Learning,* the
De Augumentis Scientiarum, sees as the twofold division of "the Doctrine
concerning Negotiation," that is, "*the Doctrine concerning Scattered Occasions*" and "*the Doctrine concerning Advancement in Life,*" such prose was to
be written with the authority of experience. The form and style must
convey the social occasion and "the variety of business" needed for "the

improvement of a man's own fortune"; the literary form must act as "a private notebook or register of his own affairs" (5:35). In fact, because "actions in common life are dispersed, and not arranged in order, dispersed directions do best for them" (4:451).

When the second 1612 edition of Bacon's *Essays* appeared, with its twenty-eight new essays and the original ten revised, they were re-dedicated, this time to Bacon's brother-in-law, Sir John Constable, to whom Bacon pays the tribute of "straight friendship and societe, and particularly of communication in studies" (6:539). The printer's title shows the new and more public direction of the text: "The / Writings of / Sr ffrancis Bacon Knt: / the Kinges Solli- / citor Generall: / in Moralitie / Policie, and / Historie." The threefold variety promised in the title had resulted from expansion in the text of topics and the methods for exploring them. They would still contain, however, the same tension of an aphoristic base that focused thought or "meditacion" and the dispersed progressing structure embodied in the sequence of essays.

The third and final edition of Francis Bacon's "most literary-looking work," in Brian Vickers' phrase,[7] adds eighteen essays and revises the originals from the first two volumes, to make fifty-eight essays in all. This definitive English form of Bacon's *Essays* appeared in 1625. Its dedication is to none other than the King's favorite George Villiers, the Duke of Buckingham, and its printer's title reveals its basic dialectical structure: "*THE / ESSAYES / OR / COVNSELS, / CIVILL AND / MORALL, / OF / FRANCIS LO. VERVLAM, / VISCOVNT St. ALBAN.*" In this edition and form, Bacon's *Essays* would influence English-speaking cultures (and European cultures) for the next three centuries.

There is another edition of the essays dedicated to George Villiers, a Latin version. This posthumous edition of Bacon's *Essays* is virtually unknown today but was significant in Bacon's own trajectory of texts. In 1638 Bacon's literary executor, William Rawley, published the Latin edition of the essays with the significant title that marked it as part of the newly expanded program Bacon set himself during his last five years: *Sermones Fideles sive interiora rerum.*[8] Especially in their Latin form, the *Essays* would perform as part of Bacon's final strategy. In that *quinquennium*, he would prepare all his work for the largest possible audience. Because of his intent, if there were any relationship between Bacon's *Essays* and the larger program of the Great Instauration or Renewal, the final Latin version would have made it more explicit. But the connection is tenuous. In fact, Bacon's essays offer the only point in his integrated scheme where subjectivity and ambiguity of self rather than the objectivity of science might be revealed. For this reason, as Bacon writes the Venetian priest Fulgentius at the end of his life, his essays would remain in some sense separate from the order of his Instauration, not naturally in the order but interjected into it or interposed: "atque hic tomus (ut diximus) interjectus est, et non ex ordine 'Instaurationis'" (14:531).

When the Latin essays appeared in the 1538 *Operum moralium et civilium tomus*, twelve years after his death, the increasingly popular Bacon found immediately a continental audience. This was what Bacon had desired when on June 26, 1523, he first mentioned his Latin translation to his close friend Sir Tobie Matthew in a letter to him in Spain. In this letter Bacon also reveals the place of Latin in any transmission of his texts to new audiences: "These modern languages will at one time or other play the bank-rowtes with books; and since I have lost much time with this age, I would be glad as God shall give me leave to recover it with posterity" (14:429). In his letters to Father Fulgentius, Bacon remarks that he works for future generations: "quia posteritati (saecula enim ista requirunt) inservio" (because I work for posterity; these things requiring ages for their accomplishment). For this reason he is translating his major works into Latin, he says, including the essays already published in Italy "which in your language you have called *Saggi Morali*." In Latin he will give the *Essays* "a weightier name," *Sermones Fideles* or "Faithful Discourses, or the Inwardness of Things," and "these discourses will be both increased in number and much enlarged in treatment" (14:531–3). In the 1538 volume with these Latin *Essays* was his Latin work of myths, *De Sapientia Veterum*. By no accident then, Bacon is even more confident in his dedication to Buckingham in 1625 of both his English and forthcoming (so he thought) Latin editions: "I do now publish my Essays; which, of all my works, have been most current; for that, it seems, they come home to men's business and bosoms. I have enlarged them both in number and weight; so they are indeed a new work. . . . [And] I do conceive that the Latin volume of them (being in the universal language) may last as long as books last" (6:373).

How to Read Bacon's *Essays* (and Almost Anything Else by Bacon)

As odd as it may seem to modern readers, this interest in Latin generated Bacon's hope for the transformation of English and European society. In the late Renaissance, at a moment of universal cultural collapse, at least as Bacon saw it, he could bring not just reform but deliverance itself. The means would be Latin. Latin would provide the larger instrument of this reform (and from Descartes to Richelieu to Leibnitz and especially to Kant, Europe understood Bacon's message of deliverance because of this instrument). Only in that universal culture could his texts be perceived as revealing the restitution of archaic knowledge or at least a restatement so now it seemed revolutionary. By no surprise, the fundamental Latin basis of his culture also led to Bacon's fundamental conception of style. The power of Latin stayed in the control that only a language almost two thousand years old could give, the levels of nuance and verbal gesture needed in a new world where nothing could be assumed as natural and no metaphysics taken for granted. Style must be controlled, self-conscious, even theatrical, for, in a time of breakdown, the stage must be bare and all voice and gesture calculated if it intended to survive. In this sense of language as theater or oratory, Bacon responded at his deepest level to that classical humanism bequeathed him by his culture in general but specifically by his brilliant mother and his Reformist schoolmaster grandfather Cooke. What they understood from their own visions of reality and deliverance—expressed in Latin— Bacon absorbed and then took his linguistic strategies a step further.

Thus, if there is any secret to reading Bacon's *Essays* or almost anything else Bacon wrote, it lies in this sense of a performative art whose assurance in performance rose from controlled language. For Bacon, soteriological purpose for a text demands a soteriological style and language. Like the Calvinist preaching Bacon's mother admired, language and style could never be less than staged performance in an unstable discontinuous world. In fact, Bacon's conception of language begins, as in Bacon's mother's view of reality, in the inherited human tragedy of disjointed time. The immediate result of such a fall from the Garden— the originating moment of time—left for the powers of human language little more than broken representation. Bacon's inherited history is, in fact, so fallen and cracked that it calls for restitution not as a means for originating solutions but for survival and sheer continuance in the onslaught of time, the moving river in Bacon's beloved Heraclitus' aphorism: "You could not step twice into the same river; for other waters are ever flowing on to you."[9] Throughout all of Bacon's canon, as Paolo Rossi remarks, "a basic, unchanging aspect of [his] philosophy" is that the human being "renounced . . . original power with the Fall." The force of breakdown thus permeates his texts, as Rossi notes: "Bacon's doctrine of scientific knowledge is entirely conditioned by his conception of the universe as a labyrinth and forest filled with 'so many ambiguities of the way,' 'deceitful resemblances of objects and signs,' 'natures irregular in their lines and so knotted and entangled.' "[10] Bacon's poem, "The World's A Bubble" (a text Hobbes may have given Aubrey) lacks a single human consolation for the relentless pain of existence, least of all Christian transcendence: "What then remaines? but that we still should cry / Not to be borne, or, being borne, to dye."[11] If the language echoes *Lear*, for Bacon, as for Hamlet, the dialectic of history remains always between a broken world (and therefore broken knowledge and false history) and the restitution of that world, a matter of action. Even then, as in *Hamlet*, there are no guarantees for making it right.

In fact, the horror of the Fall is only another way, as in Calvinist theology, of confirming the perennial plunge all being has taken from the first moment in the Garden. In the paradox that follows such a conception of history, discontinuity actually emphasizes that first continuous moment before the fall into time. Present corruption continually implies that an archaic perfection once existed. Just as Bacon's universe of discontinuity and constant free-fall parodies the original fall from the Garden in the Bible, so in a Baconian dialectic there is always the memory of what the human mind fell from. Michael McCanles has defined this archaizing process in Bacon that the English Franciscans William of Ockham and Duns Scotus had prefigured and set the terms for. As McCanles argues, the central place in Baconian methodizing is the ideal intuition that may come at some point between initial sensual awareness and the actualization of the method—not unlike, one might add, a modern conception (ironically, such as Karl Popper's) of scientific hypothesis. As this recaptured intuition is also expected to emerge in its visionary fullness at the end of the hexemeral stages of the Great Instauration, it drives all stages of Bacon's method. "There is, then," says McCanles, "an element of historical and religious primitivism in Bacon's thought, which parallels his epistemological primitivism, the ideal of unmediated intuition" (43). This intuition may not be defined exactly as Bacon's "tabula rasa" (a phrase he invented long before his admirer John Locke) but does operate, as it drives the Baconian method, with the sense of a blinding totality—an innocence before the fall of "unmediated" reality into the phenomena of the many, the contingent distinctions of the barking dogs-Scholastics, as Bacon calls them in the *Advancement* (3:287), that reduce mystery to reason. As Bacon underscores in his crucial Plan of the Great Instauration, "It [is] part of my design to set everything forth, as far as may be, plainly and perspicuously (for nakedness of the mind is still, as nakedness of the body once was, the companion of innocence and simplicity) . . ." (4:22).

It was within this dialectic between discontinuity and attempts at making and building toward the "nakedness" of the ideal intuition that Bacon wrote his texts. The dialectic applies to reading them as well. In this sense, reading Bacon is like being in the middle of a battlefield or, to use Bacon's own transcription from the Prophet Habakkuk 2:2, on the run. From this prophetic passage, itself the original Old Testament text for Romans 1:17 (the Pauline text that transformed Martin Luther), Bacon forms his new method of reading in 1605: "as the prophet saith, *he that runneth by may read it*" (3:341). Bacon takes his text from Habakkuk 2:2 in the Geneva Bible: "And the Lord answered me, & said, Write the vision, and make it plaine upon tables, that he may runne that readeth it." Coming shortly before Bacon's parodic use of Virgil's *Georgics* and the *Faber Fortunae in the Advancement*, and close to his first use of the prophecy in Daniel marking the later emblem on the first page of the *Instauratio Magna* (1620), the topos defines Bacon's new method of reading. The innovation is marked by Bacon's crucial addition of the adverb "by" to the Biblical verse. All texts are to be read in a world without leisure, a world of business, the serious business of literally redeeming society. Bacon would write for readers who would see the advantages of science and technology in the new soteriological frame of "redeming the time," as given in Ephesians 5:16 to which the Geneva translation adds: "for the dayes are euil."[12]

With such premises, any reading of time, any act of the mind for such reading of a Bacon text, must inevitably start in a broken world. In Baconian epistemology, if knowledge is making or invention, such making starts on a bare stage. Not even one's subjectivity can be trusted, although, as Bacon notes at the beginning of his *Advancement* (quoting Ecclesiastes 3:11), "God hath framed the mind of man as a mirror or glass capable of the image of the universal world . . ." (3:265). In fact, reading or making must see what this initial framing of the mind has become, the dreadful perception that is the polar opposite from that of Pico della Mirandola's Platonic anthropology. Speaking of logical fallacies in the mind of man and the need for stronger methods of logic, Bacon writes: "For the mind of man is far from the nature of a clear and equal glass [mirror], wherein the beams of things should reflect according to their true incidence; nay, it is rather like an enchanted glass, full of superstition and imposture, if it be not delivered and reduced" (3:394–5). The Renaissance mind-as-mirror metaphor operates here, one may add, as another Bacon parody, this time in deliberate interplay with "through a glass darkly" in St. Paul's first Letter to the Corinthians 13.[13]

Although this initial frame of the corrupt nature of human existence is constantly referred to throughout his canon, Bacon is extraordinarily clear about its force in an early philosophical/scientific work, dated in 1603 by his great Victorian editor James Spedding: *VALERIUS TERMINUS of THE INTERPRETATION OF NATURE: with the ANNOTATIONS OF HERMES STELLA*. As Fulton Anderson has noted, the basis of Bacon's whole philosophical (and therefore rhetorical and literary) system can be anticipated in this text.[14] In the first chapter, Bacon adumbrates one of his famous imagistic and syntactic arguments from his later *Advancement of Learning*. He gives his definition of subjectivity and the limits of the mind: if human beings turned from "the oracles of God's word," the Bible, in their search for divine truth to "the mixtures of their own inventions," so in the same manner in the search for nature, they "have ever left the oracles of God's works, and adored the deceiving and deformed imagery which the unequal mirrors of their own minds have represented unto them." Bacon is more specific in his sixteenth chapter: because of "the native and inherent errors in the mind of man which have coloured and corrupted all his notions and impressions," Bacon finds "in this enchanted glass" or mirror of the mind "four Idols or false appearances," both objective and subjective deceptions of the human mind (3:224;241–2). These "idols" or illusions have haunted intellectual history. If later in his revised myth of the Sphinx "Or Science," Bacon attacks illusion, "content with what it finds, and swelling with talk," as marking the Catholic Scholastics, who make false Aristotelian distinctions and "neglect or spurn the search after realities or works" (6:757), so in the early *Valerius* Bacon denounces as strongly as any anti-humanist or Calvinist preacher "the mind of a man": "as it is not a vessel of that content or receipt to comprehend knowledge without helps and supplies, so again it is not sincere, but of an ill and corrupt tincture" (3:245). Thus, any reading of Bacon must begin with the recognition of that permanent "tincture" that has colored the mind of all human beings and corrupted it. Bacon's is hardly less a tragically disorganized universe than those invented by Bacon's contemporary writing *Hamlet* and *King Lear* at the same time as *Valerius Terminus* was being composed.

In such a debased world, then, subjectivity is itself broken and untrustworthy, and the self haunted by idols, a term whose etymology in Bacon includes both ghosts (inward and outward) and the images of false gods (or devils). Time now takes on an urgency in which there is a kind of Baconian "readiness is all," in Hamlet's phrase to Horatio. Readers will inevitably be like the prophet Habakkuk, on the run if they would build structures of survival. In a more traditional and cyclical cosmos (the kind of time that, for example, Mircea Eliade has described),[15] the reader has time for contemplation or the leisure Bacon laments as lost to Prince Henry. Rather, in a fallen world, the new anthropology of human limitation must operate. A clearer dialectic of this operation can be found in the first aphorism of Bacon's most magisterial text, Book One of the *Novum Organum*. In the most consciously placed of all his aphorisms or statements, human limits are set: "Man, being the servant and interpreter of Nature, can do and understand so much only as he has observed in fact or in thought of the course of nature: beyond this he neither knows anything nor can he do anything" (4:47).

The Necessity for Theater

Thus Bacon's audiences are to read and understand his texts in their interplay between recognition of disjointed time as a bare stage and the urge to action to redeem that time, to build new structures and speak, as it were, on that stage by inventing new roles for the deliverance of history. Only in that dialectic or interplay can the reader enter and make history. But such making acts within liminality, the limits of the dialectic in history itself. Within such limits, ideas may move as freely as the ships passing through the Gates of Hercules in Bacon's famous emblem for the *Magna Instauratio* of 1620. There is freedom but within and through gates. That is, structures of freedom on a bare stage must be manipulated: the actor or producer must follow directions as exact as in the essay "Of Masques and Triumphs" in order to produce any show at all. On this bare stage, gesture and text are always limited to the necessities of the stage itself and the audience before it. The demands of acting with such absolute urgency Bacon had learned from the profession he practiced every day—law. In this sense, Bacon's law texts are like scenarios, the husks of the live theater that belong to the courtroom or speech forum. By no accident, such a basis in performance and theater can be found throughout Bacon's canon.[16]

Thus, no matter how they may call for humility and eschew the dramatic, Bacon's texts can only be supremely self-conscious on a stage as epistemologically bare as that for Samuel Beckett's clowns. On a stage "beyond" which the human being "neither knows anything nor can he do anything," to paraphrase the first aphorism of the *Novum Organum*, texts and actions can only be themselves. They are virtually self-begetting, no matter how they originate out of the classics and the Bible. The very way the past will be used is dramatically altered. In a sense nothing had existed (or could exist) before. On this stripped stage, for the text to survive as authentic, theater must be of the subtlest as well as boldest kind, to which Bacon adverts in his essay "Of Envy": "the wiser sort of great persons bring in ever upon the stage somebody upon whom to derive [turn] the envy that would come upon themselves" (6:396).

Such a theater also implies that the interaction of such stage actors and an audience is the only life possible in this world or any other. For this reason, the *Essays* have, unlike Montaigne's from whence the form originated, few pronouns in the first person, and most texts offer a collective self. This sense of theater and the process of playing a role could be learned, as collective experience, from a master-actor and then as a book of directions, as Bacon makes clear in his essay "Of Counsel": "It was truly said, *optimi consiliarii mortui* [the best counselors are the dead]: books will speak plain when counselors blanch. Therefore it is good to be conversant in them, specially the books of such as themselves have been actors upon the stage" (6:426). Bacon repeats this motif of his experience in the theater of the royal court or of the law courts or of Parliament. It becomes a means of "honor" still left to him in the year after his fall, when in 1621 he wrote to his old friend the Spanish ambassador Count Gondomar: "Me verò jam vocat et aetas, et fortuna, atque etiam Genius meus, cui adhuc satis morosé satisfeci, ut excedens è theatro rerum civilium literis me dedam, et ipsos actores instruam, et posteritati serviam" (In truth, already both age and fortune and even my genius, for which I have sadly not done enough, call me, so that, exiting the theatre of civil business, I shall give myself to writing, and I shall instruct the actors themselves, and I shall serve future generations) (14:285; translation mine).

Seeing the universe as one staged event (or rather event to be staged) is particularly useful in reading Bacon's *Essays*. It keeps the reader from forcing Bacon's texts into interpretations of the "sincere" and the "prophetic," entrapments that Bacon may indeed intend at high moments but only to make significant utilitarian points. Conversely, if the *Essays* are not to be read as "sincere," they are neither to be read as purely sinister, revealing an English Machiavel rotten at the heart. Rather, the *Essays* offer quite consciously staged performances for a world where meaning can only come from interactive performance and cannot be assumed from the corruption of history. The essays enact particular experiences Bacon (as stagemaster) is setting up within the particular topic of the essay or "trial" being presented. From Bacon's perspective, such staging enacts a text of social therapy, as the ancient Stoics intended (a "medicinable" text). Like many later readers, Blake could not accept such therapy or such social staging or the language of performance that would deny transcendence to human action. For him, Bacon's *Essays* were, as Blake inscribed in the title page of his copy before throwing it across the room, "Good Advice for Satan's Kingdom," adding later "This is Certain: If What Bacon says Is True, then what Christ says Is False."[17]

Bacon's Aphorism as "Meditacion" in Time

Of the three characteristics of the *Essays* that Kiernan has singled out, in many ways the most helpful for understanding their development lies in their function as extraordinary commonplace books. In this sense, Bacon's essays arise from the short pithy notes, incipient aphorisms, in his own notebooks. Both the extensive use of classical and biblical quotations in "Of Truth" and its powerful antithetical sentences come out of what the humanist Renaissance culture had become by 1561 when Bacon was born, a "notebook culture," to use Vickers' phrase.[18] In this use of *topoi* or *loci communes* the Renaissance was merely imitating Hellenic and Hebraic cultures as well as continuing medieval traditions. But there had been a significant difference with Erasmus. The difference lay in *his* most crucial notebook, the *Adagia*. This ever-growing catalogue of sayings from earlier ages had distinctive designs for Erasmus' audience. A major purpose was to make materials accessible for a culture more and more committed to an ethic of labor (as opposed to lazy monks and slothful courtiers), a culture ready to use time as fully and quickly as possible. In fact, the enormous influence of Erasmus on Luther and on the intellectual giant who was Luther's greatest disciple, Philip Melanchthon, can be evidenced by the fact that the first formulation of Protestant doctrine came in Melanchthon's 1520 *Loci Communes* or Commonplaces of the new teaching (not called Protestantism until 1529). Thus, in England, one major result of Reformation iconoclasm was the substitution, as, for example, at York Minster, of biblical aphorisms or sententiae for the smashed stained glass. In the Edwardian England of Bacon's zealot grandfather and mother, Erasmus' biblical paraphrases were set on the altar table in some English churches. This combination of a concentrated linguistic form with the highest sacred purpose for a new society would not be missed on later generations who looked for the right form to reinvent their world.

Bacon recognized this social, even cosmic power of the aphorism from the beginning. He kept from the 1590s a commonplace book entitled *Promus of Formularies and Elegancies*, the curious title using the Latin figure for one who distributes or keeps, like a librarian, linguistic forms that suit rhetorical occasions. Such a notebook as Bacon began on December 5, 1594, would be especially useful for a young lawyer or, later, a middle-aged solicitor moving from one social and legal crisis to another, especially at a royal court where timing, the right speech, and compliment required the finesse of a modern-day lobbyist. Such aphoristic quotations become, in fact, leit-motifs for all his work. These same concerns about his method and his plans for reform distinguish the only other notebook recovered from lost Bacon manuscripts. At age forty-eight, in the summer of 1608, Bacon kept a notebook in which he states explicitly the need for aphorisms in his method and the role they will play in his Instauration. Bacon called this commonplace book, now more concerned with notes for action than formulae, *Commentarius Solutus Sive Pandecta Sive Ancilla Memoriae*. The text lived up to its name, a loose commentary like the Pandecta the Roman Pliny used for his collection in his Natural History and the Emperor Justinian in his laws, all notes acting as handmaiden to memory. This surprisingly long text (for one week's notes!) has, as Spedding remarks in one of his most biographical introductions, the explicit purpose of acting as a memory bank for Bacon at a turning point of both his political and intellectual careers (11:18). Its vast survey of topics, running like a stream of consciousness among Bacon's varied life-interests, remains a treasure for any student of Bacon. Already he was indicating future works and a context for works like the *Essays*: "Qu. of an oration ad filios, delightfull, sublime, and mixt with elegancy, affection, *novelty of conceyt and yet sensible*, and Superstition" and six entries before this, "The finishing of the Aphorismes, Clavis interpretationis, and then setting foorth the book." Shortly after these entries, Bacon also proposes "an History mechanique" and for this work he would find "all observacions, Axiomes, directions" (11:64–6; cf. BL Add. Ms. 26278).

In two places, then, for the first time, the linguistic method of the 1597 essays, the aphorism, has been taken into the realm of philosophy and science. It is to express the key (*clavis*) of interpretation, the means by which his grand Instauration will be set forth, and, in fact, an early name that Bacon intended to give his *Novum Organum* was *Clavis Inter-pretationis*. Spedding considers that Bacon is perhaps thinking of an unfinished rudimentary Latin work here, one never translated, that may have adumbrated the greater work: *Aphorismi et consilia de auxiliis mentis et accensione luminis naturalis* (Aphorisms and strategms for helps to the mind and for the ascent of natural light) (3:793–4).

It should be no surprise therefore that with the exception of *The Advancement* (and the *De Augmentis Scientiarum*), all major texts of Bacon's revert, in one form or another, to the shape of the aphorism. As Rawley writes early in his life, his master's "opinions and assertions" were "rather like oracles than discourses" (1:12), and so there was always the ground-ing of Bacon's mediating/meditating language in intense and discontinu-ous form such as the aphorism. It was as though language should actual-ize those radiating points of light Bacon saw at the center of a universe in flux. In fact, at ideologically the most crucial point in the entire canon, his preface to the *Instauratio Magna*, Bacon describes the value of his method as so inherent that a linguistic form would inevitably be discov-ered to express it: "But it is the empty things that are vast: things solid are most contracted and lie in little room" (4:21).

By no accident, therefore, the text of this highest point of Bacon's Instauration, the *Novum Organum*, consisted, after a long preface, of a series of aphorisms. So too, as the method of the discontinuous aphorism was always to invite further investigation, one more step into an endless horizon or future, it was quite appropriate that Bacon's answer to Aris-totle's old *Organon* be unfinished. Bacon was, as a persistent image throughout his works makes clear, a trumpeter (*buccinator*) of a new era. His linguistic forms of brevity were to open up that era.

In what is probably his earliest theoretical statement about the apho-rism, Bacon finds the form, not surprisingly, as rising both from the practice of law and, for one of the most original Latin stylists in the European Renaissance, from the ancients. As Peter Stein has remarked, what made a "proposition a maxim" in Bacon's time was "not so much its degree of abstraction or its epigrammatic form but the fact that it could not be challenged." In this sense, maxims formed the original structure of all law; to deny a maxim was the same as "denying the law itself."[19] If, for a humanist culture like Bacon's and for one of its bright-est students, the classics also held absolute authenticity, the aphorism offered a special authority. The classics themselves authorized a new form of intellectual revolution. Writing in his 1596 preface to his *Max-ims of the Law*, Bacon notes: "For we see all the ancient wisdom and science was wont to be delivered in that form; as may be seen by the parables of Solomon, and by the aphorisms of Hippocrates, and the moral verses of Theognis and Phocyclides; but chiefly the precedent of the civil law, which hath taken the same course with their rules, did confirm me in my opinion" (7:321). In his *Maxims of the Law* Bacon revises current practice by stating a law in Latin and then giving an aphoristic commentary—the first such series of aphorisms in Bacon's canon. In his preface for the *Maxims*, written at the same time as he was preparing the first edition of his *Essays*, Bacon writes: "whereas I could have digested these rules into a certain method or order . . . I have avoided so to do, because this delivering of knowledge in distinct and disjoined aphorisms doth leave the wit of man more free to turn and toss, and to make use of that which is so delivered to more several purposes and applications" (7:321).

Such assurance from the classical world allows Bacon to describe the use of aphorisms in another work, *Filum Labyrinthi* (The Thread to the Maze). "Antiquity," writes Bacon, "used to deliver the knowledge which the mind of man had gathered, in observations, aphorisms, or short and dispersed sentences, or small tractates of some parts that they had diligently meditated and laboured" and these aphorisms "did invite men" of the ancient world "both to ponder that which was invented, and to add and supply" (3:498). In short, argues Bacon, as the ancient world knew, the aphorism was the instrument of time, stopping in its flux for reflection or observation, but by its brevity signaling seriality or succession. It could allow thus for the latest knowledge and technology in society. In fact, as Bacon admitted in his 1603 *Valerius Terminus*, his own profession as lawyer provided him with an example of how maxims show a seriality that may "be augmented and rectified by the superior light thereof" and by "the mutual light and consent which one part receiveth of another."

In his 1605 *Advancement of Learning*, Bacon gives his most composite theory for the aphorism. The essential lines of his theory would last throughout his work. The first discussion of the aphorism in the *Advancement* is—hardly by accident—in terms of discontinuous time. Appearing in Book One in the catalogue of "peccant humors," the theory appears in Bacon's general definition of the right method of learning, as he had earlier explored it in *Valerius Terminus*. What gives this theory of the aphorism a spectacular difference in the 1605 text is Bacon's imagery. A simile unites his larger motif of the filial nature of science to a motif more physical and gender-directed: "Another error, of a diverse nature from all the former, is the over-early and peremptory reduction of knowledge into arts and methods; from which time commonly sciences receive small or no augmentation. But as young men, when they knit and shape perfectly, do seldom grow to a further stature; so knowledge, while it is in aphorisms and observations, it is in growth; but when it once is comprehended in exact methods, it may perchance be further polished and illustrate, and accommodated for use and practice; but it increaseth no more in bulk and substance" (3:292).

Thus, the true form of knowledge must be "as a thread to be spun on and where possible, *in the same method wherein it was invented*"(3:404). This form is the method of "Probation" or later of the "Initiative." Although the linguistic form is strenuous, Bacon's aphorisms would provide such a model for delivering knowledge of the probative or the experimental kind that will grow: "For first, it trieth the writer, whether he be superficial or solid: for Aphorisms, except they be ridiculous, cannot be made but of the pith and heart of sciences; for discourse of illustration is cut off; recitals of examples are cut off; discourse of connexion and order is cut off; descriptions of practice are cut off; so there remaineth nothing to fill the Aphorisms but some good quantity of observation: and therefore no man can suffice, nor in reason will attempt, to write Aphorisms, but he that is sound and grounded" (3:405). The aphorism represents, therefore, nothing less than the outward and visible sign of a truer method of knowledge itself. It represents the method of the "initiative" as contrasted to Peter Ramus' "majestral method." So Bacon argues: if "Magistral" methods "are more fit to win consent or belief, but less fit to point to action," then in what he will call the "Initiative" method, "aphorisms, representing a knowledge broken [the only kind possible in a Baconian cosmos], do invite men to inquire further" because, by disparate linguistic form, aphorisms are not complete and cannot carry, as methods, "the shew of a total" (3:403; 405).

In his 1623 Latin translation of the *Advancement*, the *De Augmentis Scientiarum*, aphorisms as "Initiative" support the new art of the Wisdom of Transmission, essential to the *Traditio Lampadis* or "the *Handing on of the Lamp*, or Method of Delivery to Posterity." From the lists and topics of *Antitheta Rerum* (Antitheses of Things) that follow this 1623 passage, Bacon developed directly two of his essays—"Of Innovations" and "Of Delays"—and indirectly fifteen more. Similarly, in the eighth book of the *De Augmentis*, dealing with "*the Doctrine concerning Scattered Occasions, and the Doctrine concerning Advancement in Life*," Bacon finds as a form to teach such doctrines "nothing any way comparable to those Aphorisms composed by Solomon the King ... springing from the inmost recesses of wisdom and extending to much variety of occasions." He then proceeds to give a list of such aphorisms with commentary. But "neither was this in use only with the Hebrews," comments Bacon, for such aphoristic form "is generally to be found in the wisdom of the ancients, that as men found out any observation which they thought good for life, they would gather it and express it in some short proverb, parable, or fable" (5:36;56). Finally, in this *De Augmentis*, Bacon concludes his theory of the aphorism with its most succinct definition: "Lastly, aphorisms, representing only portions and as it were fragments of knowledge, invite others to contribute and add something in their turn; whereas methodical delivery, carrying the show of a total, makes men careless, as if they were already at the end" (4:451).

The Aphorisms of the *Essays*

If Bacon's essays do not always have so pure a development of the aphorism as Bacon describes for his scientific and philosophical program, they do act out Bacon's basic rhetorical scenario and strategy derived from his dialectic of time and audience. "The proofs and persuasions of Rhetoric ought to differ according to auditors," writes Bacon in the *Advancement of Learning* and then quotes a famous Latin line from Virgil's *Eclogues* (8:56), translated as "Orpheus in the forest, Arion among the dolphins" (3:411). The *Essays* reflect this rhetorical strategy. They have the same sense of staged performance as Bacon's catalogue of Antitheses and Proverbs, and in their full 1625 edition they have commentary that fleshes out a more "magistral" style within the essential "initiative" basis of the aphorism. If Bacon tried in the aphorisms of his *Novum Organum* to bring the concentration in the aphorism to its most intense—but allowed many of them to expand into short essays, particularly in the second book—so in the *Essays* he incorporated more and more of another rhetorical strategy he found increasingly adaptive for his ideological needs: response to occasion as the determining form.

In the *De Augmentis*, Bacon would develop a theory for the apophthegm that sounds like the dialectical frame he used for his essays. In his appendix to the discussion of history in the 1623 text, he notes how the words of human beings and not just their actions have been preserved. Here he finds again the central place of concentrated linguistic form. Short pithy sayings in the speeches and letters of "wise men on business and matters of grave and deep importance conduce greatly as well to the

knowledge of the things themselves as to eloquence." Letters in this
respect are especially helpful "when there is a continual series of them in
the order of time," but "neither are Apophthegms themselves only for
pleasure and ornament, but also for use and action." They act as "goads"
and are "words with an edge or point, that cut and penetrate the knots
of business and affairs" (4:314), even if they have been used before. If
Julius Caesar kept such a collection (now lost), so such concentrated language may be used for expression and definition of a progressing history.
Thus, Bacon's preface to his own collection *Apophthegms New and Old*
sounds very much like his dedication of the 1612 essay to Prince Henry:
"Certainly they are of excellent use. They are *mucrones verborum, pointed
speeches*. Cicero prettily calls them *salinas, saltpits*; that you may extract
salt out of, and sprinkle it where you will. They serve to be interlaced in
continued speech. They serve to be recited upon occasion of themselves.
They serve if you take out the kernel of them, and make them your
own" (7:123).

In the *Essays*, the use of the aphorism, no matter how expanded it
may be, is neither consistent nor easily plotted as form. In fact, the same
lack of strict consistency hangs over the whole use of the aphorism in
Bacon's canon, and if he attacks an excessive Senecan use of the aphorism ("concise and sharp maxims and conclusions") in his additions to
the *De Augmentis*,[20] the attack merely confirms the importance in
Bacon's entire work of this literary form for which he had developed a
coherent theory, the first in Europe. The point is that Bacon's complex
use and lack of consistency are perfectly compatible with a rhetorical
strategy that serves, in context after context, as "Orpheus in the forest,
Arion among the dolphins." Such consistent variability for the purposes
of audience, within the continuing probability of the centering aphorism
as basic linguistic structure for the whole canon, answers somewhat Lisa
Jardine's questions about the appropriateness of the term aphorism
overall in Bacon. As she remarks, "the same condensed sentence may
function in one context as the grounds for an exploratory discussion of
an ethical or scientific point" and then in another context "prove illustration, and rhetorical force, as an example supporting a general point in
discussion."

In fact, Jardine's own exact analysis of Bacon's use of Solomonic
proverb, parable, and *exempla* demonstrates the power of these variations
and the general direction of Bacon's formal method toward concentration. Further, what Jardine views as negative, Vickers sees as positive
variations: "In the scientific works [Bacon] stressed [the aphorism's] dis-
connected, anti-systematic (or rather presystematic) quality, and its suit-

ability for containing observation; in the civil and political spheres, he valued its easily applicable flexibility (although ultimately here too it was going to help to form a system) and its direct relationship to observed human experience, mainly in the well-defined context of Renaissance politics."[21] Alvin Snider has also commented on the value of the aphorism in replacing "endlessly self-referential disputation . . . with measurably productive doubt" and "a call to action." If for Snider Bacon "envisions syntax as a means for producing eidetically clear speaking-pictures," the "aphorism provides the means for inducing recognition" in a system of induction that "functions as a heuristic, a procedure, or a routine." It performs "a therapeutic task, a way of releasing humanity from the grip of outmoded institutions."[22] This variability of the aphorism allowed Bacon, at least for Anne Righter [Barton], the kind of liberating and inclusive, if ambiguous, texture he wanted for all his texts: "It is the nature of the aphorism to mean more than one thing. In the words themselves, not merely in the progression of the sentences, Bacon contrives to gather together a whole series of different and sometimes contradictory meanings and emotions; to hold them in suspension in such a way that they react upon one another; and to explore without dictating."[23]

In light of this definition of the aphorism as the proper form of historicizing a text—that is, allowing the method of graduation within "dispersed meditacions"—the well-known revisions of the three versions of Bacon's *Essays* take on particular significance. The incremental growth from 1597 to 1625 has been meticulously traced by Edward Arber in the nineteenth century and in this century by Sister M.E. Bowman (and to some degree by Sister S. Mandeville) in unpublished dissertations and by others in a list that supplements the nearly endless studies of Bacon's essays.[24] The irony in the development and the revision of the *Essays* that many of these critics have missed is that, in the first edition of the essays, where the aphorism is made to stand out as sign of its theory of existence, the content of the essays themselves is less radical. In the elaboration and variations on the basic aphoristic base that followed in the later editions of the essays, as Fish has shown, the meaning is far more complex and ambiguous. The "methodizing" merely adds to the density of strategy and representation and the ever growing transvalorization of the subject. "The effect of Bacon's revisions," notes Fish, "is never to cancel out what had been asserted previously, but to qualify it; something assumed to be true on the basis of what now appears to be inadequate evidence is not declared false (necessarily); rather, something else is declared to be true also."[25]

From another perspective, Vickers also analyzes Bacon's great vitality in his revisions: "the care with which Bacon revised them, extending, clarifying, and focusing both observation and expression, is not the care of a virtuoso working on a display piece, but that of a thinker who wants his meaning to be fully and deeply understood."[26] Vickers' analysis of the revisions gives more evidence of a "methodizing" that led to deeper complexity and Bacon's deeper immersion into, and his fascination with, the mysterious life of his own world and time. It corresponds to the animism that fascinated him in nature. Finally, if R. S. Crane is correct to see a synthesis in all of Bacon's work, his argument that the *Essays* are an integral part of a system of Instauration is wrong, at least in any limiting sense.[27] In fact, working with an aphoristic base, both as topic moving like a "skein" to be expanded and as functional structural control at any point in the discourse, the essays find increasingly their own mysterious and often enigmatic freedom outside of Bacon's objectifying six-level system of the Great Instauration and outside the uncluttered categories of critics. Experimentation in the *Essays* is of self and time, not nature. In fact, if there is subjectivity to be found anywhere in the canon of Bacon, it is found in the experience of reading these essays. Their dialectic of a discontinuous self and a progressive history demands an encounter of the reader's subjectivity and time, if not history. As centuries of readers have discovered, whatever the theories given for the essays, they finally submit only to reading, the experience of the text.

"Of Truth"

Bacon's 1625 book of essays opens with an aphorism that soon became famous: "*What is Truth?* said jesting Pilate; and would not stay for an answer" (6:377). The aphorism represents at the absolute beginning of his text the first premise of Bacon's continuing dialectic: truth, the absolute for which all human beings search, is contingent. It exists in a discontinuous moral universe where even conversation about the absolute is not completed. Bacon's reader is immediately defined, however obliquely, in the figure of Pilate. This reader reads only on the run. Given this dialectic, it is no surprise that, in this essay written only for the 1625 edition, Bacon begins with the same first step as that of his scientific method in the *Novum Organum*: the use of the negative or of exclusion in order to find, if at all, the positive. Not even the most originating figure of modern European culture, Jesus Christ, could be recognized as truth by Pilate, the representative of the greatest of all civilizations, Rome. The lack of leisure that Bacon told Prince Henry was evident in both the writer and his readers of 1612 is typified in the thoroughly modern Pilate. The Roman executive does not wait even for an answer from, in Bacon's culture, God Himself. Right away, therefore, in Bacon's text, a dialectic is set up between the reality of a truth and the fact that it cannot be easily known, at least in a broken world by an enchanted mind. The initial aphorism announces that this whole discourse on the grand metaphysical subject of truth will be less an analysis of a matter at the heart of every human culture and its systems of reality than of the nature of lies.

Bacon is bold in beginning this first "trial" or essay in short prose discourse with the most ideological of images in his culture. Religion was at the heart of warring social reality in 1625. However religious one actually might be, religious identity in 1625 meant political identity. Indeed, the English Revolution sprang, whatever economic and social struggles, fundamentally from a crisis of religious identity. In a culture, then, absolutely and firmly tied to the belief-system that Jesus Christ was the Son of God, and Christ Himself associated, in the imagery of the Gospel of John, with light and truth, Bacon dares to identify the highest anthropological basis of his culture with his own task of defining truth. With even more boldness, Bacon proceeds to ironize it. The irony in the opening aphorism thus sets up the dialectic by which truth exists not only as the totalizing Christ that ends the essay but also as, in the ending as in the opening reference to Christ, the finding of no faith upon the earth. As a result, "Of Truth" is about the experience of lies within the framework of a Christ as total truth to whom a leap in faith is possible but not likely.

Between this leap to Christ that begins and ends Bacon's discourse, the action of the essay takes place. If, in the famous Erasmian aphorism so propagandized by the English Reformation, truth is the daughter of time (*veritas temporis filia*), so truth could only rise from the experience of time, not its abstraction. The grand metaphysical subject must naturally then be reduced to reification, a series of things. So, in the next image, not the soul but the psychology of belief itself is examined. The tone of the narrator of the experience is properly censorious of those "that delight in giddiness, and count it a bondage to fix a belief; affecting free-will in thinking, as well as in acting." Yet in another aphorism, the experience of difficulty in trying to find truth points to a terrifying psychological conclusion about human nature: "But it is not only the difficulty and labour which men take in finding out of truth; nor again that when it is found it imposeth upon men's thoughts; that doth bring lies in favour; but a natural though corrupt love of the lie itself." The transition in these ideas offers little rational link, only a grammatical linking of clauses through antithesis and isocolon, as though the link of syntax and image were quite enough. Even worse, as the narrator echoes with a reference to the ancient Greek poet (Lucian), human beings "love lies, where neither they make for pleasure, as with poets, nor for advantage, as with the merchant; but for the lie's sake" (6:377).

Without any apparent logic, except to remind the reader of his essential dialectic, Bacon then adds a disclaimer in the front of such a mystery of profound evil in human nature. He reminds his reader of the encapsulating frame of the leap to Christ by recalling the Johannine analogy of light and truth, the source of an unmediated ideal intuition: "But I cannot tell: this same truth is a naked and open day-light" and it really cannot work well in a corrupt world "that doth not shew the masks and mummeries and triumphs of the world, half so stately and daintily as candle-lights." The reader's experience comes across, however, as ambiguous. For, if truth is naked like the daughter of time emerging from its cave in a 1525 woodcut so beloved by reformed Christians, still the syntactical lingering and alliteration in the attractions of nocturnal entertainments make the sensual world of "candle-lights" attractive. Signals are getting mixed. The mixture continues in the imagery of the precious stones that follow: pearls do show best by day but the brilliant diamond or carbuncle are, after all, more expensive and do indeed show "best in varied light." Then, to complicate the reader's response even more, the narrator of the essay announces that "a mixture of a lie doth ever add pleasure"—lies and sensuality once more combined. More terribly, now the narrator drives the point home: does any reader doubt that if the lies were taken out of opinions, hopes, evaluations, "imaginations as one would," human beings would not become "poor shrunken things, full of melancholy and indisposition, and unpleasing to themselves?" Even one of the Church Fathers, a group especially important in Anglican theology, condemned poetry "because it filleth the imagination" although for Bacon only "with the shadow of a lie." Up to this point, therefore, the whole sequence of "Of Truth" has developed through a series of trenchant sentences and examples. These rhetorical devices have been Bacon's primary resources for developing the *amplificatio* of his essays, with accumulation that has the programmatic effect of Agricola's place-logic or Ramist diagrams of knowledge. Indeed, use of the figure of *amplificatio*, as here, marks one of the few places where the methods of Bacon and Montaigne are similar. To end this sequence that makes the finding of truth increasingly improbable, Bacon resorts to another antithetical aphorism: "it is not the lie that passeth through the mind, but the lie that sinketh in and settleth in it, that doth the hurt" (6:377–8).

Then, as in a therapeutic session, having taken the reader to one end of the dialectical experience, Bacon turns and restates the positive frame to which the reader can "leap": "But howsoever these things are thus in men's depraved judgments and affections, yet truth, which only doth judge itself, teacheth that the inquiry of truth, which is the love-making or wooing of it, the knowledge of truth, which is the presence of it, and the belief of truth, which is the enjoying of it, is the sovereign good of human nature." The sexual metaphor dominates here, the relationship to truth reduced to the chronology of a satisfactory love affair. Also, this unity of good and truth is expanded from the *Antitheta* in the *De Augmentis* (4:82) and follows from Bacon's view on good and enjoyment (3:230). This relaxed note then leads to the more exalted identification of light—in the continuing Christological metaphor from the Gospel of John. Here it also refers to the hexameral myth of creation popular with Protestant England. Bacon dramatizes this continuance of light/truth in a series of triplets, a favorite device. If "the first creature of God, in the works of the days," is "the light of the sense" and the last on the sixth day is "the light of reason" in the human being, then God's "sabbath work ever since, is the illumination of his Spirit." Or: "first he breathed light upon the face of matter or chaos; then he breathed light into the face of man; and still he breatheth and inspireth light into the face of his chosen" (6:378).

This shift from the emphasis on the experience of the lie to experiencing light (interestingly with no metaphysical, Aristotelian, or Thomistic definition of truth) leads to Bacon's most idealistic point, the climax of a positive sequence. Bacon reverts, in a surprising twist, not to any Christian or biblical source but to a pagan author, Lucretius, one whose metaphysics was diametrically opposite to the Christian. Quoting the pleasure of having oneself *"upon the vantage ground of Truth,* (a hill not to be commanded, and where the air is always clear and serene), *and to see the errors, and wanderings, and mists, and tempest, in the vale below"*—the condition of Epicurean *ataraxia*—Bacon renders his clearest definition of truth. Ironically, beyond Christian or Jewish theology, readers are left, once more, with a certain questioning of absolute truth. Yet even this serenity of Lucretian truth is qualified for Bacon's purposes: "so always that this prospect be with pity, and not with swelling or pride." As Moody E. Prior has shown,[28] this characteristic of pity is the foremost sign of Bacon's ideal scientist and refers to compassion for a society lacking the revelations and technologies of the Baconian method. For the Father of Salomon's House in the *New Atlantis*, for example, charity means social renewal through new inventions that spring from "truth." Bacon can now give another definition to truth introduced by his most signifying adverb and built on an astronomical Ptolemaic metaphor: "Certainly, it is heaven upon earth, to have a man's mind move in charity, rest in providence, and turn upon the poles of truth" (6:378).

Instead of ending here, as other prose meditations might have done, with a theatrical climax, Bacon carries out another rhythm. It will identify the structural trajectory of most of his essays: that is, he begins with a magnificent opening, often with a deliberately memorable sentence or sentences, and winds down slowly, with an almost alogical turning and twisting. Bacon follows the more trivializing line of actual experience (including the experiencing of startling analogies and metaphors) rather than a tight syllogistic argument (although syllogisms come and go within this loose syntactic structure). The process is not to end with a bang, however, but a whimper, certainly a reduction in meaning. Thus the only place where there is a paragraph break in "Of Truth" shows quite consciously the deflation: "To pass from theological and philosophical truth, to the truth of civil business."

Once more the reader is plunged from one end of the dialectic to the other. The lie works, the narrator appears to be saying with his paragraph break. Honesty is "acknowledged even by those that practise it not" as "the honour of man's nature" and "mixture of falsehood" works like alloy in gold and silver to embase it. Truth therefore "may make the metal work the better." That is, truth can be useful. Such windings of lies are like "the goings of the serpent" and their social shame, for those being "found false and perfidious," is like no other vice. Here, in his first essay, Bacon quotes the author of the genre. Montaigne "saith prettily," says Bacon, that a human being who lies *"is brave towards God and a coward towards men. For a lie faces God, and shrinks from man."* But, and here Bacon ends his essay abruptly, this "wickedness of falsehood and breach of faith" will never end. Is it possible such "wickedness" will "be the last peal to call the judgments of God upon the generations of men"? Christian scripture is clear. When Christ returns, *"he shall not find faith upon the earth"* (6:378–9). If the reader at the end now has a clearer and more experiential feeling of what the search for an absolute can entail, he or she also has a sense of the ambiguity of the meaning of any absolute and of its own contingency. The reader has become, in fact, through the experience of the essay, very much like Pilate. Bacon has begun his book.

Bacon's Audience: The Maker of Time

If the form of a Bacon essay can be understood as an expanded aphorism, the form exists only in dialectic with that other essential of any Baconian text: audience. In Bacon, audience originates both the occasion for any text at all and then for its performance. If the "dispersed" series of aphorisms mark the broken world that can no longer allow grand performances of language like Ralegh's *History of the World* (contemporary with Bacon's *Advancement*), for example, without terrible distortion and even absurdity, audience represents the other side of Bacon's dialectic of history that demands new representation. Bacon's contemporary and personal physician, William Harvey, who discovered the circulation of the blood, was quite right about Bacon. Harvey told Aubrey that not only was Bacon's "delicate, lively, hazel Eie" like the eye of a viper (the master observer), but that "He writes Philosophy like a Lord Chancellor."[29] Whether Harvey was sneering or not, Bacon's sense of audience and his program of action for it dominates every text. With this sense of audience, Bacon is writing in the *Essays* another kind of Renaissance "courtesy book" in the same mode as his uncle Sir Thomas Hoby's translation of Castiglione's *The Book of the Courtier* and in the mode of that other popular text for young men in the Renaissance, Cicero's *De Officiis* (written as advice book for a luckless son).

For such readers, then, Bacon's "medicinable" essays are creating, through the continuity and health of dialectical serial texts, a personality, a new maker of knowledge and history. If the subjectivity of the reader can be so controlled and shaped by texts into a new persona on the discontinuous stage of Renaissance history, then this new convert-reader will be Bacon's figuration of the *Faber Fortunae* or the Maker of Fortune or Time or History. Derived from Plautus, Livy, and Virgil,[30] Bacon's collective maker of history will move from the serial figuration of the *Essays* to the magus-Father of Solomon's House in Bacon's *New Atlantis*. For the audience, however, this new Maker of Time exists only on stage. He lives in the essays in syncopated texts moving from "Of Truth" to "Of Vicissitude of Things"—the last essay in the 1625

Essays—the process of which suggests the dialectic of history will always move from certainty to ambiguity. The *Essays* thus reveal a process that involves confrontation with the negative and evil itself: "So that we are much beholden to Machiavel and others, that write what men do and not what they ought to do" because in this world "it is not possible to join serpentine wisdom with the columbine innocency," what Christ in the gospel of Matthew had commanded his disciples to have as they went out to convert, "except men know exactly all the conditions of the serpent." Bacon analogizes from the fable of the basilisk: "if he see you first you die for it, but if you see him first he dieth; so it is with deceits and evil arts; which if they be first espied they leese [lose] their life, but if they prevent ["come before"] they endanger" (3:430–1). Only in the process of reading will the dialectical confrontation take place to offer therapy and meaning.

Thus, the individual essays provide a technology for a plural personality—a collective young man—who is moving through the fifty-eight topics of life revealed in the 1625 *Essays*. In the terms of Jardine, "basically these essays communicate precepts for the guidance of personal conduct in public affairs, based on Bacon's own political experience" and are "straightforwardly instructive, but without any attempt to justify rationally the knowledge which they transmit."[31] This justification rises, in fact, from the reading process itself and the dialectical terms that give rise to it. From such a justification greater than rationality, the experience of the essays leads to a recapitulation in actual history of the self's own dialectic with a Heraclitean flux of time.

Because this self is always changing in relationship to that history surrounding it, the shifting focus and valence of individual essays can be best illustrated by seeing them in context with each other. In context they form subtle networks influencing the reader like the argument of a master lawyer. The essays are at their most "medicinal" in this intersection with other texts, for such is the nature of discontinuous time that the human Maker of History can only be ready to confront it through interweaving therapy. Flux must fight flux. So, if subjectivity starts from an epistemology of one, it never remains there. Reality is always plural.

In the three following analyses, a central essay forms a focus for a network of other essays. This network intersects, in turn, with the complicated motion of other galaxies of meaning and structure (their intersecting analyses beyond the scope of this brief study). As always, it is the rhythm of the essays, the serial process, not necessarily the truth of ideas, that the young reader is enjoined to enter as an experience, even a dance. The syncopated therapy of the individual essay readies the reader to enter history and "deliver" it.

"Of Studies"

As the child and grandchild of militant humanists, Bacon could not but recognize that, for the maker of new knowledge, the role of proper studies was crucial. Bacon's famous opening aphorism sets this paradigm of roles for his audience within a typically tripartite division: "Studies serve for delight, for ornament, and for ability." This figure of partitio expands: "Their chief use for delight, is in privateness and retiring; for ornament, is in discourse; and for ability, is in the judgment and disposition of business" (6:497). Thus, the function of studies begins as a private matter (and will always remain a private "delight" for the self) but evolves into methods for discourse and business, basic arenas for any human society. The dialectic of the essay is set from the start.

Precisely this role of public self is defined in the same dichotomous terms in a 1625 essay, updated from 1612, "Of Wisdom For a Man's Self." Bacon opens the essay with an insect image that deflates the exalted notion of wisdom: "An ant is a wise creature for itself, but it is a shrewd [mischievous] thing in an orchard or garden." Then Bacon adds: "And certainly men that are great lovers of themselves waste the public. Divide with reason between self-love and society; and so be true to thyself as thou be not false to others, specially to thy king and country. It is a poor centre of a man's actions, *himself*. It is right earth" (6:431–3). From the insect image to the Ptolemaic image of the earth, Bacon redefines the higher position of love of society before "self-love" but with his usual inherent contradictions: are "self-love" and being "true to thyself" real equivalents? If not, then why are they placed in juxtaposition? If the essay defines, in true Ciceronian fashion, the greater worth of a human being in social identity, the question of self still remains open.

Studies or reading can bridge this gap or at least learn to use the inescapable tension of self and society to advantage. Thus, in his third sentence of "Of Studies," the author notes that "expert men" can carry projects out and "perhaps judge of particulars, one by one" (as an ant). But the ability to judge generally, to see the larger picture "and the plots and marshalling of affairs, come best from those that are learned." Yet, if those capable of generalizing have a power over the immediate, the books and studies that produce this power have their own limitations. With an abrupt shift—but far more ameliorated than the shifts at the same place in the 1597 and 1612 essays on the same topic—the author lists these dangers in an antithetical aphorism, in a building figure, a gradatio of disgust: "To spend too much time in studies is sloth; to use them too much for ornament, is affectation; to make judgment wholly by their rules, is the humour of a scholar." In another aphorism, with variations on antithetical balance, the author shows the correct balance between the intellectual and his communal world. Studies "perfect nature, and are perfected by experience; for natural abilities are like natural plants, that need proyning [pruning] by study; and studies themselves do give forth directions too much at large, except they be bounded in by experience" (6:497). It should also be noted that one of the best means to "bind in" studies by experience is in the controlled and artificial world of travel. "Of Travel" opens with just such a generality: "Travel, in the younger sort, is a part of education; in the elder, a part of experience" (6:417–8). This essay with its precise particulars reads like a Renaissance manual or a Jacobean Baedeker, but it recommends special uses like keeping a diary, the latter influencing later young Englishmen on the Continent, especially John Evelyn.)

With this recall to experience as the basis for real learning, Bacon's readers of "Of Studies" may wonder logically just where they are. How is learning to be valued? The author of the text hurries to reassure them with another series of aphorisms that carry not only syntactic figures of isocolon but a constant tension between directions forward and backward. Typically, they affirm the value of studies and then denigrate their ultimate power. "Crafty men contemn studies, simple men admire them, and wise men use them; for they teach not their own use; but that is a wisdom without them, and above them, won by observation." Even the process of reading—"read not to contradict and confute; not to believe and take for granted; not to find talk and discourse"—appears straitjacketed and leads to a frustrating act that can neither affirm nor deny but "weigh and consider."

With a turn hardly logical in connection (except to follow out the process of having to "weigh and consider"), Bacon gives one of his most famous aphorisms, a masterpiece of antithetical structure that serves the purpose here of defining the whole process of reading. It offers a discriminating labor, not particularly inviting, and the rather violent metaphor of eating books does not help. If the intent here is once more to reduce an idealistic frame to an empirical one, Bacon has followed through with his own staging. Typically he gives the metaphor, then explains it as tripartite, expecting the audience to admire both the performance of the analogy and its stylistic device, now singled out—"that is"—as though on stage: "Some books are to be tasted, others to be swallowed, and some few to be read wholly, and with diligence and attention; that is, some books are to be read only in parts; others to be read, but not curiously; and some few to be read wholly, and with diligence and attention." Bacon would immediately continue to deflate the transcendent act of gaining knowledge through reading by turning to the rather demeaning question of whether to read "by deputy, and extracts made of them by others." He recommends it "for the less important arguments, and the meaner sort of books." The reader is turned around once more, for such books can be low things and "distilled books like common distilled waters, flashy things" (6:497–8).

With one more seemingly illogical turn, Bacon offers another aphorism with its antitheses, isocolon, and asyndeton. It is one of his most famous that reveals not so much about studies or knowledge but their effect: "Reading maketh a full man; conference a ready man; and writing an exact man." Bacon can now reduce studies to a kind of therapeutic series: "And therefore, if a man write little, he had need have a great memory; if he confer little, he had need have a present wit; and if he read little, he had need to have much cunning, to seem to know that he doth not." Then, as if to give his reader a positive sense of purpose to studies, Bacon lends to studies the quality of endowing the reader with personality traits: "Histories make men wise; poets witty; the mathematics subtile; natural philosophy deep; moral grave; logic and rhetoric able to contend." He concludes with a Latin quotation (untranslated) from Ovid: studies become manners. Bacon is now free, once more, to reduce the intellectual life to the social.

With a final catalogue that stunningly reduces transcendent intellectual life, he compares problems of the mind to diseases of the body: "Nay there is no stond or impediment in the wit, but may be wrought out by fit studies: like as diseases of the body may have appropriate exercises." If bowling "is good for the stone and reins" and "shooting for the lungs and breast" and so on, "so if a man's wit be wandering, let him study the mathematics; for in demonstrations, if his wit be called away never so little, he must begin again" and "if he be not apt to beat over matters, and to call up one thing to prove and illustrate another, let him study the lawyers' cases." With the flattest of closures—"So every defect of the mind may have a special receipt" (6:498)—Bacon leaves the subject (and the reader) deliberately dangling in this unfinished, if not frustrated, state, ready to move on to the next essay.

Finally, if the placement of essays in the 1625 edition originated with Bacon himself, and there is every reason to think that it did, then the place of "Of Studies" was itself another device of structure. This essay that asserts the power of reading and intellectual growth lies between "Of Suitors" and "Of Faction," essays obviously concerned with court political life and, beyond these, on either side of them, the carefully organized and ambiguous "Of Ceremonies and Respects" and "Of Followers and Friends," more essays that stress the directions needed for success at court and in the world. Situated therefore as the fiftieth essay, "Of Studies" reminds the reader strongly of the dialectic that operates in Bacon's choice of subjects for the essays. By its appearance and place, "Of Studies" counterbalances all the political and social necessities surrounding the composite self being generated in all fifty-eight essays.

"Of Cunning"

Essential to this textual experience of balance and integration is the very fact of the social and historical experiences transforming the self inside the text and outside of it. Bacon's assertive self must confront these. His world is textualized neither as gnostic nor as angelic. In fact, the changes from the 1612 version of "Of Cunning" to the 1625 final essay show this attempt by Bacon to set up a textual basis for the experience of adaptation within the reader. For one thing, Bacon adds more detailed examples in 1625 that keep a tension and interplay between the negative view of cunning and its uses and the positive. The ambiguity is not lessened but enlarged in this third essay that completes a carefully written sequence after "Of Counsels" and "Of Delays." The reader who emerges from the "medicinable" experience of "Of Cunning" is ready, as in Stoic therapy, to encounter a world falling apart (in fact, in 1625 ready for a revolution). Bacon's opening sentence gets immediately to the point: "We take Cunning for a sinister or crooked wisdom." The verb "take" carries its meaning of "assume" and is therefore hardly absolute. The next sentence continues the ambiguity—the "certainly" is reversed by the disturbing thought at the end of the sentence that the good guy—"a wise man"—is not being referred to: "And certainly there is a great difference between a cunning man and a wise man; not only in point of honesty, but in point of ability." There are simply no easy answers: "Again, it is one thing to understand persons, and another thing to understand matters; for many are perfect in men's humours, that are not greatly capable of the real part of business; which is the constitution of one that hath studied men more than books." Neither type appears superior here; old judgments do not seem to work. These persons who cannot make the act of generalization discussed in "Of Studies" because they have lacked reading and the learning of the intellectual life are still valuable, and so, "because these cunning men are like haberdashers of small wares, it is not amiss to set forth their shop" (6:428).

With this introduction, Bacon turns to his listing of these "wares" in a figure of merismus, and his first item is his most startling, with, as Fish notes (130), its powerful use of the second person: "It is a point of cunning, to wait upon him with whom you speak, with your eye; as the Jesuits give it in precept: for there be many wise men that have secret hearts and transparent countenances. Yet this would be done with a demure abasing of your eye sometimes, as the Jesuits also do use." In this listing, there are an unusual number of references to his own time, for example, the old English trick called *"The turning of the cat in the pan"* (or what one man says to another when "he lays it as if another had said it to him") or an event of crafty discovery made in a busy thoroughfare like the main aisle in the nave of St. Paul's Cathedral in London. It should be noted that Bacon's friend Tobie Matthew had been ordained a Jesuit in 1614 and if, as Kiernan notes (221), Matthew sent a copy of the rules of the Society of Jesus to John Donne in 1619, it is quite likely that, living with Bacon, as Matthew did after his return from Spain in 1621, he would have given Bacon the same. Bacon had also tortured Jesuits, as the record of Fr. John Gerard shows but he knew and admired the breed.

Bacon completes his catalogue of "wares" by admitting they are "infinite" but that "it were a good deed to make a list of them; for that nothing doth moe hurt in a state than that cunning men pass for wise." In this dialectic, therefore, where absolute structures of good and evil do not work, Bacon has represented for the reader an experience of how to use the evil. His closure, the last sentence, quotes Solomon in Latin, a favorite aphorism that sums up the choice always before his audience: "Prudens advertit ad gressus suos: stultus divertit ad dolos" (the wise man looks to his steps; the fool turns aside to deceits) (6.428–31). In either case, cunning cannot be ignored for any transcendent principle. Indeed, no such principle exists except within such an ambiguous experience as rendered in Bacon's text. Its ambiguity thus so rendered, by no accident, the next essay in this sequence, "Of Wisdom for a Man's Self" condemns selfishness of the individual who does not make his social self the higher form of his being. Within this social imperative, dramatized in the essay, the whole question of the morality of cunning must now be re-examined.

This seeming crassness in terms of morality has marked much of the criticism aimed at Bacon's essays throughout the centuries. As often as not, such criticism does not take into account two fundamental premises, already discussed, in Bacon's reading of his world: (1) the highest identity for each human being is that of social being and (2) the utter corruption and the "enchanted glass" of the human mind at the heart of all reality. Given such premises, individual morality based on codes from the Romantics or the Enlightenment could never be a concern for Bacon. Indeed, for him, such an individual or personality so "free" may even be unimaginable. Within this cycle, therefore, of essays that stem from a dialectical matrix like that in "Of Cunning," Bacon's advice may or may not be good for Satan's kingdom, but just before the English Revolution (and later) it was thought quite good for young men from Eton or Gray's Inn or any other training center for future wheelers and dealers of the state. There may indeed be questions of whether or not the structures in essays like "Of Boldness," "Of Seditions and Troubles," "Of Seeming Wise," and "Of Honour and Reputation" admit to what was once called literary. As both Fish and Jardine[32] have shown in their analyses of "Of Simulation and Dissimulation," however, such brief discourses as those in a cycle with "Of Cunning" are quite literary by any standards of a text, both as social or political documents and within their own structural terms. Even if the essays "Of Discourse" and "Of Negotiating" appear virtually the same in their specific codes of rhetorical response and "how-to" advice, the similarity is simply another way Bacon reminds his audience that social identity determines the success of any action. In a world founded on an epistemological failure and always open to breakdown and social collapse, the only way to escape dissolution is clear: the social body must communicate, and communication does not mean a lyric poem of self.

For this reason, to the horror of modern and post-modern readers, an essay like "Of Ceremonies and Respects" appears quite natural and useful. Indeed, this essay comes after "Of Faction," with its Roman, modern Italian, and French examples, and the opening aphorism in "Of Ceremonies and Respects" is an attack on all forms of "sincerity" and individuality: "He that is only real, had need have exceeding great parts of virtue; as the stone [jewel] had need to be rich that is set without foil."

If this opening can also be read as praise for honesty, the ambivalence sets the Baconian dialectic, and what sounds reasoned is merely suggested, as Jardine notes.[33] Ceremonies are neither good nor bad, but if used lightly and "continually in use" they can serve a young courtier's or young lawyer's cause: "Therefore it doth much add to a man's reputation, and is (as Queen Isabella said) *like perpetual letters commendatory*, to have good forms" (6:500).

Also, by no surprise, the cue to good ceremonies and respects is timing: "Some men's behaviour is like a verse, wherein every syllable is measured; how can a man comprehend great matters, that breaketh his mind too much to small observations?" If advice here is generally the positive through the negative, so is any question of timing: only through what is not possible in limited time can one tell what is possible. As Bacon implies in his closure of two aphoristic statements, learning control from the experience of the essay can give readers freedom because they learn the right timing. Such timing is expressed now in the closing aphorisms of a proverb and an apophthegm: "A wise man will make more opportunies than he finds. Men's behaviour should be like their apparel, not too strait or point device, but free for exercise or motion" (6:500–1). If manners and character are here reduced to clothes, the analogy may be unsettling to an outrageous style- and clothes-conscious late twentieth-century world (because it implies there is any connection at all). To Bacon's first audiences, the shock came from the reduction. Ceremonies carry no transcendence in themselves, Bacon is saying. They are no more than clothes. The point of this essay, as all those in the cycle focused in "Of Cunning," then, is the social freedom that ceremonies allow the new Maker of Time and History—if, however, such ceremonies are controlled. They are, in fact, nothing more than instruments for control. The flatness of the final image proves the triviality of instrument: gesture as transcendence is dead.

The whole subject of ceremonies as debated and experienced is thus a perfect setup for the three essays that follow, "Of Praise" (the right kind); "Of Vainglory" (its dangers); and "Of Honour and Reputation" (crucial for a courtier, lawyer, or citizen in 1625). In turn, by no accident, they lead to the final sequence of the whole book. This sequence builds on an analysis of social order as seen in "Of Judicature" followed by dissection of a dangerous subjectivity as in "Of Anger" before the cosmic limits of all human life in "Of Vicissitude of Things."

"Of Adversity"

In this essay, presented early on as number five in the 1625 volume, Bacon reveals the basic structure of all his *Essays*. In them, hope remains, although the realities to be found in a negative examination of human life "are to be admired"—that is, in the Latin etymology, wondered at. Such wonder is for Bacon in the *Advancement of Learning* "the seed of knowledge" so that "having regard to God" there is "no perfect knowledge, but wonder, which is broken knowledge" (3:266–7). If wonder can only come from discontinuity or the broken, then negative realities must be recognized. The negative may express, in fact, opportunity for learning, as Bacon's second proverbial sentence in this text points out: "Certainly if miracles be the command over nature, they appear most in adversity." True greatness consists, Bacon finds in a quotation from Seneca, in having the fraility of a human being and the security of a god, and the strange myth of Hercules who sailed to save Prometheus "in an earthen pot or pitcher" illustrates this power. Having certified the moral life by citing pagan examples, Bacon then transforms the "lively" Hercules image so that it describes "Christian resolution, that saileth in the frail bark of the flesh thorough the waves of the world." Even this pagan illustration made Christian is undercut, however, and deconstructed: Seneca's noble definition of human nature "would have done better in poesy, where transcendences are more allowed" (6:386).

Early on in his book, therefore, Bacon has described to his audience his dialectical method of examining possibilities, of moving between poles of reality that may be uncomfortable but necessary and "medicinable." This painful motion between poles will not end even in the final essay of his 1625 volume, "Of Vicissitude of Things." In another enactment of the nature of time itself, Bacon opens the last essay with dramatic evocation of one of the Bible's most spectacular statements, the epanodos on time, in the Book of Ecclesiastes: "Salomon saith, *There is no new thing upon the earth.*" The audience is reminded at once, here at the end, that all is passing and, in Bacon's second sentence, quoting from Plato, "*all knowledge was but remembrance.*" Another aphorism in the last essay marks this same point of vicissitude: "Certain it is, that the matter is in a perpetual flux, and never at a stay." Deluges, earthquakes, fires, the larger cosmic disasters that determine history, are to be balanced by the human disasters. The latter are, for Bacon in 1625 (who was, no doubt, aware of the danger of civil war), most focused in "the vicissitudes of sects and religions." After giving particulars of the problems of sectarianism, he then turns to the "changes and vicissitudes of wars" and the inevitability of empires to collapse amid the force of new weapons and the conduct of war. After tracing a chronology of learning from child to "old age, when it waxeth dry and exhaust," Bacon abruptly ends his book. The same apparent indecision and lack of dramatic closure typical of almost all the other essays obtains here too when Bacon writes: "But it is not good to look too long upon these turning wheels of vicissitude, lest we become giddy. As for the philology of them, that is but a circle of tales, and therefore not fit for this writing" (6:512–7). The reader should not linger, Bacon seems to be saying, with this text or with contemplating the terrors of living in discontinuous time but move on from such transcendences and "tales." What counts in history is action.

If Bacon's actual ending for his book of essays deliberately intends to be unliterary, pointing the reader toward the world of natural fact, not poetry and mind, there is one essay that reverses the regular order of Bacon's series. "Of Adversity," the shortest of Bacon's essays, moves unlike the others from a rather flat beginning to a closure worthy of a lyric poem. "Of Adversity" sums up, in fact, all of Bacon's conceptualization of the form and genre of the essay. So, it is natural, after quoting Seneca, Bacon follows a familiar pattern. Switching (as in his first essay "Of Truth") in the phrase "but to speak in a mean," Bacon continues his series of expanded aphorisms (less expanded here than in longer essays), each of which acts and interacts with particulars from history or nature or some other aspect of common life to give the experience of adversity itself.

What is being developed in this associative and alogical structure (which may in fact use syllogisms and enthymemes) is a linguistic transformation: the individual text and then the book as a whole are performing like some natural phenomenon that will itself possess, with its uncontrollable and ambiguous but fascinating energy, a life to be tried and experimented within a process of survival, that is, textualization. Bacon's readers are to act like the new scientists of induction and experiment. In other words, this text, with its staged discontinuities, brings hope and possible survival if read as an experimental text for new Makers of History and Fortune and then enacted in their worlds. If such "trial" as this essay and the networks of essays around it are read through to the last essay "Of Vicissitude," they can lead to enlightenment, some recapturing of the archaic ideal intuition that motivates and drives the series. A new *Faber Fortunae* might be born. Birth will be a matter of the right textual dialectic. "Prosperity is the blessing of the Old Testament," Bacon concludes in his essay, cheering his reader on; "Adversity is the blessing of the New; which carrieth the greater benediction, and the clearer revelation of God's favour." In this ideological certainty, only the experience of the negative can produce the positive: "Certainly virtue is like precious odours, most fragrant when they are incensed or crushed: for Prosperity doth best discover vice, but Adversity doth best discover virtue" (6:386).

It is probably true that Bacon's *Essays* offer an experience of reading like nothing else in literature. For those who have learned to read the essays and to live them, that is, to follow the performative texts as Bacon wrote them, the experience remains quite different from any other reading, more like a post-modern text than a Victorian prose discourse. Not always pleasant or even interesting, the experience of Bacon's *Essays* is always *sui generis* and originating, as four centuries of readers have proved. Ironically, this phenomenon of longevity would have typically interested the Lord Chancellor himself. Bacon would have immediately set out to investigate it.

Chapter Three

Actual Makers of Time: The Experience of *Henry VII* and Bacon's Law Texts

The method of the *Essays*, with their special dramatization of human experience trapped in Bacon's dialectic of time, led to *The Historie of the Raigne of King Henry the Seventh*, "the first major historical biography in the English language."[1] The logic of this development came, once more, from Bacon's attempt to represent the world as it actually existed or, as he wrote in one of his earliest texts, the "true and inward" sources of reality that originate in the ordinary, "the smaller passages and motions of men and matter," for "such being the workmanship of God, that he hangs the greatest weights upon the smallest springs" (4:304). Any theory of historiography must begin therefore in the particular, even if the subject is the highest person in the realm such as Henry VII. Further, with Stoic roots, Bacon's text would incorporate into its particularizing representation a kind of therapeutic reading. Like the *Essays*, Bacon's biographical text of the first Tudor monarch, in no sense hagiographical, would lead a renewed reader to return to the world of actuality. There readers could either endure terrible tensions, the harshest agons of their own theater, or reform them, or in Bacon's revision of classical Stoicism, actualize both endurance and reformation.

Bacon's only finished history, the first of a cycle based on Renaissance monarchs that he intended to write, was immediately popular, as the gossiping John Chamberlain noted.[2] It influenced court and university intellectuals ranging from Lord Herbert of Cherbury to John Selden (in one version of Bacon's will, an executor). In fact, Bacon thought it so important that, in his last days, with the *Essays* and the *Advancement of Learning*, he was supervising its translation into Latin. It had been the first fruit of his *quinquinneum*, as Bacon described his last five years (14:297), and he had sent it to the King in 1621 for approval before he published it the next year as proof of his continuous influence on his time. The King made a few changes, not in the least noticing the revo-

lutionary nature of what he read. Bacon had written the text in exile at
Gorhambury from the libraries and archives of London, and at its end
the text shows hasty writing (lapsing into the style of the annalist). Nevertheless, Bacon had invented the first psychological history in English—a clear prelude to the novel. What had been discussed in Bacon's
Advancement of Learning as a desideratum for human nature and enacted
as composite experience in the *Essays* was now focused in this new
genre of English biography. Such an experience Bacon's text could offer
readers as it revealed a narrative with the ranging dialectic of a twentieth-century post-modernist text. The story begins with Richard III's
defeat and then renders the transformation of the outlaw Henry Tudor
into a rich, unloved, but quite stable King Henry VII, an actualized
Maker of History and Fortune. Bacon's *Faber Fortunae* has moved from
theory to living reality, a figure brooding over the ambiguities of time
and the pain of subjectivity trying to control its history, as early in the
Bacon's text: "But King Henry, in the very entrance of his reign and
the instant of time when the kingdom was cast into his arms, met with
a point of great difficulty and knotty to solve, able to trouble and confound the wisest King in the newness of his estate; and so much the
more, because it could not endure a deliberation, but must be at once
deliberated and determined" (6:29). Bacon's text thus reversed all the
presuppositions of his world with its concept, for example, of the Great
Chain of Being. Bacon had declared that history is the first of the three
divisions of all human knowledge in his *Advancement of Learning*.[3] It was
therefore essential that history be represented as it was. That is, to portray his world as it actually existed, Bacon had to manipulate the subject-object relationship in a special way. Bacon must textualize a portrayal of subjectivity that rules supposedly objective reality. As in the
Essays, the deepest involvement with the objective world actually
springs from subjective responses to "occasions"—in this case, the
responses of the frightened mind of a king with its own "idols" and
enchantments. The King himself becomes little more than an ambiguous subject encountering the ambiguities of history. As Edward Berry
notes, "Whether in the Perkin Warbeck episode, in his dealings with
successive Parliaments, or in his negotiations with the French, both the
successes and failures of Henry's policies are almost invariably traced to
a source in his [Henry VII's] own mind." In this sense, even history
becomes subjectivity as "political problems resolve themselves into psychological ones." The "contrapuntal progression" in narrative shifts
between a world as it is and a will that is attempting to control that

world or be killed, as Henry Tudor himself had billed Richard III.[4] This sense of a progressive and inescapable dialectic in the nature of social reality continually inscribes the structure of Bacon's historical text. Thus Bacon begins with the old-fashioned humanist and negative figuration of Richard III (one of a number of critical resemblances of this text with that of Thomas More's equally ambiguous hero). Bacon borrows from the old techniques of allegory with ironic results. What appears, with its categorical imperatives and stiff posturing, performs with a strange nemesis: by the end of the text, the young Tudor hero who has responded and borne within himself the terrible burdens and chimeras of his time has himself become a monster of history not unlike Richard III.

Therefore, Bacon's portrayal of so subjective a King as the ruler of objective reality was an ironic reversal of all previous heroic encomia and a deflating of all secular authority as a heroic or holy Other. Bacon even goes a step further than the ironizations of Shakespeare's history plays when he details in a special narrative style the desacralization of royal reality. For this desacralization, the portrayal of a world as it is—the negative state necessary before positive probabilities can be considered—Bacon develops a special literary strategy. It would be a variation on his "initiative" style as described in the 1605 *Advancement of Learning*: "but yet nevertheless, *secundum majus et minus* [according to more or less], a man may revisit and descend unto the foundations of his knowledge and consent; and so transplant it into another as it grew in his own mind" (3:404). In this process of transplanted experience (the metaphor from Bacon's beloved processes of gardening), the reader's subjectivity can enter into the objective history Bacon is unfolding through his particularized or "initiative" style. This objectivity of such style portrays, in turn, the subjectivity of a model figuration.

Thus, particular facts from a specific history would "transplant" the reader, not generalizations. In such particularizing method, as Bacon comments in his 1623 *De Augmentis Scientiarum*, "the difficulty" in writing good Civil History is "as great as the Dignity" ("Ad dignitatem rei accedit difficultas non minor").[5] In this definition Bacon inscribes a revolutionary premise for historiography: the dignity of history rises from its difficulty of particular facts and not necessarily from its harmony. "Civil knowledge," writes Bacon in his 1605 *Advancement*, "is conversant about a subject which of all others is most immersed in matter, and hardliest reduced to axiom" (3:445). To "reduce" such "matter" or facts to the forms of writing, therefore, the new historian must have the right eye, the right observation. This facility of shrewd observation is the reason why Bacon prefers the Latin historian Tacitus to abstract philosophical systems of the ancients, as he notes in his early work *Temporis Partus Masculus* (The Masculine Birth of Time): "the ethics of Plato and Aristotle are much admired; but the pages of Tacitus breathe a livelier and truer observation of morals and institutions."[6]

Once his reifying history is established, such "reduced" facts in the narrative could open up the reader's subjectivity to the subjectivity of the King but only through a second step. The facts must exist in a seriality or a collectivity of text. Here the style must center on the mind of Bacon's new hero as revealed in the series of facts. A total psychological history could be initiated but only through Bacon's "initiative" style that allows facts to reveal their discontinuity and their intractability before the brooding self, both the King's and the reader's. Their relationship or dialectic of one to the other marks the point of reading Bacon's text. If subjectivity appears too much a twentieth-century term for this self, Bacon has his own Thomistic nomenclature for his blend of the mental and the physical, the self and historical facts, or his version of the subject-object dichotomy. "Above all things," Bacon writes, defining the nature of history in his 1623 Latin translation of the *Advancement*, "(for this is the ornament and life of Civil History), I wish events to be coupled with their causes" (4:300–1). He would have the reader meditate on the dispersed occasions of the narrative. In fact, because of Bacon's theory of a mixed history—event and self—Leonard Dean sees Bacon as "one of the most important English advocates of what may be called the Polybian or Florentine theory of history-writing,"[7] one based on psychological fact. In no sense, then, can the search for true causes come from abstract moral philosophy. Rather, like Machiavelli's history, Bacon's must also focus on "what men do and not what men ought to do" (3:430). As George Nadel argues, for Bacon "history, its insights psychological, its method inductive, must replace conventional moral philosophy in the instauration of learning." The new historian, like the new scientist, can, in the new inductive and particularized logic of historiography, "reveal the seen and unseen springs of human behavior."[8] Bacon himself defines this new task: "For to carry the mind in writing back into the past, and bring it into sympathy with antiquity; diligently to examine, freely and faithfully to report, and by the light of words to place, as it were, before the eyes, the revolutions [motus] of times, the characters of persons, the fluctuations of counsels, the courses and currents of actions, the bottoms of pretences, and the secrets of governments; is a task of great labour and judgment—the rather because in ancient transactions the truth is difficult to ascertain, and in modern it is dangerous to tell" (4:302).

For such a fluid, plural rendering of reality, Bacon must develop a loose style, open to realistic analysis of the discontinuous event. In his masterful treatment of the Perkin Warbeck episode, Bacon allows, for example, the reader to see a dual vision through a special stylization: first, the reader's view of the objective Henry VII and then the King's fearful eye looking on the male beauty of the young imposter bewitching most of Europe and, in Henry's terror, bewitching the King in a virtual dance of death. This dance or narrative of deception is rendered in a special associative sequence, with looser and more asymmetrical sentences (evident already in the opening passage of the book), with clausal and phrasal subordination often sacrificing grammatical clarity for mental processes. Thus, when the handsome and vulnerable Perkin finally believes his own lie, Bacon writes: "Nay himself with long and continual counterfeiting and with often telling a lie, was turned (by habit) almost into the thing he seemed to be, and from a liar to a believer." Then, in another example, Bacon writes how the "wise, stout, and fortunate" King is sucked into the intrigues of the young man, and, after his capture, "from his first appearance upon the stage in his new person of a sycophant or juggler, instead of his former person of a Prince," Perkin is watched secretly by the King "out of a window or in passage" as the King sets up a kind of "may-game" for taunting the imposter. Then, when Henry VII finally makes an "end of this little cockatrice [Perkin] of a King, that was able to destroy those that did not espy him first" (spying and seeing a key image-pattern in the entire text), the whole event is metonymic of Bacon's entire narrative. It has become "one of the longest plays of that kind that hath been in memory, and might perhaps have had another end, if he had not met with a King both wise, stout, and fortunate" (6:203).

For this kind of realistic and ambiguous analysis, the more ranging style of Montaigne—what Morris Croll calls the "loose Senecan"[9]—replaces the aphoristic (as Berry notes, there are only four true aphorisms in the text[10]). Montaigne's own theorizing about his style can also be applied to Bacon's text on Henry VII. "I cannot keep my subject still," he writes in "Of Repentance," and that freedom inherent in such particularity leads the insouciant Montaigne to his special assertion of content and form: "I do not portray being; I portray passing" with "a record of various and changeable occurrences, and of irresolute, and when it so befalls, contradictory ideas." Sounding like Henry VII at the opening of Bacon's text, the French essayist continues: "If the mind could gain a firm footing, I would not make an essay, I would make decisions; but [the mind] is always in apprenticeship and on trial."[11]

Set, therefore, in such a living style, the particularities of Bacon's text form a network of objective realism surrounding his royal subject. For this novelty of textual realism (clearly adumbrating the English novel), Bacon apologizes in the dedication of his 1622 English text to Prince Charles. Although Henry VII as authorizing ancestor of Charles I and all the Stuarts (through Mary Queen of Scots' grandmother, Henry VII's daughter) "was a wise man, and an excellent King," still the first Tudor's "times were rough, and full of mutations and rare accidents." Following Bacon's own theory from "the wiser sort of historians" that "a character so worked into the narrative gives a better idea of the man, than any formal criticism and review can," Bacon sees King Henry VII in a "commixture" with the King's own time, of "actions both greater and smaller, public and private." This mixture describes the best sort of "Lives," a major division of history in Bacon's scheme of knowledge and learning in his *Advancement of Learning* (3:334). Thus, working with such conscious theory, Bacon's method of composition has been no accident, as Bacon tells the young Prince of Wales in a metaphor of painting: "I have not flattered him, but took him to life as well as I could, sitting so far off, and having no better light" (6:25).

Bacon is right about his own text: his "commixture" of events and characters provides a dialectical framing for any reader's interpretation. In this "commixture," Henry VII becomes less the objective *Faber Fortunae*, the founder of England's greatest dynasties, and more the mystery of human epistemology itself—the self seeking and making knowledge in terrorizing encounters with time. For Bacon, the reader can discover these encounters and, reading them, gain the endurance and survival of the self in one's own special serial narrative.

The Law Works: Texts of Professional Experience

In his essay "Francis Bacon, Inquisitor," Kenneth Cardwell comments on one aspect of Bacon's law career that epitomizes the two actualizing and originating forces behind his major law texts: (1) their total immersion in the matter of time and society and (2) their hortative or propaedeutic framing—that is, their desire to transform the common laws of Elizabethan and Jacobean England into more rationalizing language (whether Roman civil law or not) or at the least into linguistic structures that would liberate society from the burdens of time and law. "During his legal career," notes Cardwell, "Bacon meditated on the inquisitorial practices of Privy Council—whether formalized by subsequent arraignment and trial in the Star Chamber or in another central court; or non-judicial, as in the hearing that dunned poor Whitelocke," a special case Bacon as Solicitor-General had tried in June 1613 (11:348–57). What came out of this "meditation" that occupied Bacon's entire life (his work on law texts had begun in the 1580s and continued into the Latin translations of the *quinquennium*) was a further synthesizing of knowledge. Out of one practice Bacon could frame a general principle and so transfer one area of knowledge into another. This transfer within areas marks all Bacon's law texts as we have them (none were published in Bacon's lifetime). This "meditation" on the methods of inquisition brought about, as Cardwell argues, one more improvement on, and revision of, old forms and language: "Seeing the old linkage of the verbal arts of controversy to the practice of adversarial courts, Bacon excogitated a new verbal art of uncontroversial speech modeled on the inquisitor's submission to his examinee's response."[12]

Thus the problem of destructive controversy discussed at length throughout Bacon's canon, especially in the first book of the *Advancement of Learning*, became analogized here from philosophy and science to law. Ernst Cassirer has noted this transfer in reverse: "Bacon sits as a judge over reality, questioning it as one examines the accused." Cassirer comments how Bacon will "resort to force to obtain the answer desired, that nature must be 'put to the rack.'" For Cassirer, "this procedure is not simply observational but strictly inquisitorial."[13] In short, in Cassirer's terms, it is quite possible that some of Bacon's most extraordinary scientific breakthroughs came from his professional experience in law.

Thus, in the 1600 Lenten vacation at Gray's Inn, in his *Reading on the Statute of Uses* (a text that proves, as Sir William Holdsworth notes,[14] what a superb reader of the law Bacon was for his students and audiences at Gray's Inn), Bacon is concerned about the effect of time on the common law. He proposes remedies for such mutability, one being the proper procedure to investigate such received common law: "The nature of an use is best discerned by considering first, what it is not; and then what it is: for it is the nature of all human science and knowledge to proceed most safely by negative and exclusion, to what is affirmative and inclusive" (7:398). In his fullest explanation of scientific method in the 1620 *Novum Organum*, Bacon uses exactly the same procedure of the negative. It is first adumbrated here in a law text itself revolutionary. This text is, as Daniel R. Coquillette comments, "the first systematic treatment" of the process by which a drafted statute "would then be shaped by judicial action, customary application, and equitable relief" —in short, "the first set of principles for progressive statutory interpretation in the history of Anglo-American jurisprudence."[15]

Similarly in his 1597 *Maxims of the Law*, where he had developed a crucial theory of the aphorism, Bacon had developed the kind of transferring within the fields of law as he would later develop in science, philosophy, and rhetoric. His maxims run the gamut from torts or contracts to the two types of ambiguity in the language of any case: *patens* or open, "which appears to be ambiguous upon the deed or instrument"; and *latens* or hidden, "or that which seemeth certain and without ambiguity for any thing that appeareth upon the deed or instrument, but there is some collateral matter out of the deed that breedeth the ambiguity" (7:385). The language of these twenty-five maxims—more had been promised—resembles that of Bacon's scientific and philosophical treatises, as, for example, in the first maxim, Regula I, *In jure non remota causa, sed proxima spectatur* (in law the cause is seen not as remote but immediate). As Paul Kocher has noted, although these legal aphorisms generalize from particular common law experiences, they are still not legal rules of the highest class but "rather, they seem to be generalizations or axioms of that middle order which Bacon throughout his philosophical writings describes as the most fruitful for works." Or to make the analogy: "in natural science the utility of the middle axiom is to state a rule applicable to new physical situations. In jurisprudence the utility of the maxim is similarly to provide the premises by which new cases can be decided, contradictions in existing cases erased, and analogies more safely carried out." Thus, the maxims as axioms act "to effectuate and protect the broad human rights when they reach the state of litigation" by establishing "practical ties between basic human rights and the ordinary court-room scene without which the former would remain uninstrumented airy platitudes."[16] Such a systematic attempt to explore in a series the determining variant, as here through a system of middle axioms, was set up in the *Novum Organum* as part of its system of induction. From Bacon's system, a varying induction has been argued through theories of probability and inference,[17] especially by L. Jonathan Cohen, as consequential for the functioning of a moral epistemology. The experience of this early law text thus provided a matrix for Bacon's later development.

Indeed, the basic informing principle in Bacon for such transfers of knowledge had remained the same basic *philosophia prima* (first philosophy) described in the 1605 *Advancement*. With such a universal base, induction was the method that would, for Bacon in his *Novum Organum*, "embrace everything. For I form a history and tables of discovery for anger, fear, shame, and the like; for matters political; and again for the mental operations of memory, composition and division, judgment and the rest" (4:112). This use of induction was particularly central for the development of law texts because, for Bacon, Aristotle had been right to see the use of examples as the rhetorical equivalent of the inductive method in logic. The law case and the law maxim that stemmed from Bacon's rhetorical matrix of the aphorism thus became the means by which a living Maker of Fortune, the ideal for a young law student at Gray's Inn in London, could be formed. As in Bacon's own life, so in his texts the practical and the actualizing new form combined.

Such a form coming out of ambiguity could have a clear purpose. In fact, Bacon's provided what Holdsworth calls "the first critical, the first jurisprudential, estimate of English law which had ever been made."[18] In three texts particularly, Bacon wanted the actualizing new form to lead to a progression of self-consciousness in law itself. This consciousness would be revealed in clearer linguistic expression. In his 1597 *Maxims* Bacon attempted a cleansing of English common law with their emphasis on the particular. In a fragment only recently discovered (possibly brought to Chatsworth by Hobbes), the *Aphorismi* (1615–22) turned toward the kind of generalizing and rationalizing typical of the Roman civil law, its union with native English common law being, as Bacon wrote his friend Buckingham, essential for the understanding of foreign policy if nothing else (13:27). In this dispute over English common law, Bacon was viewed, however erroneously, as the Roman antagonist to his personal enemy and rival, Sir Edward Coke, who favored English common law. Bacon's widest influence came, in his rationalizing aphorisms on the law, in a third text entitled *A Treatise on Universal Justice or the Fountains of Equity* in Book Eight of his 1623 *De Augmentis Scientiarum*. The ninety-seven enlarged aphorisms of the *Treatise* were the same middle axioms Bacon had sought in 1597. Now they built less on English common law and moved toward the greater systemization of Roman civil law but without formality, simply as aphorism. The aphoristic form had thus freed the legal instance to act as both particular fact and universal directive.

Even in so cursory a survey as this, the reader cannot but be daunted by the legal texts that emerged from the profession that occupied the greater part of Francis Bacon's every day. Coquillette's study of Bacon as man of law provides resources for any reader to follow (in chronological sequence) this career of infinite details. Such a career shows clearly, as Huntington Cairns remarks, that there can be no question of Bacon's power as a lawyer: "His little tract on *The Maxim of the Law*, his *Reading on the Statute of Uses*, his *Ordinances in Chancery*, his *Arguments of Law* leave no doubt as to his technical competence." Further, "his knowledge of Roman law permitted him to escape from the insularity of the precepts of his native legal system," and "altogether, his practical experience as a common law lawyer and chancellor imparted to his legal philosophy the concreteness and applicability to use which is its chief characteristic."[19] The result of Bacon's experiencing texts is that he became, as Coquillette notes, "the first truly analytical and critical jurist in the Anglo-American tradition." He anticipated the utilitarian jurisprudence of the modern world and "was the father of secular instrumentalism in Anglo-American legal theory." Furthermore, in his lifetime, Bacon played all the major legal roles, unlike many jurists of his day (and today). Such a breadth of experience gave his legal texts, where the structural formalities would allow, the same techniques of organization and linguistic precision as his *Essays*: that is, his rendering of language gave directions for law within a historical dialectic of ambiguity. As Coquillette delineates, Bacon moved from mere practitioner to senior posts at Gray's Inn, preparing "the required technical 'readings' on English statues with great skills." He was also "a 'hired gun' advocate"[20] in some sensational cases of his day, including *Slade's Case, Chudleigh's Case*, and the *Post-Nati* (*Calvin's Case*), the latter having to do with the tricky problem of the nationality of those born after James I became King of England *and* Scotland. In such cases, Bacon learned to press arguments in a case about which he may or may not have had passionate commitments, terrible roles as demanding as those in any theater. These included his roles as royal prosecutor against former friends like Essex, Somerset, and Ralegh. A member of Elizabeth I's Learned Counsel, Bacon also became a special advocate for James I whom he served as Solicitor-General and then Attorney-General. Bacon's highest legal position, that of one of the great judges of the kingdom, came upon his appointment as Lord Keeper of the Seal and shortly after that as the Lord Chancellor. He presided over the Court of Equity in the Star Chamber (the role Wolsey had played with such efficiency a hundred years before).

Out of that full life and almost forty years in Commons, Bacon desired reforms. In the world of law—the analysis of which can never originate in anything but discontinuous reality—Bacon saw breakdown, both linguistically and conceptually. The old systems would no longer work. The human pain that had resulted demanded a man of pity with the look of the Father of Salomon's House in the *New Atlantis*. One of Bacon's earliest works, his masque *Gesta Grayorum* produced during Twelfth Night 1594 had a fifth Counselor to advise "the Prince of Purpoole." This counselor had been specific about legal breakdown: "Then look into the state of your laws and justice of your land; purge out multiplicity of laws, clear the incertainty of them, repeal those that are snaring, and press the execution of those that are wholesome and necessary" (8:339). Bacon's mighty attempts to bring greater certainty, like his *Digest of Laws* to which the *Maxims* would be ancillary, could only be partial and unfinished. By no accident, therefore, the experience of these law texts reveal the same ambiguous manipulation of experience as in the *Essays*, albeit in more technical details.

If Bacon worked to codify, or at least to simplify through his own power of language, the disaster of human relationships expressed in the laws of his time, then it appears ironic that in his famous *Proposition Touching the Compiling and Amendment of the Laws of England*, written in 1616 as Attorney-General, Bacon refused to allow a total rationalization or codification of case law. As Bernard McCabe has noted, Bacon "places himself squarely in the English legal tradition by largely avoiding abstraction about the nature of law."[21] In his *Proposition*, Bacon refuses the ordering of heads and titles in the manner of the Roman Civil Law. Rather, "customs are laws written in living tables" and as "in all sciences, they are the soundest that keep close to particulars." In this case, "the work which I propound tendeth to proyning [pruning] and grafting the law, and not to ploughing and planting it again." What Bacon does insist on, however, in this odd protection of the ambiguity of texts, is that case digests always be chronological, preserving the sequence of the Year Books. Thus, retaining the historical order—"a narrative of the laws" (5:104)—and not an abstract coding, Bacon would follow the incremental method of time, which is, as he had written in his early 1592 "Praise of Knowledge," "to discover truth." As Bacon observes in his Aphorism 76 in the *De Augmentis*, such "judgments" made from time will "give light to a wise judge" (5:104). In Bacon's new chronological series of digests, new inductive axioms could be essayed or tried out. New laws themselves might originate out of the greater healing systems of history and time.

What was needed, therefore, was a new method of certainty based on these healing systems. In Aphorism 8 in the *De Augmentis*, Bacon announces that "certainty is so essential to law, that law cannot even be just without it." He then quotes from the first of the Pauline letters to the Corinthians (14:8), "For if the trumpet give an uncertain sound, who shall prepare himself for battle?" Bacon's law texts suggest a method of certainty in this healing of time; it would involve, as Huntington Cairns has shown,[22] analogies and examples. It would be a method of time in which the art of discovery itself will lead to discovery, as Bacon says at the end of his first book of the *Novum Organum*. The right legal maxim or aphorism will lead to new experimentation and growth, in law a "heroic work" and a new "instauration" (5:100–1)—or if not, as Bacon analogizes about the old laws in his *Proposition*, using an image from the *Aeneid*: "the living lie in the arms of the dead" (13:65). For the law texts, the method of time would be a process of cleansing laws of the living dead. It would then reshape, through a progressive series, a new kind of history of law. Then, there would be a second step: building a new history or a new series of living texts.

Already inherent, therefore, in the actual is the probable. Experiencing the world as it is through the reading of *Essays, Henry VII*, and the law texts, Bacon's audience can watch Bacon unfold the probable always implicit in these works, although they primarily teach survival in the world as it is. In new texts, the central texts of his career, Bacon would represent the world as it might be. In their power of language, the probable could be read as the actual.

PART TWO

Bacon's World as It Might Be

Chapter Four
The Great Instauration

In 1620, at the height of his political power as Lord Chancellor of the kingdom of Great Britain, Wales, Scotland, and Ireland, Francis Bacon, Baron Verulam, now Viscount Saint Albans, published what he considered his greatest work, the Latin text entitled *Franciscus de Verulamio Summi Angliae Cancellaris Instauratio magna*. The text included, in its opening, his proemium or general statement of purpose. This introduction was written, like the *Gallic Wars* of Julius Caesar, in an imperial third person, and was followed by the grand dedication of the book to James I and then by Bacon's longer preface in which all the directions, motifs, and significances of his life-work are summed up. Next came the plan or program, the strategies, of the whole Great Instauration or Renewal of human learning that Bacon had been planning all his life. This vision of a world that might be was revealed to readers in six stages that would model themselves on the six days' work of creation in the Book of Genesis, a literary strategy that would parody one of the most popular works of modern Europe, the French Protestant poet Du Bartas' epic *Divine Weeks* translated by Sylvester in the same year the *Advancement* appeared. The cultural equations Bacon thus set for himself and his task were breathtaking, if not impenetrable to most of his public. In fact, most courtiers probably shared the opinion of Bacon's prime audience, James I, the hope of all financial support, who announced that he found the Lord Chancellor's masterwork like the peace of God: it "passeth" all understanding.

After these four introductory chapters, Bacon turned in the rest of his 1620 text to the second part of his Great Instauration, the actual new method for science. He skipped over the first part of the six stages because the second book of the 1605 *Advancement* that Bacon was then translating, with the aid of amanuenses like Thomas Hobbes into the *De Augmentis Scientiarium*, would act as the first part of his Instauration. Although it may be true, as Spedding conjectures (1:146), that in 1620 Bacon may have been thinking of an entirely new work for this first stage, one Bacon had already begun in Latin but intended to enlarge, *Descriptio Globi Intellectualis* (Description of the Intellectual World), he did not develop it. In any case, enough had been done with the 1605 *Advancement* to allow its translation into the universal language of Latin. The *De Augmentis* could become the key starting point of his Great Renewal or Restoration.

The second part of his Great Instauration was already in Latin, having been worked out through a series of earlier incomplete texts. For this second part, as in his general parody of the Biblical hexameral account and of Caesar's style, Bacon selected another grand tradition. He parodied no one less than Aristotle. He would write his own *Organon*, a *Novum Organum*, his own central text of philosophy. Thus the 1620 text of the *Instauratio Magna* is completed by the *Novum Organum*. After his short but penetrating preface, Bacon's aphorisms of Book One perform the task of preparing the mind for the true method or *Organum* to come in Book Two. Although Bacon's second book begins to analyze what he intends his method to be and important signposts are depicted, the analysis and the frame of its logic remain incomplete and unfinished. It would be the same for all the other stages of Bacon's grand scheme for restituting a world as it might be.

The trajectory of Bacon's masterwork did not miss its aim, however. It offered, in a dramatic hexameral frame, a full exposition of what the world might become if the world as it is could be adjusted or re-formed. In this sense, renewal does not adequately translate Bacon's term "instauratio," as Charles Whitney has demonstrated.[1] This classical term as derived from Cicero and Livy does carry the meaning of restoring the past but through erecting structures and building life anew. In other words, for Bacon, the future dominates any real instauration, not an attempt to reproduce the past. If a tension did exist between a purer past and a corrupt present, such a dialectic existed only to enable the future, with all its promise of becoming, to emerge.

Nowhere is this image of the future clearer than in a visual emblem at the start of Bacon's 1620 text (1:119). Here the title of the book appears between two grand columns powerfully projecting a liminality against a limitless sky and horizon. One of the most influential emblems in later Renaissance and early modern society, the figuration held for a Jacobean audience the force of a religious icon. The old Catholic devotion to transcendent visual images had imprinted English and European culture and had operated in England for a millennium before the Reformation eighty years earlier. But habits of reading pictures hermeneutically, that is, for interpretation, had not vanished. Bacon thus starts with an icon that, like the book it introduces, stages a performance. The emblem enacts a superb theater precisely set to arrest the reader's attention from the start.

For his audience, Bacon places an aphorism at the base of this printed icon, above the date and the publisher's name on the title-page. It recapitulates ideologically the basis of both Bacon's present and future society. The Daniel text explains the whole point and direction of the book: "Multi pertransibunt & augebitur scientia" (many will pass through and knowledge or science will increase). As Bacon had written in his notebook of 1608, *Commentarius Solutus*, "ut religiones solent" (as religions do), so here Bacon would draw the new out of the old in a method of religious parody. The apocalyptic Book of Daniel (12:4) was a text from one of the Jewish prophets especially beloved by Protestants. As set in the emblem, especially with Bacon's misquoting for sharper rhetorical and propagandistic focus, the Latin aphorism would catch his audience's eye immediately. At the same time the aphorism would locate the picture in the popular Renaissance tradition of emblem books familiar to Bacon's readers and provide a prophetic ideology fully acceptable to his English audience as well as the Continental audience Bacon also sought.

Language thus becomes visual reality. The process of ideas in the emblem promises the future (and the book ahead). A ship is moving through two enormous pseudo-Doric columns from a vast ocean; another ship in the distance, near the borders of the picture and the horizon, is also returning. Both returning ships mean that knowledge will be decidedly increased because of this arrival from the unknown world. In fact, in the icon, fish or monsters from the deep ocean look up in amazement as the ship (nearer the reader) is returning from the limitless world to the specific world of the columns. With their liminality, the columns also represent the world of steady if ambiguous history, to which all personal freedom must return. Beyond them, however, lies the promise of unambiguous probability—made actual in the text that follows as the greater freedom of science and learning, greater technology, the hope of "a land unknown," as the Father of Solomon's House tells his new convert in Bacon's last work. In this central hermeneutical action of the returning ship, Bacon is making a politically bold parody. He is revalorizing the emblem Charles V had set for the Holy Roman Empire almost a hundred years before: two columns and a view of the ocean beyond leading for Charles V to his New Spain and the motto of hope "plus ultra" (more beyond)—a motto signifying the greatness of the Holy Roman Empire that then spread from Russia to the shores of Peru and Mexico. For Bacon, there would be another empire for the human mind to embrace—now restored through his New Instauration and its method, a world that might be.

A proof that his audiences understood exactly the meaning of his iconic and symbolic transference is that "plus ultra"—nowhere on the emblem (although used as motif in Bacon's texts)—soon became the rallying cry of new scientists and philosophers for the next two hundred years. In this sense of increase or "augebitur," Bacon intended that his audience recognize that the two ships are returning (the set of the full-blown sails is the hermeneutical clue). The future *can* be realized, and the thick clouds above the limitless ocean are the same thick clouds first sighted in the land of Bensalem in the *New Atlantis* before its riches are revealed. Such a theater piece acted, therefore, as a rhetorical and visual masterstroke: whatever the abstruse philosophical and scientific arguments of the text, especially the second book of the *Novum Organum*, the simplest audience had a picture of the redemptive direction of the entire work. This staged opening thus begins a text of philosophy and science (set as metaphor and visual image) unlike almost any other in Western culture, a synthesis of rhetoric and philosophy that intends all European society as its audience. As revealed by the dedication of Immanuel Kant of his crucial second edition of *The Critique of Pure Reason* to Bacon, the "Verulamium" who had dared to write his new text, Bacon succeeded dramatically in converting such an audience to the hope of his emblem.

Proemium

The proemium that follows the emblem is equally staged. Its intense solipsism might have been expected where staging of self is the only way to focus such a new proleptic program. William Harvey was right: the Lord Chancellor at the height of his immense political power is promulgating science. If anywhere in Bacon, in this text subjectivity transforms itself into history. At the same time, if the whole of Europe is the final audience for this highly self-conscious performance, Bacon must be plural, not the man himself. The dramatized self is speaking for society itself at an exalted intellectual moment. Thus, the "FRANCIS OF VERULAM" that begins the special typeface that Bacon utilizes for this passage invites the reader to join his or her subjectivity as it tries to define European history. The plural self continues as Bacon moves to a smaller but heightened line "REASONED THUS WITH HIMSELF" and then into the smallest type for the next three lines also set as though in a title: "and judged it to be for the interest of the present and future generations that they should be made acquainted with his thoughts."

The conceit, if not arrogance, in the bold type continues with the long Ciceronian sentence that begins this most majestic of Bacon's texts: "Being convinced that the human intellect makes its own difficulties, not using the true helps which are at man's disposal soberly and judiciously [sobrie et commode]; whence follows manifold ignorance of things, and by reason of that ignorance mischiefs innumerable; he thought all trial should be made, whether that commerce between the mind of man and the nature of things, which is more precious than anything on earth, or at least than anything that is of the earth, might be by any means restored to its perfect and original condition, or if that may not be, yet reduced to a better condition than that in which it now is" (4:7).

It was a restoration devoutly to be wished, but "the errors that have hitherto prevailed" will continue "(if the mind be left to go its own way)." From "primary notions of things" that are "overhastily abstracted from the facts" to "the secondary and subsequent notions" also "arbitrary and inconstant," one central conclusion can be reached: "the entire fabric of human reason which we employ in the inquisition of nature, is badly put together and built up, and like some magnificent structure without any foundation." In such a fundamental disorientation of the mirror of man's mind, "there was but one course left, therefore,—to try the whole thing anew upon a better plan, and to commence a total reconstruction [Instauratio] of sciences, arts, and all human knowledge, raised upon the proper foundations."

As terrible as this task will be, at least it would promise an "exitus" or end of some kind, not the "agitatio perpetua et circulus" (agitation perpetual and circular) typical of knowledge in 1620. "And although he was well aware how solitary an enterprise [experimentum] it would be and how hard to build up faith in such an enterprise," nevertheless, "he did not think of abandoning either the project or himself but would try and enter on that one road that is open to the human mind." Indeed, in a line that explains Bacon's own compositional method throughout his canon and particularly in his book of 1620, he argues "It is better to make a beginning of what will lead to something" than to deal with contentious matters that have no end or purpose.

So, as with Hercules at his own crossroads, there are two paths for Bacon's audience. The one is tough and difficult at the start but "leads out at last into the open country" and the other, easy at first, "leads to pathless and precipitous places." In order to direct his reader's choice, Bacon narrates his own struggle, his own personal stake in the project: "Because [Bacon] knew not how long it might be before these things would occur to any one else, judging especially from this, that he has found no man hitherto who has applied his mind to the like," he has published his book. He has no ambition for himself but "solicitude for his work" [4:7–8]. He may be dying soon (he was in his sixtieth year); he wants at least some design and direction of what he intended and also some "signum" [sign] published of his own honesty and desire to improve human society. All other human ambition is thus small in comparison to the work at hand.

Dedicatory Epistle to James I

The dedication to the English King picks up this same theme of self, society, and the meaning of Bacon's text and all his work. In what is probably his most significant dedication, Bacon begins with a kind of joke: "Your Majesty may perhaps accuse me of larceny, having stolen from your affairs so much time as was required for this work." The joke has the inverse effect of reminding the King how many hours Bacon *has* given the King, time stolen by the monarch from the text. If anything has been lost by Bacon, it "may perhaps go to the memory of your name and the honour of your age," that is, "if these things [Bacon's text] are indeed worth anything." This humility *ethos* Bacon had developed in a number of speeches and orations and in some legal texts. Here it allows him not only to congratulate himself but also to lead to his real point, the value of what he is offering in his book. These ideas in his text are quite new ("Sunt certe prorsus nova"), in fact, "totally new in their very kind" but, says Bacon arguing once more from his primitivist theory, "they are copied from a very ancient model; even the world itself and the nature of things and of the mind."

With this fundamental sense of an evolving progression of time out of a genuine archaic past, Bacon gives a definition of his work that will become a motif in his canon: "And to say truth, I hold this work as more a birth of time than of intellect [hoc opus magis pro partu temporis quam ingenii]." The only wonder is that the ideas came into "any man's mind." Although there is probably more accident and luck in what human beings think as well as in what they do and say (in contrast to the assumption of transcendent essentializing teachings), the right history or method can control these accidental workings of the mind. Bacon's method or achievement can be "ascribed" not to luck but to the "infinite mercy and goodness of God and to the felicity of your Majesty's times," a period of history in which Bacon has "been an honest and affectionate servant" and to which, after his death, Bacon hopes to become "the kindling of this new light in the darkness of philosophy" and make "this age famous to prosperity," for "surely to the times of the wisest and most learned of kings belongs of right the regeneration and restoration [Instauratio] of the sciences." Praise and flattery lead to Bacon's final request of a King whom he sees as similar to Solomon in four ways—"in the gravity of your judgments, in the peacefulness of your reign, in the largeness of your heart, in the noble variety of the books which you have composed." Bacon can only wish James I would follow the Solomonic example and support the scientific project of "collecting and perfecting of a Natural and Experimental History, true and severe (unincumbered with literature and book-learning), such as philosophy may be built upon" so that finally, after many ages, "philosophy and science may no longer float in air, but rest on the solid foundation of experience of every kind, and the same well examined and weighed." In his closure, Bacon is more direct: "I have provided the machine, but the stuff must be gathered from the facts of nature" (4:11–12). The promise of his world to be has concrete needs in the world that is.

The Meaning of the Great Instauration

In his general preface to his *Instauratio Magna*, Bacon expounds on the emblem at the start of his book. He refers to "the pillars of fate set in the path of knowledge," namely, that human beings either exaggerate "the value of the arts which they possess," such as the study of logic, Aristotelian or otherwise, or they spend their time in "small matters" because they underestimate their abilities to reform. The problem is "opinion" and the great respect society pays to the Greeks, "the boyhood of knowledge," where boys "can talk" but "cannot generate" being only "fruitful of controversies but barren of works." These concerns become frequent motifs in Bacon, with different imaging. Thus the myth of Scylla as the current state of learning, "head and face of a virgin" but with a "womb" holding "barking monsters, from which she could not be delivered" (4:13–4). Bacon draws the contrast between such old schools of philosophy and the mechanical arts, which "are continually growing and becoming more perfect," whereas contentious schools elaborate positions of inventors, not inventions. Bacon then repeats his theory of a time, always in process and incomplete: "neither the births nor the miscarriages of Time are entered in our records." So, concludes Bacon, in an image refined from his 1605 *Advancement*, "Time is like a river, which has brought down to us things light and puffed up, while those which are weighty and solid have sunk" (4:15).

Joining the deductive philosophers like Aristotle, who have survived time, with the empiricists who have only "dwelt upon experience and the facts of nature" and noting all those who have sought "experiments of Fruit, not experiments of Light," Bacon models his solution for science on the method found in another Greek myth. In Bacon's "universe" which "to the eye of human understanding is framed like a labyrinth; presenting as it does on every side so many ambiguities of way, such deceitful resemblances of objects and signs, natures so irregular in their lines, and so knotted and entangled," the "steps" of the true method "must be guided by a clue." That clue, like Ariadne's thread in the Theseus myth, must be attached to a strategy, "a sure plan." Like the compass that has led human beings from coasting "along the shores of an old continent" into the open sea, "a more perfect use and application of the human mind and intellect" needs to "be introduced" (4:16–17).

Having analyzed the problem at hand, Bacon can now dramatize himself as the new prophetic seeker whose subjectivity is offering this method of salvation: "For my own part at least, in obedience to the everlasting love of truth, I have committed myself to the uncertainties and difficulties and solitudes of the ways and relying on the divine assistance have upheld my mind both against the shocks and embattled ranks of opinion, and against my own private and inward hesitations and scruples, and against the fogs and clouds of nature, and the phantoms flitting about on every side; in the hope of providing at last for present future generations guidance more faithful and secure" (4:18–9).

If Bacon has done anything, it has been through "the true and legitimate humiliation of the human spirit." But what has distinguished this noble hero, whose subjectivity corresponds to that of the reader's and thus offers a probable model for all future scientists? How can his image of self lead to the intended conversion of the reader? The answer lies in the very nature of his trial or his humble method of experimentation. Unlike those philosophers who have glanced "upon facts and examples and experience," Bacon says about himself: "I, on the contrary, dwelling purely and constantly among the facts of nature, withdraw my intellect from them no further than may suffice to let the images and rays meet in a point, as they do in the sense of vision; whence it follows that the strength and excellency of the wit has but little to do in the matter." This emphasis on the need for distancing of self in investigation will generate Bacon's strategies in *Novum Organum*. This "same humility which I use in inventing" he will also use in teaching.

Bacon then prescribes the proper method of didactic instruction, his recapitulation of the standard humanistic topos of teaching by reverting to the text itself. Like the older philosopher's method of teaching in the early *Redargutio Philosopharium*, Bacon's method appears quite new: "for I do not endeavour either by triumphs of confutation, or pleadings of antiquity, or assumption of authority, or even by veil of obscurity, to invest these inventions of mine with any majesty" but rather "I lead them to things themselves and the concordances of things [rerum foedera], that they may see for themselves what they have, what they can argue about, and what they can add and contribute to the common good." Thus, "I so present these things naked and open [res nudas et apertas], that my errors can be marked and set aside before the mass of knowledge be further infected by them; and it will be easy also for others to continue and carry on my labours." And what will be the result of Bacon's method founded on such a profound humility? "I suppose that I have established for ever a true and lawful marriage between the empirical and the rational faculty"—seeing and thinking, world and self—"the unkind and ill-starred divorce and separation of which has thrown into confusion all the affairs of the human family" (4:19).

From this motif of family and ordered sexual generation as images of true science, Bacon can turn to the divine. He prays to the Christian trinity that "remembering the sorrows of mankind and the pilgrimage of this our life wherein we wear out days few and evil, they will vouchsafe through my hands to endow the human family with new mercies." Here Bacon repeats motifs and arguments from other works, including the essay "Of Atheism," to effect the separation of human knowledge from the divine, "that the understanding being thereby purified and purged of fancies and vanity, and yet not the less subject and entirely submissive to the divine oracles, may give to faith what is faith's" and "the mind of mind" not "to sell" but rather to "cultivate truth in charity." In the next paragraph, repeating the same motifs of separation of human and divine knowledge, Bacon ends with his praise for this human social interaction that he sees as redemptive (in another parody of I Corinthians 13): "For it was from lust of power that the angels fell, from lust of knowledge that man fell; but of charity there can be no excess, neither did angel or man ever come in danger by it."

In his closure, with characteristic humility, Bacon launches into a proclamation of his personal aims. He does want his audience to "be well assured that I am labouring to lay the foundation, not of any sect or doctrine, but of human utility and power [amplitudinis]." He asks readers to put aside "all emulations and prejudices in favour of this or that opinion" and join him "for the common good." They must also "be of good hope" and not "imagine this Instauration of mine is thing infinite and beyond the power of man, when it is in fact the true end and termination of infinite error," for, although it cannot be "altogether completed within one generation," Bacon's renewal has a method that "provides for its being taken up by another." Bacon's method thus "seeks for the sciences not arrogantly in the little cells of human wit, but with reverence in the greater world." Finally, the Lord Chancellor asks his audience to judge him carefully and not "with premature human reasoning," for "I cannot be fairly asked to abide by the decision of a tribunal which is itself on trial" (4:20–1).

Distributio Operis: Six Strategies for Bacon's Instauration

The plan and outline that follow in the *Distribution of the Work* concretize the general statements of the preface. In his program and its strategies, Bacon wishes to be as clear as possible. He reflects the original clarity of "naked" intuition that is guiding him. "It being part of my design to set everything forth, as far as may be, plainly and perspicuously (for nakedness of the mind is still, as nakedness of the body once was, the companion of innocence and simplicity), let me explain the order and plan of the work. I distribute it into six parts."

1. "The Divisions of the Sciences." Here Bacon will exhibit "a summary or general description of the knowledge which the human race at present possesses." In setting up this first section of his Great Instauration, Bacon will "take into account not only things already invented and known, but likewise things omitted which ought to be there." In fact, "there are found in the intellectual as in the terrestrial globe waste regions as well as cultivated ones." The analogy here of globes is one, in fact, of Bacon's most persisting and innovative, the earth as globe just over a century old. Bacon will not only mention the omissions but will give "directions" for finding how to correct the loss. In this first part Bacon will not be passive in his precise and even tedious details, "for I do not propose merely to survey these regions in my mind, like an augur taking auspices, but to enter them like a general who means to take possession" (4:22–3).

2. "The New Organon; or Directions concerning the Interpretation of Nature." If the first part of the Great Renewal has "coasted past the ancient arts," Bacon continues his voyaging metaphor in the second, "the next point is to equip the intellect for passing beyond." Here Bacon discusses what he calls his "kind of logic." It will help human reason examine and learn from nature so that "(as far as the conditions of mortality and humanity allows) the intellect may be raised and exalted, and made capable of overcoming the difficulties and obscurities of nature." If both the old logic and Bacon's new logic "prepare helps and guards for the understanding," Bacon's differs dramatically from the old in three ways: "in the end aimed at; in the order of demonstration; and in the starting point of the inquiry." He then contrasts his method of induction and that of the syllogism. The latter he rejects, "as acting too confusedly, and letting nature slip out of its hands." The failure of syllogisms is that they consist of propositions, propositions of words, and words are simply "the tokens and signs of notions." Because such "notions of the mind (which are the soul of words and the basis of the whole structure) be improperly and overhastily abstracted from facts, vague, not sufficiently definite," not surprisingly "the whole edifice crumbles."

Revealing his linguistic theory here as well as conceptions of epistemology and logic, Bacon turns to a definition of the truer method of induction: "for I consider induction to be that form of demonstration which upholds the sense and closes with nature, and comes to the very brink of operation, if it does not actually deal with it." This kind of inductive method, unlike the "puerile" form that "proceeds by simple enumeration," would build from axiom to axiom in a pyramid-like fashion so that "the most general are not reached till the last," not the jumping "from the sense and particulars up to the most general propositions." In this inductive search for truth, when "notions" are arrived at, "nature would really recognise" them "as her first principles, and such as lie at the heart and marrow of things" (4:24–5). Because the old logic depends on the senses as a start, "the testimony and information of the sense has reference always to man, not to the universe" and so cannot be "the measure of things." Bacon's induction allows for such distortion: "not so much by instruments as by experiments," methods and controlled processes, "for the subtlety of experiments is far greater than that of the sense itself, even when assisted by exquisite instruments." The experiment "itself shall judge of the thing."

In this objective process Bacon finds a new role for his subjectivity: "And thus I conceive that I perform the office of a true priest of the sense (from which all knowledge in nature must be sought, unless men mean to go mad) and a not unskillful," he adds with a calculated figure of litotes, "interpreter of its oracles." Thus, "while others only profess to uphold and cultivate the sense, I do so in fact." Bacon has offered such provisions "for finding the genuine light of nature and kindling it and bringing it to bear," and they would be quite enough if, says Bacon, in his famous image Locke would appropriate, the human intellect were even, and "like a fair sheet of paper with no writing on it [tabulae abrasae—in genitive case]." Sadly, the mind of man is possessed by "idols, or phantoms" and "like an uneven mirror" that so "distorts the rays of objects" according to the mind's "notions" that it "mixes up" with "the nature of things." Thus "there is no true and even surface left to reflect the genuine rays of things." Bacon must then "lay down once for all as a fixed and established maxim, that the intellect is not qualified to judge except by means of induction, and induction in its legitimate form." In fact, the mind must be expurgated and cleansed by a three-fold method (largely the work of the first book of the *Novum Organum*): "the refutation of the Philosophies; the refutation of the Demonstrations; and the refutation of the Natural Human Reason." If the mind can then be purified in a "true relation" with the nature of things, it will be, in a simile that builds on the popular Renaissance and classical tradition of the epithalamion, "as the strewing and decoration of the bridal chamber of the Mind and the Universe, the Divine Goodness assisting." "Out of which marriage," concludes Bacon in his sexual image for this second part of his Instauration, "(and be this the prayer of the bridal song) there may spring helps to man, and a line and race of inventions that may in some degree subdue and overcome the necessities and miseries of humanity" (4:26–7).

3. "The Phenomena of the Universe; or a Natural and Experimental History for the foundation of Philosophy." In this third part of his Great Renewal, Bacon announces: "I design not only to indicate and mark out the ways, but also to enter them." This stage will include what will be the major scientific work of Bacon's last five years: his gathering of specific natural histories and then his general collection of observations in his *Sylva Sylvarum* (The Forest of Forests). In schoolroom logic, especially Agricola's place-logic, a storehouse for *inventio* was called a forest or *sylva*. Such natural histories as forests for later invention will then "serve for a foundation to build philosophy upon" and keep the mind on the track of true experimentation with "things." Scientists "who aspire not to guess and divine, but to discover and know; who propose not to

devise fables and false images of their own, but to examine and dissect the nature of this very world itself; must go to the facts themselves for everything." Indeed, "it is in vain that you polish the mirror"—correct the defects of the mind—"if there are no images to be reflected; and it is as necessary that the intellect should be supplied with fit matter to work upon, as with safeguards to guide its working."

Bacon's natural histories will be different from the medieval or classical. They are "not so to delight with variety of matter or to help with present use of experiments, as to give light to the discovery of causes and supply a suckling philosophy with its first food." But there can be no hurry, "for though it be true that I am principally in pursuit of works and the active department of the sciences, yet I wait for harvest-time, and do not attempt to mow the moss or to reap the green corn." Bacon will not be drawn away by immediate rewards as, in the Greek myth, Atalanta is drawn from her race by a golden apple. Bacon knows well that "axioms once rightly discovered will carry whole troops of works along with them, and produce them, not here and there one, but in clusters." In fact, Bacon desires a history not only of nature "free and at large" but, as he will also describe it in his interpretation of the Homeric myth of Proteus or Matter, "much more of nature under constraint and vexed," held down like Proteus in order to tell his secret, "that is to say, when by art and the hand of man she is forced out of her natural state, and squeezed and moulded." To be sure, "the nature of things betrays itself more readily under the vexations of art than in its natural freedom" and so "all experiments of the mechanical arts" and "the many crafts which have not yet grown into arts" will be included.

Bacon would thus include all kinds of natural histories but only those founded "on the faith of the eyes" and not on fables: "I interpose everywhere admonitions and scruples and cautions, with a religious care to eject, repress, and as it were exorcise every kind of phantasm." Finally, in the writing of these natural histories, Bacon would add "observations of my own, being as the first offers, inclinations, and as it were glances of history towards philosophy; both by way of an assurance to men that they not be kept for ever tossing on the waves of experience, and also that when the time comes for the intellect to begin its work, it may find everything the more ready" (4:27–30).

Bacon began on this third part of his *Distributio* immediately. In fact, included in the same 1620 *Instauratio Magna* with the *Novum Organon* was the text of what Bacon called *Parasceve ad Historiam Naturalem et Experimentalem*, a title Spedding translates as "Preparative Towards a

Natural and Experimental History." The Greek roots of *parasceve* carry more than the concept of a preparation, however; the word means the day of preparation for the holy sabbath and, as such, actualizes one more parody of the Hebraic and biblical worlds that served Bacon as a means of focusing his new text. The subtitle of the *Parasceve*, "Such As May Serve for the Foundation of a True Philosophy," is more inclusive in Latin, "Qualis Sufficiat et Sit in Ordine ad Basin et Fundamenta Philosophae Verae," where it indicates the role of the natural histories as the basis for the New Logic and all the Experiments of Light and Experiments of Fruit that would follow. Furthermore, because "a history of this kind, such as I conceive and shall presently describe, is a thing of very great size," needing "great labour and expense" and, in fact, "a kind of royal work," Bacon adds it to his master text in 1620 to encourage others when his "own strength (if I should have no one to help me) is hardly equal" to the task. Without such a history, "no progress worthy of the human race" can be made. With it and "added to it such auxiliary and light-giving experiments as in the very course of interpretation will present themselves or will have to be found out," time can be redeemed: "the investigation of nature and of all sciences will be the work of a few years." Again Bacon sounds his clarion cry: "For in this way, and in this way only, can the foundations of a true and active philosophy be established; and then will men wake as from deep sleep, and at once perceive what a difference there is between the dogma and figments [placita et commenta] of the wit and a true and active philosophy, and what it is in questions of nature to consult nature itself" (4:251–2).

In the ten expanded aphorisms "on the composition of the primary history" that follow this general statement, Bacon repeats motifs already developed and adumbrates others to follow. Thus he sees nature "in three states" and "subject as it were to three kinds of regimen": free and developing "in her own ordinary course"; or "forced out of her proper state by the perverseness and insubordination of matter and the violence of impediments"; or "constrained and moulded by art and human industry." These three lead to three conditions in nature: the *"species* of things"; *"monsters"*; and *"things artificial."* In this latter condition, nature "takes orders from man, and works under his authority" so that "another universe or theatre of things" comes into view. Making can become knowledge. Thus a natural history must examine "the *liberty* of nature, or the *errors* of nature, or the *bonds* of nature" and these became histories of *"Generations,* of *Pretergenerations,* and of *Arts."* This last Bacon calls *"Mechanical* or *Experimental* history" and, as he will indicate, such a history or collection, both in actuality and theory, would be quite original in Western culture. Such natural histories can be either for their own sakes, with the fascination inherent in such collections (increasing in Bacon's time and even more after Bacon's texts were read), or "as the primary material of philosophy and the stuff and subject-matter of true induction." The latter is the true purpose of any collection and, as such, differs from the purposes of all the famous natural histories of the ancient world, from Aristotle and Theophrastus to Pliny, as well as the overly erudite histories of Bacon's contemporaries.

In this *Parasceve*, Bacon adds three cautions for the purpose of "true axioms": "away with antiquities, and citations and testimonies of authors"; cut "superfluidity" in descriptions and curiosities; avoid "all superstitious stories." All such caution will lead to the proper writing style itself although, in a sexual metaphor, "this kind of chastity and brevity will give less pleasure both to the reader and writer." In fact, the correct metaphor for his history would be "a granary or storehouse of matters," not pleasant to stay in but useful for the occasion "when anything is wanted for the work of the *Interpreter*." And, says Bacon in his sixth aphorism that adumbrates a democratic realism, nothing should be omitted from this collection, not even "the most ordinary" and "things mean, illiberal, filthy, . . . things trifling and childish (and no wonder, for we are to become again as little children); and lastly, things which seem over subtle, because they are in themselves of no use." Indeed, such a collection should "be compiled with a most religious care," says Bacon in his ninth aphorism, because it deals with "the book of God's works" and "a kind of second Scripture." With this kind of supply, the new scientists will "be no longer kept dancing within little rings, like persons bewitched, but our range and circuit will be as wide as the compass of the world" (4:253–7). In fact, as Bacon notes in his seventh aphorism, "it is works we are in pursuit of, not speculations; and practical working comes of the due combination of physics and mathematics." As he comes to his last aphorism, Bacon apologizes for the catalogue that ends his text: "I have at present so many other things to do that I can only find time to subjoin a Catalogue of their titles." In the vast list that ensues, Bacon offers 130 possible histories from the history of comets to a "History of Venus, as a species of Touch," to the history of honey to the history of ticking and feathers to the history of the natures and powers of numbers. For Bacon, the task would stretch on and on. The lawyer Bacon would examine, "(according to the practice in civil causes) in this great Plea or Suit granted by the divine favour and provi-

dence (whereby the human race seeks to recover its right over nature),"
nothing less than "nature herself and the arts upon interrogatories." In
Bacon's method, nature herself is on trial (4:257–70).

Two years later, in 1622, Bacon proposes to write six natural histories: History of the Winds; History of Dense and Rare and of the Con-
traction and Expansion of Matter in Space; History of Heavy and Light;
History of the Sympathy and Antipathy of Things; History of Sulphur,
Mercury, and Salt; and History of Life and Death. He will dedicate to
Prince Charles the first volume containing only the History of the
Winds and the general preface with its proposals. The book is elaborately entitled in Latin translated as *Natural and Experimental History for
the Foundation of Philosophy or Phenomena of the Universe: Being the Third
Part of the Instauratio Magna*, the whole surmounted with the titles *Francis, Baron of Verulam and Viscount St. Albans*. It was another staged performance as shown in his letter to the future Charles I (he had dedicated
the text of his Instauration to Charles' father James I): "The first fruits
of my Natural History I most humbly offer to your Highness." Bacon
makes now another parody of the Bible, here from one of the most
famous parables of Christ. Bacon's text is "a thing like a grain of mus-
tard-seed very small in itself, yet a pledge of those things which by the
grace of God will come hereafter." He will complete one such history,
binding himself "as by a vow every month that the goodness of God
(whose glory is sung as in a new song) shall add to my life." He hopes
his example will stir others to "like industry" and, of course, the royal
family to support such a collection. The preface that follows builds on
similar religious imagery ending in a staged rhapsody modeled on
Hebrew prophets and psalmists: "For this is the sound and language
which went forth into all lands and did not incur the confusion of Babel;
this should men study to be perfect in, and becoming again as little children condescend to take the alphabet of it into their hands, and spare no
pains to search and unravel the interpretation thereof, but pursue it
strenuously and persevere even unto death" (5:127–31).

In this 1622 preface Bacon reveals as nowhere else the literary strategy of his last years. Before the final elaborate prayer, Bacon indicates he
has abandoned further work on the New Logic: "For although not a few
things, and those among the most important, still remain to be completed in my Organum, yet my design is rather to advance the universal
work of Instauration in many things, than to perfect it in a few." In all
this, "ever earnestly desiring, with such a passion as we believe God
alone inspires," that he will not attempt this great task in vain, Bacon

looks to "the many wits scattered over Europe, capacious, open, subtle, solid, and constant." Would such intellects "enter into the plan of my Organum and try to use it"? In fact, says Bacon, in a complex analogy, if such "wits so vigorous" that they could build "out of a mere plank or shell" of natural evidence ships "of philosophy, of admirable construction," there can only be "good hope" if "they have obtained proper material and provision" for "much more solid structures." And such solidity cannot come only from Bacon's New Organon, though it be the best Europe had to offer in 1622. It needs the Natural History that "would advance" the sciences "not a little," even without a completed Organon (5:131–3).

In the histories that follow and in the dozen or so documents to which Bacon gave the title of "Inquisition" or "History or Inquisition" (including the *Historia et Inquisitio de Animato et Inanimato* recently discovered and analyzed by Graham Rees[2]), the primary stylistic device is the use of the example or topic or some variety of expanded aphorism. The organizations of the histories may change, but primarily, as Bacon says in this same 1622 text in his "rule of the present history," they have a similar order: after the title and introduction in such histories comes "Particular Topics or Articles of Inquiry" that are to be investigated and also to "stimulate further inquiry" because "questions are at our command, though facts are not." Then follows "the History and Experiments" that may be collected "into tables." Bacon also includes "admonitions and cautions" as well as his own "observations" and "speculations," even "rules or imperfect axioms" set down if "only provisionally" because they are "useful." Such natural histories then not only serve the third part of the Great Instauration but anticipate the fourth, "by reason of the titles from the Alphabet" of Nature Bacon appends in this text as well as "the Topics," and even anticipates the sixth and final stage.

Four years later in 1626, the year of Bacon's death, his chaplain Dr. Rawley would also dedicate the *Sylva Sylvarum or Natural History in Ten Centuries* to Charles I. For its form and the style of the work, Bacon would once more revert to Aristotelian example as the rhetorical form of induction, although typically, with bold transfer, the series of examples perform for Bacon not as rhetorical devices but as logical proof. The "centuries" or loosely structured series thus perform as logical form, induction itself. Rawley also has a crucial preface to the reader that repeats the main motifs of Bacon's prefaces to his project of the natural history, motifs "fundamental to the erecting and building of a true phi-

losophy." Bacon's intention was that "men's minds . . . would not think
themselves utterly lost in a vast wood of experience" but have some
direction in his chapters or "Centuries" "till true axioms may be more
fully discovered." Most of all, says Rawley almost with defiance, the
book "hath nothing of imagination." Writing such a natural history during his last five years was a humbling task: "I have heard his lordship
speak complainingly, that his lordship (who thinketh he deserveth to be
an architect in this building) should be forced to be a workman and a
labourer, and to dig the clay and burn the brick" and like the Israelites
in Egypt, even "gather the straw and stubble over all the fields" in order
to burn the bricks.

For the reader who has worked through all ten "Centuries" of the
Sylva Sylvarum as well as the various histories and the ancillary inquiries
into light, the magnet, the ebb and flow of the sea, and then fragments
like the *Abecedarium Naturae*, the most striking feature is their rhetorical organization, no matter how inchoate the material. Metaphors or
images or figures of speech inherited from the classical world have
merged into varying uses of concentrated language more or less resembling the form of the aphorism but always cataloguing and summariz-
ing before listing again. This listing and the fragmentary efforts at
place-logic would indeed collapse in this text (as they would in so many
imitations of Bacon to come) if it were not for a central fact found also
in the best imitations of this Baconian style such as Burton's *Anatomy of
Melancholy* and Sir Thomas Browne's *Pseudodoxia Epidemica, Hydrio-
taphia; Or Urne Buriall* (and to some degree, the *Religio Medici*): a powerful response to the life being observed ties all the disparate items of
Bacon's catalogue together into a compelling style. The authoritative
passion enacted in the language takes the reader on a seemingly endless
trip of brilliant or tedious or surprising episodes, experiments, anec-
dotes, observations, or unmediated contacts with phenomena. The passion abounds, for the world is essentially animistic to Bacon, a concept
he will develop in his doctrine of the spirits inherent in matter as given,
for example, in Rule IV in the *History of Life and Death*. It is probably
this section of his Instauration that made Bacon the fascinating model
for Charles Darwin when he wrote about his own method for the collections of *The Origins of the Species*: "I worked on true Baconian principles."[3]

4. "The Ladder of the Intellect." This stage and the next of the Great
Instauration remain the most problematic. In this "Ladder," Bacon
"would set forth examples of inquiry and invention according to my

method, exhibited by anticipation in some particular subjects," and then Bacon adds vaguely: "choosing such subjects as are at once the most noble in themselves among those under inquiry, and most different one from another; that there may be an example in every kind." He does not mean illustrations, he is careful to note, but "actual types and models, by which the entire process of the mind and the whole fabric and order of invention from the beginning to end, in certain subjects, and those various and remarkable, should be set as it were before the eyes." Although in closing Bacon says that this fourth part will simply apply the findings of the second part of the Instauration, he gives, in fact, no example nor further details, except possibly, as Anderson conjectures, the fragment *Scala intellectus*.

5. "The Forerunners; or Anticipations of the New Philosophy." This stage of the Great Renewal is also vague in what it intends, and can only be found in the extant works, if at all, in the fragment *Prodomi*, as Anderson also speculates.[4] Although Bacon analogizes this fifth part, "for temporary use only," as "interest payable from time to time until the principal be forthcoming," he hints only at a hodgepodge of what may be called middle axioms—conclusions "not however according to the true rules and methods of interpretation." They "will serve in the meantime for wayside inns, in which the mind may rest and refresh itself on its journey to more certain conclusions." Bacon will "not make so blindly for the end of my journey, as to neglect anything useful that may turn up by the way." At best, these provisional "conclusions" perform as a refinement of what Bacon would call *Experientia Literata*, a term that, as Spedding notes (10:82), refers to an order of experimentation in which one experiment leads to another, "making the answer to one question suggest the question to be asked next."

6. "The New Philosophy; or Active Science." This final stage, the sixth day in Bacon's parody of Genesis and his re-creation of the world as it might be, has traditionally been viewed as existing in the fiction of Bacon's utopia, the *New Atlantis*. Bacon himself evokes just such a possibility when he asserts that his philosophy in its final form is "a thing both above my strength and beyond my hopes," but may be derived from "the legitimate, chaste, and severe course of inquiry which I have explained and provided" to which he has offered only a start: "a beginning, as I hope, not unimportant:—the fortune of the human race will give the end-result." It is a beginning few of his time could have conceived. Bacon's is thus a radically new view of anthropology as well as of the old epistemology—as Bacon tells his reader. As proof of that new

view, Bacon gives here what he will soon present as the first aphorism of his New Organon: the human being can do no more than serve and interpret nature. All history begins in a new dialectic of man and nature for human existence and human labor: "beyond this he knows nothing and can do nothing." What will be developed and illustrated later in the text Bacon generalizes here: "for the chain of causes cannot by any force be loosed or broken, nor can nature be commanded except by being obeyed." The result is that "those twin objects, human Knowledge and human Power, do really meet in one" if "the eye" of the self is "steadily fixed upon the facts of nature" and so receive "their images simply as they are." When Bacon moves toward his peroration and conclusion, he shifts to the most authoritative level of ideological transfer that he could make: "For God forbid that we should give out a dream of our own imagination for a pattern of the world; rather may he graciously grant to us to write an apocalypse or true vision of the footsteps of the Creator imprinted on his creatures."

This call for prayer leads, in fact, to a closure of direct prayer. Bacon's prayer does not refer at all to Christ but beseeches a more Hebraic and Islamic image of the deity: "Therefore do thou, O Father, who gavest the visible light as the first fruits of creation, and didst breathe into the face of man the intellectual light as the crown and consummation thereof, guard and protect this work, which coming from thy goodness returneth to thy glory." Picking up one of Luther's most powerful images, a georgics motif he will use again, Bacon asks for help through a kind of bargaining dialectic: "Wherefore if we labour in thy works with the sweat of our brows thou wilt make us partakers of thy vision and thy sabbath." Through these communal "hands" Bacon asks for the ultimate solution for the cultural breakdown he has found in European history. Such a solution forms the purpose of the Great Instauration. It is the redemption to be found in the renewal of community through new forms of learning and a new science and technology: "thou wilt vouchsafe to endow the human family with new mercies" (4:32–3).

Chapter Five
The Advancement of Learning

Writing in 1605 to his intimate friend Tobie Matthew, the oldest son of the Anglican Bishop of Durham and a future Jesuit, Francis Bacon comments on his latest offspring: "I have now at last taught that child to go, at the swaddling whereof you were. My work touching the *Proficiency and Advancement of Learning* I have put into two books, whereof the former, which you saw, I account but as a Page to the latter." Matthew, then living on the continent, had seen the growth of the work and had "more right to it than any man, except Bishop Andrews, who was my Inquisitor" (4:254). Bacon's reference here to his other close friend, the famous Lancelot Andrewes, who was translating sections of the King James Bible at this time and was chosen as the Anglican intellectual to debate at the Jacobean court with the Roman Catholic representative, Cardinal Bellarmine, helps date the letter and the publication of Bacon's first major text. Andrewes became bishop on November 3, 1605. The text came out after that date.

As Bacon's letter suggests, he had been developing the ideas over a period of years, and in the gap after James I's accession in 1603, Bacon had time to write them with the experimenting style he wanted (he was receiving no preferment from the new court). When James I's first Parliament opened on March 19, 1604, Bacon became quite busy, however, and the writing of the second part of his book shows this. As Spedding notes, the grand catalogue of the successes and deficiences in the current stage of knowledge in this second part is "much less careful and elaborate than the first, and bears many marks of hasty composition" [3:256]. For this reason, the first book is not only more complete in itself as an extended kind of oration[1] but commands a unity that has made this text one of the most important, not just in English but in European cultural life. It idealizes a radically new structuring for Western culture with specific tasks to carry out that structuring, the secular specificity quite new.

The *Advancement* is, in many ways, far more revolutionary than the more affected and staged text of the *Instauratio Magna* and the *Novum Organon*. In fact, Bacon's only philosophical text in English to be published in his lifetime has special power because of its native prose that is also less mannered than the language of the *Essays*. Its power as intellectual text derives directly from its power as rhetoric, and that rhetorical force derives in turn from the extraordinary organization of its ideas and topics—all set with the calculation of a master of intellectual theater. This theater may rise, in fact, to the level of myth in ways that only a Renaissance audience would understand. Ramification—the motion of a constantly branching tree of knowledge—may appear today as only dry and trivializing. To Charles Williams, the organization of the *Advancement* resembles the cosmic, the stretching tree of Igdrasil found in the Scandinavian myth,[2] and it is likely that Bacon's audience also held this view. In terms of its calculated form alone, Bacon's *Advancement* signifies nothing less than a turning point in Renaissance English prose and the history of English prose style. The whole concept of linguistic representation shifted in the change brought on by Bacon's vision of a world that might be. Ramification, the technology of "things," is in this text as much a vision of the future as any personal cosmic vision such as in the Biblical Apocalypse. Furthermore, translated into the 1623 *De Augmentis Scientiarum*, Book Two of the 1605 *Advancement* became stage one of Bacon's Great Instauration, and a newly identified style of technology pointed to a newly realized historical moment for Western culture.

The Title

The title of Bacon's major philosophical work in English revealed to its 1605 audience its radical difference from other texts of philosophy: *The Twoo Bookes of Francis Bacon: Of the Proficience and Advancement of Learning, Divine and Humane*. Bacon knew his audience would be cultivated readers from court and university who would recognize the innovative grammar, etymology, and syntax in this title. "Proficience" derived from the Latin deponent verb *proficiscor*, of whose present participle the first word in his title would derive. The word could mean in a more comprehensive language like Latin a setting out or traveling, as in Bacon's journey motif, as well as an originating act. On the other hand, "Advancement" was, with late Latin roots through Old French, a rather new word, first used in English in Robinson's translation of Sir Thomas More's *Utopia*. The shock is that both nouns would have been employed, with their sense of progression and motion, to qualify the concept of learning or knowledge, both divine and human, a concept abstract and not considered tangible. Even more potentially startling to readers was a concept of history or chronology—"advancement"—brought to knowledge (including religious thought), as though questions of time did relate to eternal realms, making them contingent, even mutable.

In this shock, Bacon adds his own linguistic coup de grâce. The prepositional phrase in the title directs the meaning of this forward movement in time: its object is not knowledge or wisdom, solid nouns of stasis, but a gerund "learning" derived from a strong Anglo-Saxon verb. Its hybrid nature ambiguous, "learning" expresses time and motion not only by its progressive -*ing* form but its completion of the two nouns in the title, themselves derived from verbs. No such gerund had before appeared in the title of a major work in English. No such manipulation of syntax to show a new conception of time and history had been used. Bacon's audience would not miss the dialectic of the old and new at play in his title. They could not but be aware of the radical transformation of history implied in the language of the title. The shock was not only of a recognition that had been developing for centuries but of the dangerous but exhilarating freedom it now brought to Bacon's Renaissance reader.

Dedication to the King

Because of this shock, Bacon is quite careful in his opening dedication to the King to outline a conservative framing. From the first sentence, Bacon identifies his text with the old Hebraic law, the solid world of the Old Testament, on which he will draw heavily for the figuration of the *New Atlantis*. Under that "Law (excellent King) both daily sacrifices and freewill offerings" were made. So to a King Bacon has made his sacrifice, "according to my humble duty and presents of affection." So "for the later, I thought it more respective to make choice of some oblation which might rather refer to the propriety and excellency of your individual person, than to the business of your crown and state." Bacon then praises the King in a series of hyperboles that climax in his assertion that James I is a reborn Hermes Trismegistus, with "the power and fortune of a King, the knowledge and illumination of a Priest, and the learning and universality of a Philosopher." Such a "miracle" as King James deserves not just the fame of his time or the future "but also in some solid work" that will carry the "signature" of such a King. The better to honor him, Bacon's "oblation"-book will have two parts, the first "concerning the excellency of learning and knowledge, and the excellency of the merit and true glory in the augmentation and propagation thereof" and the second, "what the particular acts and works are which have

been embraced and undertaken for the advancement of learning, and
again what defects and undervalues I find in such particular acts." And
what is the purpose of these two divisions? To "excite your princely cog-
itations to visit the excellent treasure of your own mind, and thence to
extract particulars for this purpose agreeable to your magnanimity and
wisdom" (3:261–4).

In this dedication, Bacon provides a preface to his book, outlining his
method. Thus, as Bacon explains to the King in 1605, he chooses, for
the first part or book of his text, the method of exclusion. Bacon will
"clear the way, and as it were to make silence to have the true testimonies concerning the dignity of learning to be better heard without
the interruption of tacit objections." The purpose of using what will be a
familiar method of the negative in all his work will allow Bacon "to
deliver" learning "from the discredits and disgraces which it hath
received . . . from ignorance; but ignorance severally disguised; appearing sometimes in the zeal and jealousy of divines, sometimes in the
severity and arrogancy of politiques, and sometimes in the errors and
imperfections of learned men themselves" (3:264).

Erasmus had early identified "ignorance" as the prime enemy (and
other early humanists had followed, including Queen Catherine Parr). In
using this term, therefore, Bacon's framing of his whole book, from the
dedication to the King to its smallest topic, derives from his special use of
humanist analysis, what one might call his special parody of humanism.
Bacon too conceives of human society as evolving from knowledge, the
right language and books. Thus, after the enemy of ignorance has been
revealed in tripartite structure and then in a catalogue of "peccant
humors" in contemporary learning, Bacon moves on to a standard
humanist listing of types or examples—in this case, of those who gave
positive impetus to study and learning, from Jewish-Christian figures to
Greek and Roman (especially emperors). He then ends his first book with
two supreme examples of "excellency" in power and learning: Alexander
the Great and Julius Caesar. His closure on private virtue builds on three
crucial quotations from Virgil and Lucretius before the final paragraph in
which Bacon appears to be imitating the wit and lightness, the sprez-
zatura, of Sidney's closing for his *Defense of Poesy*.

Book One

The first of Bacon's attacks on ignorance, that of the religious establishment, became one of Bacon's most authoritative. Bacon's subtle reduction of church to state in even greater Erastian fashion than under

Henry VIII attracted many followers. It was not knowledge in itself that
led to the Fall, as some churchmen have said, argues Bacon, but "the
proud knowledge of good and evil" and the temptation for each human
being to give a law "unto himself." Indeed, Bacon rewrites (as elsewhere)
his mirror imagery here to support the idea that the mind is divinely set
to reflect and know "the universal world." But this knowledge must
have the "corrective spice" of charity, and here Bacon rewrites the
famous Pauline epistle on charity (I Corinthians 13): "it is an excellent
thing to speak with the tongues of men and angels," yet, "if it be severed from charity, and not referred to the good of men and mankind, it
hath rather a sounding and unworthy glory than a meriting and sub-
stantial virtue." Charity in Bacon is never anything but social; whatever
exists subjectively in terms of personal love is not altogether relevant. In
fact, all "human knowledge is confined and circumscribed" and the
"limitations are three": (1) *that we do not so place our felicity in knowledge,*
as we forget our mortality"; (2) *"that we make application of our knowledge to*
give ourselves repose and contentment, and not distaste or repining"; (3) *"that we*
do not presume by the contemplation of nature to attain to the mysteries of God."
Bacon then proceeds to argue for these positions by quoting Solomon,
Heraclitus (the first use of his "dry light" motif), Plato, and finally Job
before coming to his climactic passage that had such influence on Western culture in the centuries ahead.

   In this passage, Bacon begins by using a motif that he develops in
"Of Atheism": "It is an assured truth and a conclusion of experience,
that a little or superficial knowledge of philosophy may incline the mind
of man to atheism" but going beyond second causes, "which are next to
the senses," the mind will see dependent causes and "the works of Providence" and as in "the allegory of the poets, he will easily believe that
the highest link of nature's chain must needs be tied to the foot of
Jupiter's chair." If the text attempts to show the value of religion, Bacon
ambiguously enacts in this passage, as in his essays, an undercutting
that is devastating: the Christian religion is reduced to the language of
poets and mythology. Knowledge can only come from "the contemplation of God's creatures and works"; only "having regard to the works
and creatures themselves" with "regard to God," there can never be
"perfect knowledge" but only "wonder, which is broken knowledge."
The supposed compliment yet actual deconstruction led, in turn, to the
famous image of two books that adumbrates the whole process of sever-
ing in the Western world between religion and society, faith and reason.
For learning, the liberated reader of 1605 can now choose. The realm of
religion and the realm of nature are now equal: "To conclude therefore,

let no man, upon a weak conceit of sobriety or an ill-applied moderation, think or maintain that a man can search too far or be too well studied in the book of God's word or in the book of God's works; divinity or
philosophy; but rather let men endeavour an endless progress or proficience in both; only let men beware that they apply both to charity, and
not to swelling; to use, and not to ostentation; and again, that they do
not unwisely mingle or confound these learnings together" (3:265–8).

In his second attack, that is, on "the severity and arrogancy of politiques," Bacon answers the charge that learning "doth soften men's
minds," keeping them from honor, warfare, and good government service through pleasure and a readiness to argue. He then gives a catalogue of learned politicians from classical history and even from the
papacy, climaxing with his praise of both "two so learned princes, queen
Elizabeth and your Majesty, being as Castor and Pollux, *lucida sidera*,
stars of excellent light and most benign influence" (3:168;274). In the
third attack on learning, on "learned men themselves" or the academy,
Bacon provided his audience with another shock. He attacks humanism
itself, the very method he is using. He would force humanist-readers
also to recognize their vulnerability and the basic human condition of
the "enchanted" mind, even in the liberated and liberal, as so many
humanists saw themselves. In fact, their kind of failure "commonly
cleaveth fastest."

In Bacon's tight organization of Book One, the importance of this
section can be seen in its intricacy of topic, sub-topic, and sub-sub-topic.
Thus learned men bring disgrace to learning through three means:
"either from their fortune, or from their manners, or from the nature of
their studies." The first "is not in their power; and the second is accidental; the third only is proper to be handled," but, because in "popular
estimation and credit" the first two are important, Bacon will deal with
them. As for the first, "the derogations therefore which grow to learning
from the fortune or condition of learned men" can be sub-divided into
three: no money; too private a life; too mean an employment. As for the
second, "the manners of learned men," Bacon finds it "a thing personal
and individual." Bacon takes up four disgraces, generally defending the
eccentricity of academics, but he closes this section by giving examples
of those who "have wronged themselves and gone too far"—although
even here the example of Diogenes proves such manners justified.

For the third disgrace that learned men have given learning, Bacon
makes three sub-sub-topics. These he first calls "three vanities in studies,
whereby learning hath been most traduced" and then names "three dis-

tempers" or fevers "of learning," in the first of his anatomical metaphors for the sick body of learning (3:282). These "vanities"—the false or frivolous in learning—can be found where (1) learning has "no truth or use" or (2) persons involved in the process "are either credulous or curious" or (3) this "curiosity" or over-subtlety or high elaboration is beyond the needs of either "matter or words," that is, of content or form. To focus this crucial section, Bacon narrows the image: "so that in reason as well as in experience, there fall out to be these three distempers (as I may term them) of learning; the first, fantastical learning; the second, contentious learning; and the last, delicate learning; vain imaginations, vain altercations, vain affectations," and then Bacon adds abruptly, "and with the last I will begin."

The section that follows is one of the first analyses in the Renaissance of the Renaissance itself. History now views itself subjectively and self-consciously, with the same analysis as Puttenham had done in his historicizing of style in the 1589 *Arte of English Poesy*. Bacon takes all style out of the realm of the transcendent or sublime (his ironizing aside "no doubt" helps to serve that effect). He places linguistic style instead squarely in a process of time. In a corrupt world, nothing is capable of rising above itself; all human life, especially its language, responds to the political, social, and physical forces of time: "Martin Luther, conducted (no doubt) by an higher Providence, but in discourse of reason finding what a province he had undertaken against the Bishop of Rome and the degenerate traditions of the church, and finding his own solitude, being no ways aided by the opinions of his own time, was enforced to awake all antiquity, and to call former times to his succors to make a party against the present time; so that the ancient authors, both in divinity and in humanity, which had long time slept in libraries, began generally to be read and revolved."

As Bacon must have known quite well, what matters in this erroneous account of the formation of humanism and of the Renaissance (he omits any Italian origin) is its power as audience-gambit, not as factual truth. In 1605 Bacon must convince his English audience of the empirical and political facts behind transformations of style. He must develop in his audience a consciousness of history, something even beyond their own exalted Protestant origins, in order to make his point: bad style results from even the best social events, however—"no doubt"—divinely inspired. Thus, from Luther's historical necessity sprang "a more exquisite travail in the languages original wherein those authors did write," not only a labor to understand the classical authors themselves but to generate "the better advantage of pressing and applying their words," their own social and political agenda, even "taking liberty to coin and frame new terms of art to express their own sense and to avoid circuit of speech" without regard to "(as I may call it) lawfulness of the phrase or word." This dangerous process toward a more personal and less social language—"eloquence and variety of discourse, as the fittest and forciblest access into the capacity of the vulgar set"—had its own four-stage chronology: "admiration of ancient authors, the hate of the schoolmen, the exact study of languages, and the efficacy of preaching," all leading to "an affectionate study of eloquence and copie of speech, which then began to flourish" and the most terrible of all consequences for learning: "men began to search more after words than matter" (3:282–3).

To this dismal history, Bacon adds names of early Renaissance humanists, Continental and English, who were chief offenders. Although Bacon has chosen "an example of late times," he historicizes that all times have had such mistakes. In his Latin version in 1623, Bacon adds further sections that stress the historical necessities for language of this kind and then condemns another excrescence besides the Ciceronian prose style of Luther and others. In one of the few new passages for the *De Augmentis*, he attacks the late Renaissance vogue of the Senecan style, another "kind of hunting after words" (*Advancement*, tr. Wats, p. 18). To cap his attack on this kind of "learned ignorance" of language, Bacon incorporates two Hellenic myths: "Pygmalion's frenzy is a good emblem or portraiture of this vanity" and then the response of Hercules on seeing an image of Adonis in a temple: "Nil sacri es [you are not holy]." Bacon can now make his synthesis and show his heroic figure of the new scientist as a new kind of Hercules. Hercules will be a persistent motif in Bacon's texts, as John Steadman has demonstrated,[3] and "so there is none of Hercules' followers in learning, that is, the more severe and laborious sort of inquirers into truth, but will despise those delicacies and affectations, as indeed capable of no divineness" (3:283–5). This kind of attack on a false linguistic style for the new type of European hero would not be missed in the centuries ahead, not least by the Royal Society in England and in Bishop Sprat's 1660 directions for the proper prose style for the modern English elite.

The second "distemper" or fever of the sick body of learning is worse than the first, as "vain matter is worse than vain words." Quoting St. Paul, Bacon sees this vanity in either too much novelty of terms or too strict positions. Bacon here launches his strongest attack on the Catholic schoolmen, and his insect and animal imagery dramatizes his assault: "Surely, like as many substances in nature which are solid do putrefy and corrupt into worms," so "good and sound knowledge" breaks up into "vermiculate questions, which have indeed a kind of quickness and life of spirit, but no soundness of matter or goodness of quality." Such "degenerate learning" among "the schoolmen" came from their social conditions: "sharp and strong wits" with "abundance of leisure, and small variety of reading," so that "their wits being shut up in the cells of a few authors (chiefly Aristotle their dictator) as their persons were shut up in the cells of monasteries and colleges; and knowing little history, either of nature or time; did, out of no great quantity of matter, and infinite agitation of wit, spin out unto us those laborious webs of learning which are extant in their books."

This early analysis of the sociological conditions of learning made Bacon a pioneer in fields like sociology and anthropology, as Robert Merton has shown.[4] Here it leads to his definition that further divides the realms of religion and nature: "For the wit and mind of man, if it work upon matter, which is the contemplation of the creatures of God, worketh according to the stuff, and is limited thereby; but if it work upon itself, as the spider worketh his web, then it is endless, and brings forth indeed cobwebs of learning, admirable for the fineness of thread and work, but of no substance or profit." These schoolmen, with "their great thirst of truth and unwearied travail of wit," might have "proved excellent lights, to the great advancement of all learning and knowledge," but they are, like dogs pent up in darkness, "fierce with dark keeping." This graphic metaphor allows Bacon to make a scoring point with his Protestant audience: as in religion the Catholic scholastics' "pride inclined to leave the oracle of God's word," the Bible, so in learning, "they ever left the oracle of God's word and adored the deceiving and deformed images which the unequal mirror of their own minds or a few received authors or principles did represent unto them." Thus Bacon's implied question to his audience: do *you* want to be like *them*?

The third "vice or disease" or fever of learning attacks "the essential form of knowledge," which is, says Bacon in a key definition, "nothing but a representation of the truth: for the truth of being and the truth of knowing are one, differing no more than the direct beam and the beam reflected." Knowing and being are the same; therefore, for Bacon, making and being are the same, and inventors (and even mechanics) are great metaphysicians and philosophers. In this section Bacon discusses at length the errors of science that have come from bad uses of history,

either the "illusions" of ecclesiastical history or of natural history from
Pliny on, or from false studies such as astrology, natural magic, or
alchemy. For this latter, Bacon draws another motif, the analogy of
Aesop's fable about gold in a vineyard and the indirect good results of
alchemy. Thus, too much credit has been given to these early "authors in
sciences" when "in arts mechanical the first deviser comes shortest, and
time addeth and perfecteth," as exemplified by "artillery, sailing, printing" (3:287–90) or gunpowder, the compass, and the printing press,
three recent technologies of European society (3:284–90).

At this point in his progressive argument, Bacon leaves the three
fevers of learning but continues his anatomy-motif. He turns to a catalogue of illnesses almost as life-threatening as the fevers but not completely destructive. In learning "There are some other rather peccant
humours [unhealthy dispositions]," writes Bacon, "than formed diseases" that he will introduce "under a popular observation" of a serial
catalogue of ten items and then one last to be developed in Bacon's most
elaborate simile. The series will function, therefore, as a means to reca-
pitulate succinctly, as though in expanded aphorisms, large topics and
motifs that permeate the whole book.

"The first," says Bacon in a punning example of polyptoton, "is the
extreme affecting of two extremes," of antiquity and "novelty" or newness of concept. In this "the children of time" imitate the father Saturn,
"for as he devoureth his children, so one of them seeketh to devour and
suppress the other." For Bacon, antiquity is envious of the new, and the
new "cannot be content to add but it must deface." The Jewish prophet
Jeremiah was more correct with his image of the way and the choices
there: one should stand on the road of the old ways and "when the discovery is well taken, then to make progression." Bacon adds his own
invention of a new Latin aphorism, the Latin giving it authority but the
content quite revolutionary, reverberating for the next centuries: "And
to speak truly, *Antiquitas saeculi juventus mundi* [antiquity in age is the
youth of the world]." The most modern time is the ancient world.

Almost all of the next "peccant humours" reflect the concern of finding the right forms for surveying and working with time and history.
Thus the second "error" comes from the first: "a distrust that any thing
should be now to be found out, which the world should have missed and
passed over so long time." Here Bacon continues his reversal of the oldest of traditions—the reverence for the past—in order to originate in his
text a concept of progress. This will be revisionism of a profound order
for Western culture. Such a reversal is possible because of the heroic

example of Alexander the Great who (reported by Livy) dared to conquer the world because he despised vain fears of the future. As this section will be more developed in the *Novum Organum*, so will the famous motif originating here: "And the same happened to Columbus in the western navigation." The third evil "humour" follows: "the best hath prevailed" and nothing can be added. To answer this "humour," Bacon gives his most classic statement of a famous motif: "time seemeth to be of the nature of a river or stream, which carrieth down to us that which is light and blown up, and sinketh and drowneth that which is weighty and solid." In the fourth "humour," Bacon points out a consequence for this theory of time: the right method for science is not "the over-early and peremptory reduction of knowledge into arts and methods" (from which science does not grow) but, as young men who early have their shape do not grow taller, "so knowledge, while it is in aphorisms and observations, it is in growth."

In his fifth "peccant humour" Bacon calls for universality in scientific method, the rising from "a flat or a level" to a higher principle. The sixth "humour" carries a harsh attack on the humanists themselves: "another error hath proceeded from too great a reverence, and a kind of adoration of the mind and understanding of man" so that, quoting Heraclitus about the little world of human beings, Bacon notes that "intellectualists" now "disdain to spell and so by degrees to read in the volume of God's works." If this section and the others here are more elaborately developed in the aphorisms of the first book of the *Novum Organum*, here their serial brevity increases the pace and progression of Bacon's narrative of Book One and sharpens its purgative effect. In the seventh error, personal "conceits" are infused into arguments, as with Plato and theology, Aristotle and logic, and Bacon's contemporary Gilbert with the bad philosophy brought into his discovery of the magnet; in the eighth "humour," impatience and haste to judgment vitiate all results when the better of the two ways of the ancients points toward a path "rough and troublesome in the entrance, but after a while fair and even" so that "if a man will begin with certainties, he shall end in doubts." In his ninth "humour" Bacon returns to this question of method—"the manner of the tradition and delivery of knowledge, which is for the most part magistral and peremptory, and not ingenuous and faithful; in a sort as may be soonest believed, and not easilest examined" (3:290–3).

Bacon then relates "other" less developed "errors" only to lead to his resplendent climax of this sequence: "But the greatest error of all the

rest is the mistaking or misplacing of the last or furthest end of knowledge." For his eleventh and final "peccant humour" Bacon writes an
elaborate simile based on six analogies from architecture: "for men have
entered into a desire of learning and knowledge, sometimes"—this
adverbial qualifier used throughout until the last two images—"upon a
natural curiosity and inquisitive appetite" that is compared to seeking
"in knowledge a couch, whereupon to rest a searching and restless
spirit"; the second "sometimes to entertain the minds with variety and
delight" and its analogy, "a terrace, for a wandering and variable mind
to walk up and down with a fair prospect"; the third, "sometimes for
ornament and reputation" and analogy, "a tower of state, for a proud
mind to raise itself upon"; the fourth, "sometimes to enable them to vic-
tory of wit and contradiction" and analogy, "a fort or commanding
ground, for strife and contention"; the fifth, "most times for lucre and
profession" and analogy, "a shop, for profit and sale"; and then the climax: "and seldom sincerely to give a true account of their gift of reason,
to the benefit and use of men" and the analogy, "not a rich storehouse,
for the glory of the Creator and the relief of man's estate." This long
complex simile is not conjoined in the text but separates its first section
of the term to be compared in a rising figure of gradatio. Bacon then
repeats this rising figure in the second term, the comparison, in order to
emphasize a basic principle at work in the composition of his *Advancement*. That is, the theatricality of his arguments inscribes an oratorical
form judicial in intent, defending true learning and condemning the
bad, but deliberative in effect, converting his audience to greater labor
in time and history. The simile leads to the closure of this major part of
Bacon's first book of the *Advancement*. The closure ends with another
simile that completes Bacon's network of sexual imagery: "But as
heaven and earth do conspire and contribute to the use and benefit of
man, so the end ought to be, from both philosophies to separate and
reject vain speculations and whatsoever is empty and void, and to preserve and augment whatsoever is solid and fruitful; that knowledge may
not be as a curtesan [whore], for pleasure and vanity only, or as a bond-
woman, to acquire and gain to her master's use; but as a spouse, for
generation, fruit, and comfort" (3:293–5).

   The rest of Book One of Bacon's *Advancement* takes a different strategy, a rather more conservative one of typology. Once more, Bacon's
parody of a known form—Christian typology—sets up his own series of
cultural heroes that have exemplified the honor of learning. From "the
attributes and acts of God" Himself to those of the angels and all the

heroes of the narratives in the Hebrew Bible that fascinated the Renaissance to those of "our Savior" and "the Holy Spirit" (both together given one paragraph) and the examples of St. Paul, the Church Fathers, Reformers, and the Jesuits, Bacon turns to the "human proofs" of the Hellenic and Roman world, especially six emperors, and so on to Elizabeth I. Then at some length he discusses the examples of Alexander the Great and Julius Caesar and finishes his typology by generalizing on the progression "from imperial and military virtue to moral and private virtue," using key aphorisms from the ancients, notably Virgil and Lucretius (3:295–318).

But, when Bacon closes the organized but digressive discourse of the first book of his *Advancement*, he writes a tightly concluding paragraph. Its wit and allusion echoes the end of Sidney's *Defense of Poesy*. "Nevertheless I do not pretend," begins Bacon in a distinctly personal confiding tone to his reader, "and I know it will be impossible for me by any pleading of mine, to reverse the judgment either of Aesop's cock, that preferred the barleycorn before the gem." His text may not really convert. Then using either-or dichotomies, Bacon launches into a series of such examples of bad judgment, whether the judgment of Midas deciding between Apollo and Pan or that of Paris, or of Nero's mother Agrippina who preferred that her son kill her rather than lose an empire, or of Ulysses, who chose an old woman before immortality, ("being a figure of those which prefer custom and habit before all excellency,") or any other number of "popular judgments." If such bad judgments and their like will always continue, so also will that "whereupon learning hath ever relied, and which faileth not," namely, the sense of generation to be found in true learning. In the Latin phrase that ends his text, directly copied from his commonplace book, the *Promus of Formularies and Elegancies*, Bacon reveals what he wants: an audience of real "sons" and disciples. By them his text will be justified (the word carries its parody of Luther's famous "justification by faith alone"). Thus Bacon ends the text with the Old Testament aphorism "Justificata est sapientia a filiis suis" (wisdom is justified by her own sons) (3:319).

Book Two

One of the most eloquent passages of Renaissance English prose occurs at the opening of the second book of the 1605 *Advancement*. Once more, Bacon dedicates his work to James I, but this passage by the forty-four-year-old Learned Counsel adumbrates all the museums, galleries, and foundations for research of the next four centuries, setting for the first time in a major European work the necessity of such social centers for learning. Bacon's powerful English prose gives permission, so to speak, for his culture to return to corporate social endeavours, as with the monasteries of old, that will support intellectual life as they renew and reform human society. As Bacon praises James I, he also asks him directly, in his typically tripartite form: "Let the ground therefore be laid, that all works are overcome by amplitude of reward, by soundness of direction, and by the conjunction of labors" and these will have a triple effect: "the first multiplieth endeavour, the second preventeth error, and the third supplieth the frailty of man." Because "the mean is more effectual than any inforcement or accumulation of endeavours," there is labor to be carried out with specific directions: "works or acts of merit toward learning" deal with "three objects: the places of learning, the books of learning, and the persons of the learned." Just as water raining on earth needs to be collected, so with "this excellent liquor of knowledge" or it too will be dissipated.

Further, in this dedication that serves as a preface for the second book, Bacon wants the King (and his implied reader as king) "to look unto that part of the race which is before us [rather] than look back to that which is already attained." Consequently, he will examine—true to his method—the current defects in the social structures of such learning about him. First, in the contemporary "great foundations of colleges in Europe," Bacon observes "they are all dedicated to professions, and none left free to arts and sciences at large"; salaries are too small for lecturers; there is a need for support for experimentation whether "appertaining to Vulcanus or Daedalus, furnace or engine, or any other kind; and there-fore as secretaries and spials of princes and states bring in bills for intel-ligence, so you must allow the spials and intelligencers of nature to bring in bills, or else you shall be ill advertised"; there are also needs for proper government of "universities" or proper "visitation" by "princes or superior persons" and for more of "a fraternity in learning and illumina-tion" and, finally, for researchers—"writers and inquirers"—to deal with areas of knowledge that are deficient.

With this last concern, Bacon opens the door for himself and the task of his book. Now "the removing of all the defects" that Bacon has listed comprise nothing less than an "*opera basilica* [works for a king] towards which the endeavours of a private man may be but as an image in a crossway, that may point at the way but cannot go it." Toward this end,

Bacon will now inscribe "a general and faithful perambulation of learning, with an inquiry what parts thereof lie fresh and waste, and not improved and converted by the industry of man." Bacon is aware of the tremendous scope of his task, but, as Solomon wrote in Proverbs 22:13 *Dicit piger, Leo est in via* (the lazy person says, a lion is on the road), and as Virgil praised, in the *Aeneid*, the feats of the athletes at the funeral games by noting *possunt quia posse videntur* (they are able to do because they seemed to be able), so now: "I shall be content that my labours be esteemed but as the better sort of wishes; for as it asketh some knowledge to demand a question not impertinent, so it requireth some sense to make a wish not absurd" (3:322–9).

The Survey of Human Knowledge

In opening the second book of his 1605 *Advancement* Bacon is direct in his tripartite division of "man's understanding, which is the seat of learning": "history to his memory, poesy to his imagination, and philosophy to his reason." Divine learning also has a triple arrangement: history of the church, parables, and holy "doctrine or precept," with prophecy as only "divine history," except that "narration may be before the fact as well as after." In the expansion of this first section of his survey in the first chapter of the *Descriptio Globi Intellectualis*, a short unfinished text written around 1612, and in the first chapter of the second book of the 1623 *De Augmentis*, Bacon elaborates on this basic structure for his second book; and in 1623 he is clear that, in the case of divine learning, he will postpone discussion.

Any approach to the second book and its vast encyclopedic scheme, even in so cursory a summary as this, must begin with the large framework. If the framework is that of a Renaissance encyclopedia, the actual intent of the work is virtually anti-encyclopedic, not to survey all knowledge but only areas where knowledge does not exist. Nowhere is the grand soteriological purpose of his text more evident than in the extraordinary rhetorical organization of Bacon's topics and ideas in the second book. This reifying of purpose into linguistic structure is developed even more in Bacon's translation of his book into Latin in 1623. Here Bacon worked to implement even more of a Ramist logical structure. Such power of representation in these texts was recognized in Bacon's own time. His chaplain and executor, Dr. Rawley, alludes to these rhetorical strategies the year after Bacon's death: "As for his lordship's love of order,

I can refer any man to his lordship's Latin book, *De Augmentis Scientiarum*; which (if my judgment be anything) is written in the exactest order that I know any writing to be" (2:37). Although here no close comparison between the 1605 English text and the 1623 Latin text can be made, the reader can still see the larger cohesive structure at work by following Bacon's own organization in a form and frame that would anticipate all the later volumes of modern encyclopedias and instructional manuals.

Thus the first of the structures of "understanding" to be examined is history, and it has its own sub-divisions of "natural, civil, ecclesiastical, and literary." The last term means the humanist study of language and arts and so for Bacon it represents the heart of any kind of learning enterprise. Yet this fourth kind of history Bacon finds deficient. Demonstrating deficiencies in current methods of learning is, of course, the primary purpose of his survey. So Bacon would subject the exalted world of learning to the same reductive historicizing—"described and represented from age to age"—as in histories natural, civil, and ecclesiastical. What would be the point of showing the rise and fall and then resurgence of learning in time? It would "make learned men wise in the use and administration of learning" (3:329–30). It would shift the emphasis from transcendent to empirical.

Natural history is itself sub-divided into three topics: "of nature in course, of nature erring or varying, and of nature altered or wrought" (3:330). The third history is one more source for a history of mechanical arts and inventions and a general upgrading of a formerly despised (at least by intellectuals) form of human endeavor. What Bacon calls "civil history" also has a tripartite sub-division, "not unfitly to be compared with the three kinds of pictures or images," for if the second division may be "perfect histories," the first and third are not: "memorials are history unfinished, or the first or rough draughts of history, and antiquities are history defaced, or some remnants of history which have casually escaped the shipwreck of time" (3:333). Under "perfect histories," Bacon has five sub-sub-divisions, at least in the Latin translation: chronicles (itself sub-sub-sub-divided into ancient and modern); lives; narrations; annals; and "cosmography" (a rudimentary form of sociology and anthropology), in all of which Bacon finds varying deficiences. Finally, ecclesiastical history is sub-divided into church, prophecy, and what Bacon calls "providence." For the 1605 and 1623 texts, literary history forms a kind of appendix with examples of orations, letters, and apophthegms. (3:333–43; 4:300–14).

The second division of "man's understanding" or "poesy" is also divided into three groups: "narrative, representative, and allusive." Although Bacon finds no deficiency here, this brief section of the 1605 *Advancement* enlarged in 1623 has proven the source for theory after theory of Bacon's imagination, his attitude toward poetry and literature in general, and his conception of art. Correctly marked by commentators as a source for Bacon's whole epistemological scheme, the passage describes a psychological process: "And therefore [poetry] was ever thought to have some participation of divineness, because it doth raise and erect the mind, by submitting the shews of things to the desires of the mind; whereas reason doth buckle and bow the mind unto the nature of things." In this definition, it is clear how Bacon's concept of subjectivity functions in a broken universe, because poetry, in a passage echoing Sidney, "doth truly refer to the imagination; which, being not tied to the laws of matter [as true science is], may at pleasure join that which nature hath severed, and sever that which nature hath joined, and so make unlawful matches and divorces of things," not the true generative marriages of genuine science or induction. Thus such "feigned history" as poetry allows will "give some satisfaction to the mind of man in those points where the nature of things doth deny it," the objective world being in poetry always inferior "in proportion" to one's shaping subjectivity freed of the subject-object dichotomy.

Consequently, "there is agreeable to the spirit of man a more ample greatness, a more exact goodness, and a more absolute variety, than can be found in the nature of things." Only "allusive or parabolical" poetry, "a narration applied only to express some special purpose or conceit," carries positive possibilities for exploring the objective "nature of things." Already in 1605, Bacon is outlining the kind of text he will write in his 1609 book of Hellenic myths, *De Sapientia Veterum*, and in his 1623 scientific text based on myth, *De Principiis atque Originibus secundum fabulas Cupidinis et Coeli*. As "parabalical texts," these are among Bacon's most sophisticated works. Finally, poetry is, in another gardening image, "as a plant that cometh of the lust of the earth, without a formal seed," but no matter what its popularity and its "expressing of affections, passions, corruptions, and customs," says Bacon concluding this section, "it is not good to stay too long in the theatre." He would now pass on "to the judicial place or palace of the mind" (3:343–6), and the greatest of the parts of human learning, philosophy.

"Palace of the Mind"

In the 1623 *De Augmentis Scientiarum*, this third division of Bacon's encyclopedic survey is greatly enlarged (in fact, its Chapters 3–9 contain the
discussion of philosophy and conclude the text). The schemes more simply stated in the 1605 *Advancement* are still in place, however. Once
more, Bacon has a tripartite division as his main structure for analysis:
philosophy as divine, as natural, and as human. In the first Bacon discusses not so much theology as his theory of the unity of all secular
knowledge, what he calls "*Philosophia Prima*, Primitive or Summary Philosophy," although he rehearses piously again his arguments against
atheism with a paragraph on "the nature of angels and spirits." With a
kind of incipient psychology, Bacon commends the study of devils, for
"it is no more unlawful to inquire the nature of evil spirits than to
enquire the force of poisons in nature, or the nature of sin and vice in
morality," although he would "challenge" previous writings as too "fab-
ulous and fantastical."

For the second division, Bacon sub-divides natural philosophy "into
the mine and the furnace" or into speculative and operative or into "natural science or theory" and "natural prudence." The first of these is further divided into "physic" and "metaphysic," or "that which is inherent in
matter and therefore transitory" and "that which is abstracted and fixed,"
the two divisions rising from Aristotle's four causes, material and efficient
on the one hand, and, on the other, formal and final. Bacon will render,
of course, his own variations on Aristotle. For him, "physic" relates to the
first two causes, that is, "in a middle term or distance between natural
history and metaphysic"; and Aristotle's formal cause or "metaphysic"
reduced to a kind of formula in physics is to be used in experiments,
where nothing is transcendent. Aristotle's real metaphysics, that of final
causes, is for Bacon a kind of misplaced rhetorical term, causing difficulty
in science as "remoras and hinderances" that "stay and slug the ship from
further sailing." Just as all final causes in Plato are mixed too much with
theology, so in Aristotle with logic. But, in the discussion of metaphysics
(enlarged in 1623), Bacon sees two positive strengths for such universal
learning: (1) it will "abridge the infinity of individual experience" by generalizing toward some end, as in the pyramid of knowledge itself, at the
peak of which is "the summary law of nature"; and (2) "it doth enfran-
chise the power of man unto the greatest liberty and possibility of works
and effects." At this point of discussing highest abstraction, Bacon introduces mathematics and its study. If misused, mathematics could hinder

the true advancement and progression of knowledge. If, from the seventeenth century on, Bacon has been attacked for this failure to appreciate the role of mathematics in the development of science (a failure heightened by his failure to produce his own non-mathematical logic), in his denial of such a role for mathematics Bacon has been consistent. Mathematics is one more instance of that tendency of the human mind to become an "enchanted glass."[5]

The more operative part of natural philosophy or "natural prudence" is also sub-divided into three parts. They correspond to the three parts involved in the dichotomy of natural science: "experimental" like the natural history needed for any work in physics; "philosophical" like physics or the knowledge of physical causes; and "magical" referring to Bacon's theory of empirical metaphysics. Although Bacon condemns the latter, "far differing in truth of nature from such a knowledge as we require, as the story of king Arthur of Britain, or Hugh of Bourdeaux, differs from Caesar's commentaries in truth of story," he spends more time discussing it (at least in 1605). At the end of his discussion of natural philosophy, Bacon is careful once more to define himself and his text: "for my part, as I affect not to dissent, so I purpose not to contend." Rather, originating an image that George Herbert would use as the frame for one of the great poems of the later Renaissance, Bacon defines one of the commanding strategies of this work.

> And as Alexander Borgia was wont to say of the expedition of the French for Naples, that they came with chalk to mark up their lodgings, and not with weapons to fight; so I like beter that entry of truth which cometh peaceably with chalk to mark up those minds which are capable to lodge and harbour it, than that which cometh with pugnacity and contention.[6]

To his natural philosophy, Bacon would add three collections that would facilitate the process he has just defined: a *"calendar of doubts"* that scientists would develop as a kind of addendum as they worked; in the same manner, a *"calendar of popular errors"*; and finally "some collection to be made painfully and understandingly *de antiquis philosophiis*, out of all the possible light which remaineth to us of them." Then Bacon summarizes where he is in the development of his second book of the *Advancement*: "Thus have we now dealt with two of the three beams of man's knowledge: that *Radius Directus*, which is referred to nature, *Radius Refractus*, which is referred to God, and cannot report truly because of the inequality of the medium." Bacon now moves on to the last of the areas of knowledge to be surveyed, the most crucial for his 1605 audience: "There resteth *Radius Reflexus* whereby man beholdeth and contemplateth himself" (3:351–66).

Human Creativity and Work: The Human Being as "Segregate" and "Congregate"

"We come therefore now," says Bacon in his final section of the 1605 *Advancement*, "to that knowledge whereunto the ancient oracle directeth us, which is *the knowledge of ourselves.*" For this analysis of self Bacon is at his most objective: this sub-division of the last major division of "man's understanding," that is, philosophy, is itself divided into "man segregate, or distributively" and "congregate, or in society," or "Simple and Particular, or Conjugate and Civil." Then "humanity particular consisteth of the same parts whereof man consisteth," body and mind, first considered together, "in regard of the knowledge concerning the *sympathies and concordances between the mind and body.*" Bacon's fervor for such sympathy further subdivides itself into the sub-sub-sub dichotomy of "discovery" and "impression." The first is divided into the sub-sub-sub-sub topics of "two arts, both of prediction or prenotion," one from Aristotle's "physiognomy" or "disposition of the mind" foretold by shape of the body, and the other "exposition of natural dreams," which Hippocrates examined. "Impression" itself breaks down into a dichotomy of effect of bodily "humours" on mind and "passions or apprehensions of the mind" on the body. Then Bacon returns to the larger dichotomy of body and mind, and begins his analysis of the body by adding four sub-sub-sub-sub topics for the "health, beauty, strength, and pleasure" or the knowledges of medicine, cosmetic art, athletics, and "art voluptuary."

If this organization appears almost painfully complex, it was actually quite simple in comparison to the branching outlines of analyses in Ramist logic and in other texts of the day with their elaborate visual "trees." What informs all of Bacon's emphasis on detail, however, is a passion that sees the larger relationships of objects and processes within a whole. This fervor is never missed in so composed and detailed a work as the 1605 *Advancement* and the 1623 *De Augmentis*, in which Bacon would so attempt to relate part to whole that Dr. Rawley would hold the text up to the Caroline audiences of the late Renaissance as a model. In the *Sylva Sylvarum* and in the natural histories, Bacon simply lists and catalogues his observations. But in 1605 and 1623, Bacon's text in its organization would actualize his theory of form and instantiate the organic unity for which he was calling in his theory. In his actual text Bacon would attempt a synthesis of part to whole. In fact, at the opening of the last section of his *Advancement*, he addresses this problem of the exceedingly organized strategy he will use: "And generally let this be a rule, that all partitions of knowledge be accepted for lines and veins, than for sections and separations; and that the continuance and entireness of knowledge be preserved. For the contrary hereof hath made particular sciences to become barren, shallow, and erroneous; while they have not been nourished and maintained from the common fountain" (3:366–7).

Noting deficiences in the bodily knowledges, Bacon then turns to the mind. Immediately he sets up another dichotomy, "*the substance or nature of the soul or mind*" and "*the faculties or functions thereof*" (3:379). It is the second that concerns Bacon and in the 1605 *Advancement* Bacon turns to this second topic, "the faculties of the mind" at once subdivided into another dichotomy, "the one respecting [human] Understanding and Reason, the other [human] Will, Appetite, and Affection; whereof the former produceth Position or Decree, the later Action or Execution." At this point, in his introduction to what will be a lengthy discussion, the faculties of the mind under human knowledge "segregate"—in the *De Augmentis* the analysis will run for over three whole books (five, six, and seven). Bacon gives one of his crucial definitions. He inscribes the place of the human imagination. Although the kind of synthesis that Bacon sees this faculty performing is hardly Coleridgean, it still has a powerful function, the role of "an agent or *nuncius* in both provinces, both the judicial and the ministerial." Imagination is a bonding agent: "For Sense sendeth over to Imagination before Reason have judged; and Reason sendeth over to Imagination before the Decree can be acted; for Imagination ever precedeth Voluntary Motion." Then, as another image to underscore argument, Bacon uses a classical myth: "saving that this Janus of Imagination hath differing faces; for the face towards Reason hath the print of Truth, but the face toward Action hath the print of Good." Furthermore, Bacon's imagination is not passive, "simply and only a messenger; but is invested with or at leastwise usurpeth no small authority in itself, besides the duty of the message." Imagination influences greatly "matters of Faith and Religion," but "as for Poesy, it is rather a pleasure or play of imagination, than a work or duty thereof," and both here and in 1623, there is, as Spedding notes, no separate "place for Imagination among the parts of knowledge which concern the faculties of the human mind" (3:382–3). For this reason poetry as a product of imagination in the inquiry that deals with "the faculties of the human mind" cannot be considered as a part of knowledge, but, as Bacon has shown elsewhere, in the larger frame of human experience, poetry is central to knowledge.

"Intellectual Arts"

Far more crucial to knowledge than poetry are what Bacon calls intellectual arts, those concerning reason. Ironically the four that Bacon names are borrowed directly from the modes of rhetoric to be found in any Renaissance textbook: invention, judgment, memory, and delivery, "for man's labour is to *invent* that which is *sought* or *propounded;* or to *judge* that which is *invented;* or to *retain* that which *judged;* or to *deliver over* that which is *retained*." Bacon is making here one of his most radical parodies, as Wilbur Samuel Howell has noted,[7] a special kind of transfer and reduction in the position of reason, making it more efficient than transcendent in its functioning. Rhetorical terms now describe the true work of reason. This section is considerably more developed in the *De Augmentis* than in the 1605 *Advancement*, but in the earlier text Bacon clarifies his general lines of analysis with a special English gusto, as in his discussion of "the West-Indian Prometheus" where he is virtually inventing academic disciplines like social anthropology and cultural historiography.

Thus, in 1605, invention is under the intellectual arts as a function of the mind, mind itself under the "segregate" aspect of "human" philosophy, "human" itself under the general topic of philosophy as one of the three parts of "man's understanding"—to repeat Bacon's pyramidical strategy. Invention is sub-divided into two subjects, "much differing": "arts and sciences" and "speech and arguments." The first is not only deficient in using the syllogism with its dependence on words but deficient in a special way explained by legal and commercial analogy: "as if in the making of an inventory touching the estate of a defunct it should be set down *that there is no ready money*" (3:384–5). To remedy this deficiency, the two stages of Bacon's true method in his *Novum Organum* will be required: *Experientia literata* (or Learned Experience) and *Interpretatio Naturae* (or Interpretation of Nature). In his 1623 *De Augmentis* Bacon still has hopes of finishing what he had begun in his *Novum Organum*: "Of the New Organon I say nothing, nor shall I give any taste of it here; as I propose by the divine favour to compose a complete work on that subject,—being the most important thing of all" (4:421). But he did not. As Jardine has shown, it is doubtful whether Bacon ever proceeds beyond the first of these methods, the Hunt for Pan or Learned Experience, described as the fourth part of Bacon's *Distributio Operis*.[8]

In the opening of his analysis of the second part of invention, Bacon accomplishes one of those linguistic miracles that seem so natural that the transformation can be missed. He redefines the term "invention" taking it out of a strict Latin etymology, the act of coming on or upon, and out of its rhetorical context, that is, of looking up topics or materials to be used for an oration from a promptuary or commonplace book, or what Bacon will now call "Preparation and Suggestion." Rather, in 1605, for the first time (at least in a major text,) Bacon's invention takes on its modern meaning, the hallowed term that honored the litany once learned in all American grammar schools of modern inventors of technology, such as Edison, Bell, and Whitney. "The invention of speech or argument is not properly an invention: for to invent is to discover that we know not, and not to recover or resummon that which we already know." Nevertheless Bacon does explore the older usage and points out, by suggestion, that there is a deficiency of topics, especially particular topics to indicate areas of investigation in "every particular knowledge" and therefore "things of great use." The principle to be used here is as in his Greek myth of the Hunt for Pan: *Ars inveniendi adolescit cum inventis* (the art of discovery grows with discoveries) (3:389–92)—the crucial aphorism that ends the first book of the *Novum Organum*.

The second of the intellectual faculties, "the arts of judgment, which handle the natures of proofs and demonstrations," finds its deepest significance at once, as Bacon notes, "which as to induction hath a coincidence with invention; *for in all inductions, whether in good or vicious form, the same action of the mind which inventeth, judgeth; all one as in the sense.*" Induction is truly the child of time. Otherwise, all proof is by labored syllogism. All of Bacon's consequent Interpretation of Nature begins and ends in such a conceptualizing of the process of induction. In the second method of judgment called "by way of caution," Bacon is more precise, dealing with the force of the Greek *elenches* or series of refutations. In turn, this "caution" leads Bacon to his definition of the weakness of the human mind itself, which he now calls "an enchanted glass," whose fallacies Bacon sees here as "idols" or "false appearances," the full description of which will be climaxed in the *Novum Organum*. Bacon's third intellectual faculty, "the custody or retaining of knowledge," subdivides into writing and memory, the former with "characters" and their nature and then what Bacon calls "the order of the *entry*," with the latter further subdivided, in Bacon's branching tree of knowledge, into the "intentions" of "prenotion" and "emblem." If the former helps to focus memory, the latter has a more distinct purpose: "Emblem reduceth conceits intellectual to images sensible, which strike the memory more" (3:392–9). It thus facilitates the more practical use of axioms with more illustrations of such given in the 1623 Latin text.

The final section of Bacon's four intellectual faculties, "which is transitive, concerning the expressing or transferring our knowledge to others" is termed "Tradition or Delivery" (3:399). It is considerably more developed in the 1623 Latin text where it comprises the entire Book Six. There are three parts. (1) Either as speech or writing, this "organ" for such "tradition" (or "that which is passed on" in its Latin past participle root) offers, in a generalized description, an incidental but fascinating look into the nature of characters and ciphers. (2) The more critical analysis lies in what Bacon calls the "Method of Tradition," which he sees as deficient and stemming from logic "as a part of Judgment." (3) In what Bacon calls "the Illustration of Tradition," where Bacon develops his theory of rhetoric. All of these sections are more copiously illustrated in the 1623 *De Augmentis*.

In analyzing the second, his method of delivery, Bacon makes a crucial distinction between delivery or "tradition" for "the *use* of knowledge" and for "the *progression* of knowledge," both within his fundamental conception of knowledge as serial: "for since the labour and life of one man cannot attain to perfection of knowledge, the wisdom of the tradition is that which inspireth the felicity of continuance and proceeding." From this distinction derives Bacon's two methods of the "magistral" and "the other of Probation," or in 1623 the "initiative." This dichotomy leads to Bacon's definition of the best method of delivery as "a thread to be spun on" and in the same mode as that in which the initial invention was made, the whole definition illustrated by organic plant imagery. In the what Bacon calls "Another diversity of Method," the "Enigmatical and Disclosed," Bacon continues his "sons" motif. In another "diversity" he re-asserts his theory of the aphorism and the value of a linguistic form that offers "knowledge broken" (the same metaphor earlier used for "wonder" or the true knowledge of God) that "do invite men to enquire farther." The other diversities or distinctions of the method of delivery state, at least in the catalogue of 1605, themes and motifs found throughout his canon of works. They function always as particular methods, avoiding generalities. Otherwise, knowledge will be vague "and no more aiding to practice, than an Ortelius' universal map to direct the way between London and York" (3:403–8).

Rhetoric

In his third section, "Illustration of Tradition," Bacon defines his "Rhetoric, or Art of Eloquence; a science excellent, and excellently well laboured." It is a critical passage for understanding Bacon's own strategies of representation. Although rhetoric "is inferior to wisdom," as Solomon illustrates, "with people it is the more mighty" and it "prevaileth in an active life." For Bacon, both Aristotle and Cicero "exceed themselves" in their texts on rhetoric. Bacon here notes deficiencies not in the "rules or use of the art itself" but offers "some collections which may as handmaids attend the art." First he would give a general definition of rhetoric that relates to Bacon's larger conceptions of "man's understanding": "the duty and office of rhetoric is *to apply reason to imagination* for the better moving of the will." Because Bacon's next major section of examination in his *Advancement* will be on the human will, the study of rhetoric here performs a transition. For Bacon, "the end of logic is to teach a form of argument to secure reason, and not to entrap it; the end of morality is to procure the affections to obey reason, and not to invade it; the end of rhetoric is to fill the imagination to second reason, and not to oppress it." Indeed, "reason would become captive and servile, if eloquence of persuasions did not practise and win the imagination from the affection's part, and contract a confederacy between the reason and imagination against the affections." Affections "carry ever an appetite to good, as reason doth," but with a critical difference: "*affection beholdeth merely the present; reason beholdeth the future and sum of time.*" Result: if "the present" fills "the imagination more, reason is commonly vanquished; but after that force of eloquence and persuasion hath made things future and remote appear as present," as happens in Bacon's utopia the *New Atlantis*, "then upon the revolt of the imagination reason prevaileth" (3:409–10). This definition of the power of the imagination would have strong impact on later conceptualizings of the imagination in future centuries.

As a consequence of Bacon's definition, "rhetoric can be no more charged with the colouring of the worse part, than logic with sophistry, or morality with vice." At this point, Bacon reinvests Zeno's famous aphorism: "it appeareth also that logic differeth from rhetoric, not only as the fist from the palm, the one close, the other at large; but much more in this, that logic handleth reason exact and in truth, and rhetoric handleth it as it is planted in popular opinions and manners." In another subtle transformation, Bacon has redefined not only the nature of rhetoric but the nature of logic. Logic has become, on one level, another method, however grand its purpose, of rhetoric, another delivery system. It carries nothing inherently transcendent. Thus, for Bacon, Aristotle was right to place rhetoric "participating of both" between logic and "moral or civil knowledge"—the next sections of his text—for, although logical proof is "toward all men indifferent and the same," still "the proofs and persuasions of rhetoric ought to differ according to the auditors" and here Bacon quotes his repeated line from Virgil's *Eclogues*: "Orpheus in the woods, Arion among the dolphins." It only remains for Bacon in his 1605 text to add to the deficiency of this art by adding his own "collection of *the popular signs and colours of good and evil, both simple and comparative*, which are as the Sophisms of Rhetoric," and to deal with what he calls the "Critical" and "Pedantical" traditions of knowledge, or some brief notes on how to read well and teach well (3:411–3). With this section Bacon ends his discussion of the intellectual faculties and also, in the *De Augmentis*, completes his sixth book.

The Human Will and the Need for a New Georgics

The next section on the moral nature of the human being, still under the rubric of the individual or "segregate," will comprise all of the seventh book of the 1623 Latin text and there, as in 1605, will bring Bacon to his theory of the "Georgics of the mind," or the Virgilian concept of heroic labor. This section, then, on "the Appetite and Will of Man," begins appropriately with the Latin quotation from Solomon that expresses a classic subject-object relationship. The young man is to look after his heart before all else, for from it, from his subjectivity, proceed all the actions of life in the objective world that surrounds him. With such inward concerns, investigators have "despised to be conversant in ordinary and common matters" and so the corrective model of Virgil is all the more crucial. For Bacon, this greatest of poets, a moral authority for over 1600 years, advises the reader to look at the negative, the small, and the laborious in order to build any grand vision of the future: "Neither needed men of so excellent parts to have despaired of a fortune which the poet Virgil promised himself, (and indeed obtained,) who got as much glory of eloquence, wit, and learning in expressing the observations of husbandry, as of the heroical acts of Aeneas:—'Nec sum animi dubius, verbis ea vincere magnum / Quam sit, et angustis his addere rebus honorem' [Nor am I doubtful of how hard it is to conquer these things in the right words and bring honor to low things]. And surely if the purpose be in good earnest not to write at leisure that which men may read at leisure, but really to instruct and suborn action and active life, these Georgics of the mind, concerning the husbandry and tillage thereof, are no less worthy than the heroical descriptions of Virtue, Duty, and Felicity" (3:418; translation of Virgil mine, not Spedding's).

Within this "Georgics" frame, Bacon subdivides his topic: "the main and primitive division of moral knowledge seemeth to be into the Exemplar or Platform of Good, and the Regiment or Culture of the Mind; the one describing the nature of good, the other prescribing rules how to subdue, apply, and accommodate the will of man thereunto" (3:418–9). Bacon sub-divides again: the nature of the good, subdivided into (a) the private, itself divided into the active and passive (and the latter into the conservative and perfective), and (b) the relative or the human being as a citizen and then as social being; and then the nature of moral culture or the rules "to accommodate the will of man." The result is an elaborate essay on ethics, set in the humanist frame of classical allusion and precise annotation. In it, Bacon revises old theories of moral philosophy; he eschews any concept of the *summum bonum* as outside of human ethics. He also denies Aristotle's preference for the contemplative life: "But men must know, that in this theatre of man's life it is reserved only for God and angels to be lookers on" (3:421). In fact, he makes some surprising and original analogies. When he moves into (1):(b), for example, Bacon develops his conception of duty. He compares this obedience to society to personal virtue: "the term of Duty is more proper to a mind well framed and disposed towards others, as the term of Virtue is applied to a mind well formed and composed in itself; though neither can a man understand Virtue without some relation to society, nor Duty without an inward disposition" (3:428). Duty carries the same weight, therefore, as personal virtue. In this place Bacon praises King James once more, by analyzing (actually glorifying) parts of James I's own book that describe the duty of a king.

It is clear that in this section, as in the next, subtitled in the margin as "De Cultura Animi," that Bacon is developing the theoretical groundwork for the subjects, themes, and method of his *Essays*. Bacon even establishes his theory of suffering, a crucial ethical inversion of the ancient classical and Christian conceptions. "So in the culture and cure of the mind of man, two things are without our command," writes

Bacon, our natures and our fortunes. Labor or work in either is "limited and tied." Misquoting the *Aeneid* (5:710), "Vincenda est omnis fortuna ferendo" (all fortune is to be overcome by endurance or suffering), Bacon gives his own new aphorism: "Vincenda est omnis natura ferendo" (all nature is to be overcome by endurance or suffering). This revised line from Virgil, a definition of the heroic, Bacon will take into his scientific method as a definition of the scientist in the laboratory as hero. Immediately the topos functions as a marker for the inculturation of the human mind. Such a transforming process as Bacon describes not only adumbrates the disciplines of psychology and sociology but presupposes a new kind of epistemology for the human being. That is, the new human georgics figure is to think of suffering as fruitful labor, not the old suffering that was meaningless, "dull and neglected," but "a wise and industrious suffering, which draweth and contriveth use and advantage out of that which seemeth adverse and contrary"—what Bacon will call "Accommodating or Applying."

Like Machiavelli, for Bacon the first test of such a "suffering" or enduring of time is to be able to "set down sound and true distributions and descriptions of the several characters and tempers of men's natures and dispositions," especially the more radical and originating (3:433–4). In other words, living in society is itself "suffering" and for Bacon more meritorious than the purely subjective "suffering" warranted by older ethical (and religious) systems. Another test or "article of this knowledge" has to do with understanding of "the affections." Oddly, Aristotle wrote a volume on ethics, Bacon notes, but in his treatise on rhetoric, the Greek philosopher dealt only with the emotions of human beings, their psychologies. With his emphasis on the inter-receptivity of all forms of knowledge, physical and mental, Bacon sets up in his 1605 text a series of "exercises of the mind" like those of the body and then catalogues them. Their purpose will be to recognize that, like the body, the mind is "at some times in a state more perfect, and at other times in a state more depraved."

Thus the purpose of any culture of the mind, whether specific exercises or any larger training, "is to fix and cherish the good hours of the mind, and to obliterate and take forth the evil." This kind of self-analysis, perceived as mental exercise, is Bacon's subtle reduction, one among so many, of the grander earlier systems of contemplation. Reduction leads in the opposite direction: back to society, not to any transcendent reality. As Bacon comes to the conclusion of this section, the Solomonic admonition is clear: the self in the heart can train its subjectivity by objective techniques and so bring it into greater power in the objective world. For this reason, the proper ends of such an inculturation of the mind are as important as the proper habits. Bacon ends this section with another quotation from Virgil's *Aeneid*, the famous image of the two gates of sleep in the underworld in Book Six and the superiority of the one made of horn (realism) through which the true shades pass. At this point Bacon also concludes his part on human philosophy *"which contemplateth man segregate"* and notes, in closing, the analogies "between the good of the mind and the good of the body" (3:437–44).

Learning as "Congregate"

Bacon's human philosophy analyzed as "congregate" is quite straightforward in the 1605 text but is more developed in the *De Augmentis*, occupying the entire eighth book. As Bacon notes, the subject is difficult to analyze. Civil knowledge will be, at least in relationship to the subjective and the traditionally ethical encoding of society, always ambiguous. It can be examined in "three summary actions of society; which are conversation, negotiation, and government" or "comfort, use, and protection" that lead in turn to three wisdoms, those of behavior, business, and state (3:445). Quotations from the classical world and from Solomon, especially a series of aphorisms from Solomon with Bacon's commentary, lead the author to the construction of his own ideal human figuration of such civil knowledge, the Maker or Architect of Fortune, the *Faber Fortunae*. For such an ideal described elaborately here, especially through the Solomonic precepts, Bacon sets his dimensions, consciously modifying the ancient traditions.

> But as Cicero, when he setteth down an Idea of a perfect
> Orator, doth not mean that every pleader should be such;
> and so likewise, when a Prince or a Courtier hath been
> described by such as have handled those subjects, the
> mould hath used to be made according to the perfection
> of the art, and not according to the common practice: so
> I understand it that it ought to be done in the description
> of a Politic man; I mean politic for his own fortune.

In his last section on the human being "congregate," Bacon deals with government, whose processes he sees as necessarily "obscure and invisible." He notes only one deficiency in "the more public part of government, which is Laws," namely that all writers on laws have been either philosophers or lawyers but "none as statesmen," that is, those who have actually had to use laws for a higher good or for greater order in the chaos of business and society and international worlds. The point is made that such wisdom "consisteth not only in a platform of justice, but in the application thereof" (3:474–5). In the 1623 Latin text, Bacon adds a series of aphorisms that illustrate precisely this combination of theory and use, and show the practical wisdom of Bacon as master lawyer and the Lord Chancellor who presided over the Star Chamber.

Conclusion

Thus Bacon comes to the end of his section "touching Civil Knowledge; and with civil knowledge have concluded Human Philosophy; and with human philosophy, Philosophy in General" (4:476). It is time to summarize. Although Bacon will have a final section on learning in theology, "the prerogative of God," in relation to man's will and reason, this final section concludes nothing except to illustrate Bacon's own dichotomy of faith and reason. Not to have written on theology in a highly religious age would have been, however, almost impossible if not socially irregular. Bacon is thus correct to include this final section, the most strategically difficult part of his text (it will greatly change, of course, for his 1623 European audience). As a result, the final Theology section reinterprets, with a *sui generis* precision and reduction, the great themes only recently and magnificently elaborated by Thomas Hooker in his English *Laws of Ecclesiastical Polity*. Where Bacon can show originality, if any, is in his indications of the deficiencies in the government, liturgy, and service of the English church. In such a summary, Bacon's omissions appear more profound than his inclusions.

But the real conclusion to his book comes in an earlier summary to his survey of human learning. It shows Bacon in another staged auto-biographical aside: "And being now at some pause, looking back into that I have passed through, this writing seemeth to me"—and here again Bacon quotes from Virgil's *Eclogues*, this time 2:27, "if my image or vision does not fail me"—"as far as a man can judge of his own work, [it is] not much better than that noise or sound which musicians make while they are tuning their instruments." Such music "is pleasant to hear, but yet is a cause why the music is sweeter afterwards." Bacon is full of hope when he looks at his own time in the later Renaissance, "in which learning hath made her third visitation or circuit." This "circuit" he elaborates: "the excellency and vivacity of the wits of this age; the noble helps and lights which we have by the travails of ancient writers; the art of printing, which communicateth books to men of all fortunes; the openness of the world by navigation, which hath disclosed multitudes of experiments, and a mass of natural history" and all this has been combined with "the leisure wherewith these times abound, not employing men so generally in civil business, as the states of Graecia did in respect of their popularity, and the state of Rome in respect of the greatness of their monarchy." Rather, in a rising figure of gradatio, in a sentence using a special Ciceronian syntax of auxesis, Bacon points out that learning has been helped by "the present disposition of these times" and by "this third period of time." It "will far surpass that of the Graecian and Roman learning" but "only if men will know their own strength and their own weakness both," taking the "light of invention and not fire of contradiction." Bacon's time has also been helped by peace, by its "consumption of all that can ever be said in controversies of religion, which have so much diverted men from other sciences" and by the perfection of the King's own learning, and finally by "the inseparable propriety of time, which is ever more and more to disclose truth" (3:476–7).

Chapter Six

Bacon's *New Organon*
Or True Directions Concerning
the Interpretation of Nature

If the finished texts, both English and Latin, of the *Advancement of Learning* express the first stage of Bacon's Great Instauration, his Latin text *Novum Organum* represents the second stage of Bacon's world as it might be. Published with his proemium, preface, and plan for the *Instauratio Magna*, Bacon's new instrument of learning would provide in 1620 the new logic to drive the engine of the whole program of renewal and restoration. Contrasted to Aristotle's famous *Organon*, Bacon's *New Organon* would act in two stages, the first book as a kind *pars destruens*, ready to cleanse and purge the mind of the reader, and the second book to present the actual salvific method itself. It would reveal a logic ready to enter the mind and belief-system of the reader. As it turned out, the first book is, like that of the *Advancement*, the more powerful. It develops the final stages of many of Bacon's recurring systems of topics and images. Although the second book tries to represent the new method, it only approaches a certain level of demonstration. The whole text is, in this sense, unfinished.

Preface

From the outset of his preface to the *Novum Organum*, Bacon outlines his difference from other system-makers. Against "two extremes—between the presumption of pronouncing on everything, and the despair of comprehending anything" Bacon represents himself. In his personified role as guide, he is like "the more ancient of the Greeks (whose writings are lost)"—the Pre-Socratics—who, although "bitterly complaining of the difficulty of inquiry and obscurity of things, and like impatient horses champing the bit," still did "engage with nature." They thought that the question of "whether or not anything can be known," the ancient problem of acatalepsia that was haunting the later Renaissance, could be solved "not by arguing, but by trying." This Pre-Socratic method for healing or "trying" was essentially free-flow, for they trusted, according to Bacon, "entirely to the force of their understanding, applied no rule, but made everything turn upon hard thinking and perpetual working and exercise of the mind." In such a method Heraclitus' aphorism would come down to Bacon as a natural and obvious form, the aphorism standing out like a point of light in the text only to fade into silence and darkness, then to rise again. Serial aphorisms represent the method of broken time itself.

Thus, for Bacon in 1620, it was a question of the right style for his startling new ideas. Such staged indirection as the series of aphorisms were giving could become, in fact, direction. Here was not a Pygmalion style that was condemned in the *Advancement* for creating its own incestuous beloved. Rather, form and image would add, or give birth, to the emergence of a positive, if indirectly represented, argument. Style would perform as the pressure of carefully figured language interrupted by non-language (silence) in Bacon's steady encircling and entrapment of the reader's mind. Ideas would be as developed by silence as by word. In this hunt and capturing of the mind, every aphorism thus generates, in Bacon's text, a *tempus interruptum* that breaks meditation and enforces thought. This dispersed expression, then the silence that follows it, and then the rise to another aphorism in Bacon's ongoing series is nothing less than the teaching method of the whole text. Ideas are only possible through this form of rise, break, and rise again. In this style, Bacon is recapitulating a central theme of the *Essays*: interruption is the nature of modern existence—as Bacon had written to Prince Henry in 1612—and neither rounded Ciceronian certainties nor extended Senecan disjunctions of meaning that are essentially self-conscious will express it. Not even the branching tree of knowledge in the *Advancement* will work as formalizing metaphor for the new text. Rather, to explain his difficult, even shocking ideas, Bacon needed not so much an obviously organized structure as a free-flow of form, in which interruptions and silences would signal a freedom outside the authoritative text that was driving that text. The freedom, certainly the freedom of the ongoing seriality that came not only from its assertions but from its silences and humility, had to be there to challenge the authority of the text itself.

So, although retaining the same Ciceronian control of syntax and timing and with the same synthesizing method of regenerating commonplaces, Bacon's 1620 text differs radically from the 1605 *Advancement* and the 1623 *De Augmentis.* Its difference in form is made even clearer in the Latin. In this superb model of Renaissance Latin, the strategies of innovation can be seen. These nuances are often missing in Spedding's Victorian translation that omits crucial phrasing (such as the sexual motifs in Aphorism 84 in Book One and elsewhere) and cannot render the extraordinary blend of figures of speech and syntactic control (as in Aphorism 4 in Book One, for example, with its polyptoton and asyndeton and the power of its brevity and the silence operating like anacolouthon). The point of such strategic control through style was simple: to transform readers and convert their belief-systems so radically that each would view the natural duality of self and world with a different epistemological basis. They could even find some way of overcoming the inevitable dualism and the alienation of human existence. Then readers would see that truly to know was to make.[1] The dialectic of subjectivity and history could be joined in the act of invention.

Using such a form and method in another series of "dispersed meditacions," Bacon's New Logic will be, although "hard to practise," "easy to explain." Bacon's preface is clear about its purpose: it would "establish progressive states of certainty." Keeping the originating point of the evidence of the senses, but of course "helped and guarded by a certain process of correction," Bacon would now reject the rest of the "mental operation" of the old logic that "has had the effect of fixing errors rather than disclosing truth." Only a radical solution would bring learning and knowledge to "a sound and healthy condition": "namely, that the entire work of the understanding be commenced afresh, and the mind itself be from the very outset not left to its own course, but guided at every step" and the means for this guidance to be "as if by machinery," namely the New Logic.

Toward this "work," Bacon appears "merely as a guide to point out the road; an office of small authority, and depending more upon a kind of luck than upon any ability or excellency." Bacon continues such a humility ethos by arguing how his logic will neither interfere with old philosophies that had their purposes—Bacon says this with a barely concealed sneer—"for disputations or ornaments for discourse,—for the professor's lecture and for the business of life." In fact, there should be "two streams and two dispensations of knowledge" and "two tribes" of students in philosophy "bound together by mutual services" and so two methods. If the first—"*Anticipation of the Mind*"—is for the "cultivation" of current knowledge, the other—"*Interpretation of Nature*"—is for the invention of new knowledge. For those who prefer the first method, Bacon wishes the best. He himself uses "anticipations" whose goodness he distinguishes from bad "anticipations." "But if any man there be," he says with figures of auxesis and gradatio, "who, not content to rest in and use the knowledge which has already been discovered, aspires to penetrate further; to overcome, not an adversary in argument, but nature in action; to seek, not pretty and probable conjectures, but certain and demonstrable knowledge," then Bacon invites "all such to join themselves, as true sons of knowledge [tanquam veri scientiarum filii]" and pass by "the outer courts of nature" into "her inner chambers."

In his last paragraph, Bacon outlines, in a curious but effective rhetorical strategy of reversal, what his audience must do in relationship to "these speculations of mine." If they would deny his "speculations," let them apply the Baconian method of "trial" and "seasonable patience" and, when the reader becomes "master, let him (if he will) use his own judgment" (4:39–43). Thus, before presenting his arguments in the upcoming aphorisms, Bacon has already sketched for his reader a pattern of belief and acceptance, the conversion Bacon desires.

Book One

Bacon's full title for the first book of his master work contends that his aphorisms are not only for "THE INTERPRETATION OF NATURE" but also for "THE KINGDOM OF MAN." They must be read therefore in a social context, both in terms of their own collectivity and then of their public audience. They form neither legal document nor scientific fact. Bacon's anthropology emerges in the first aphorism, with its radical revision of what it means to be human: the human being is only "the servant and interpreter of Nature." If, as Spedding notes, this is a parody of Hippocrates' physician as "naturae minister," Bacon is writing not only after the Christian exaltation of a God become man but the exaltation of a man become god by a Renaissance Platonist like Pico della Mirandola. Both have failed. This new human being "can do and understand so much and so much only as he has observed in fact or in thought of the course of nature." Bacon is asserting here one more blow of what Hiram Haydn once called, in a useful phrase, the "Counter Renaissance,"[2] by denigrating the status of the human being. But Bacon is also changing the basis of Western epistemology as surely as Descartes (and in the same years), and with it, the basis of subjectivity: "beyond this he neither knows anything nor can do anything" (4:47).

Given this first shocking encounter with the text, as sharp as a baroque leap, the reader needs the first silence after the aphorism. Then the self that is the reader learns that neither "naked hand" nor the mind left to itself can do much. Both need instruments. The third aphorism strikes even deeper: the whole ancient tradition of contemplation is reduced to "human knowledge" and provides causes for effects when "human knowledge and human power meet in one." The principal point is that "nature to be commanded must be obeyed"; true human freedom "ad opera" (toward the making of works) is only a process of "admoveat et amoveat," says Bacon in a Latin pun, using figures of parison and polyptoton—putting together or putting asunder of natural bodies, for "reliqua Natura intus transigit" (Nature within itself finishes the rest). With these first four aphorisms, not only has the Renaissance ended but the centrality of Christian civilization and the analogical basis of classical and medieval culture have dramatically altered.

In this highest point of his literary (and political) career, it is not surprising, therefore, that motifs, topics, themes, and actual Latin sententiae are repeated from previous texts and brought here for a final synthesis. Thus, in this first book Bacon attacks syllogisms with the same analysis of their linguistic failure, reiterates his choice motif echoing the famous classical myth of the choices of Hercules, his Borgia/chalk motif, and his guide motif, and brings to the full his doctrine of the Idols. Beginning with Aphorism 23, Bacon contrasts the Idols of the human mind with the Ideas of the divine. Both terms are Platonic, but as Anderson has shown,[3] they are drastically revised by Bacon. This dichotomy "between certain empty dogmas, and the true signatures and marks set upon the works of creation as they are found in nature" echoes Protestant attacks on Catholic rationalizing and the Protestant view of its own endeavors as more primitive and therefore purer. Repeating his preface, Bacon also sets up a simplistic duality of evil—"*Anticipations of Nature* (as a thing rash or premature)"—and the good—"a just and methodical process, I call *Interpretation of Nature*" [4:51].

The Idols became one of Bacon's most successful rhetorical strategies, and their imagery originated early studies in the modern discipline of psychology. Bacon schematized this imagistic pattern into four segments: Idols of the Tribe, or the false conceptualizing in human nature "or the tribe or race of men"; Idols of the Cave, or the lying endemic to the individual human being; Idols of the Market-Place, or the false conceptualizing "on account of the commerce and consort of men there"; and finally, Idols of the Theatre, the latter a metaphor "because in my judgment all the received systems [of philosophy] are but so many stage-plays, representing worlds of their own creation after an unreal and scenic fashion" [4:54–5]. Bacon's reader was, of course, to remember that "idols" not only meant the false gods and false physical representations of the Gentiles in the Old Testament (and for Protestant Christians, who had early identified Catholics with the Jews, Catholic representations such as icons and statues) but, in its classical etymology, "specters" or "ghosts" and, by inference, diabolical forces.

The first idol springs from a simple fact: "the human understanding is like a false mirror, which, receiving rays irregularly, distorts and discolours the nature of things by mingling its own nature with it." From this, human thought imagines "the existence of more order and regularity in the world than it finds." It will always force agreement with itself; it is always "unquiet" and "cannot stop or rest, and still presses onward, but in vain"; it lacks Heraclitean "dry light" and instead "receives an infusion from the will and affections"; and most of all it "proceeds from the dulness, incompetency, and deceptions of the senses" as it jumps to "abstractions and gives a substance and reality to things which are fleeting" (4:54–8).

The Idols of the Cave "rise in the peculiar constitution, mental or bodily, of each individual; and also in education, habit, and accident." Transforming Plato's famous image, Bacon argues that each human being "has a cave or den of his own, which refracts and discolours the light of nature," and so "it was well observed by Heraclitus that men look for sciences in their own lesser worlds, and not in the greater or common world." Thus Aristotle was too fond of logic, and Bacon's contemporary Gilbert tried to establish a metaphysical system based on his original observations on the magnet. In this connection, there has been too great a reverence of the past and at the same time "an extreme love and appetite for novelty." Whereas some minds make distinctions well, others can connect and synthesize, and excess in either is dangerous so that "these kinds of contemplation should therefore be alternated and taken by turns" and the mind be "at once penetrating and comprehensive." For such idols Bacon therefore devises a rule harsh to all Renaissance (and for that matter, Enlightened and Romantic) concepts of the human being: "And generally let every student of nature take this as a rule,—that whatever his mind seizes and dwells upon with peculiar satisfaction is to be held in suspicion, and that so much the more care is to be taken in dealing with such questions to keep the understanding even and clear" (4:54;59–60).

For Bacon, the Idols of the Market-place "are the most troublesome of all: idols which have crept into the understanding through the alliances of words and names." Here Bacon begins the kind of empirical analysis of languages that forecasts the methods of modern linguistics. Indeed, in this section, Bacon appears almost as a poststructuralist critic: if "men believe that their reason governs words," they must know "it is also true that words react on the understanding." Because "it is by discourse that men associate," it is no surprise that "words are imposed according to the apprehension of the vulgar" and so "the ill and unfit choice of words wonderfully obstructs the understanding" and can "plainly force and overrule the understanding, and throw all into confusion, and lead men away into numberless empty controversies and idle fancies." These idols may be of "names of things which do not exist" like Fortune and Prime Mover or of "things that do exist, but yet confused and ill-defined, and hastily and irregularly derived from realities" like the word *humid* that Bacon uses as experimental example (4:55;61–2).

The Idols of the Theatre "are not innate" but "have immigrated into men's minds from the various dogmas of philosophies, and also from wrong laws of demonstration" and "are plainly impressed and received into the mind from the play-books of philosophical systems and the perverted rules of demonstration." Bacon would avoid all such systems and rules; "the course I propose for the discovery of sciences is such as leaves but little to the acuteness and strength of wits, but places all wits and understandings nearly on a level." Bacon's is a view of a technological social reality in which instruments of the mind, as Bacon argues here, make the distinction, not the human being, the rule and compass eliminating any need in drawing a circle for "the steadiness and practice of the hand." Heroism for Bacon is horizontal, not vertical. The point is to insure that "access to truth may be made less difficult, and the human understanding may the more willingly submit to its purgation and dismiss its idols" (4:55;62–3). After a review of the various systems that make "sciences dogmatic and magisterial" or introduce "*Acatalepsis*" or the despair at knowing (and therefore for Bacon, making) anything, Bacon then ends his discussion of the idols in Aphorism 68 with a call for "the understanding thoroughly freed and cleansed." In a skillful reductive parody, he adapts a famous Christian motif: "the entrance into the kingdom of man, founded on sciences, being not much other than the entrance into the kingdom of heaven, whereinto none may enter except as a little child" (4:63–9).

In the next aphorisms Bacon turns to the result of such idols, "vicious demonstrations," and discusses the need for "experiments of Light, not for experiments of Fruit." For this he uses the myth of Atalanta, who left her path for a golden apple and lost her race. Bacon then launches into an originating discourse: historicizing in terms of these "demonstrations," he argues that the best test of "signs," "more certain or more noble," will be found in "fruits." From the Greeks, who are boys (in an adaptation of Solon's quotation) and whose "wisdom abounds in words but is barren of works," onward, history has not produced one "single experiment which tends to relieve and benefit the condition of man, and which can with truth be referred to the speculations and theories of philosophy." Only by mechanics, random experimentation, or accidents in chemistry have benefits been found, whereas, "in religion we are warned to show our faith by works, so in philosophy by the same rule the system should be judged of its fruits, and pronounced frivolous if it be barren; more especially if, in places of fruits of grape and olive, it bear thorns and briars of dispute and contention." Bacon considers some of these "signs" in "the increase and progress of systems and sciences" most founded on nature and experience, like the "mechanical arts" that continually thrive and grow "as having in them a breath of life; at first rude, then convenient, afterwards adorned, and at all times advancing" (4:70–6).

Bacon now starts another sequence in his text of the *Novum Organum.* If there are positive "signs," he will now examine the negative, "the *causes* of the errors" he has been describing and their long "continuance." The reader may well wonder, says Bacon, how he has discovered what had been missing for centuries. This discovery "truly I myself esteem as the result of some happy accident, rather than of any excellence of faculty in me; a birth of time rather than a birth of wit." Here Bacon becomes the modern historian, his survey of time based on technological achievements, noting that of the twenty-five centuries that comprise all "the memory and learning of men," barely six "were fertile in sciences or favourable to their development." Again Bacon adds a metaphor that reshapes a whole discipline: "In times no less than in regions there are wastes and deserts." Here, for the first time, the word "revolution" enters a historical discourse as still carrying its Latin meaning of cycle but now set in a context of historical evolution so that, although still neutral, the term marks a stage of historical growth. There are only three such "revolutions or periods of learning": the Greeks, the Romans, and now "the nations of Western Europe; and to each of these hardly two centuries can justly be assigned." No other periods offer "rich or flourishing growth of the sciences," not even that of the Arabs or the Catholic Scholastics. Thus the first cause of "so meagre a progress in the sciences" has been "the narrow limits of the time" they have had. The second follows: in those brief periods, science received the least attention and was reduced "(unless it were some monk studying in his cell, or some gentleman in his country-house)" to the role of a servant to other learning (4:77–9).

The other negative causes follow with this generalizing historical analysis: the goal of science has been misplaced ("Now the true and lawful goal of the sciences is none other than this: that human life be endowed with new discoveries and powers"); experimentation has been considered beneath "the dignity of the human mind"; and the past is not the "advanced age of the world" but the present more "stored and stocked with infinite experiments and observations," especially when, because of the "distant voyages and travels which have become frequent in our times, many things in nature have been laid open and discovered which may let in new light upon philosophy." These generalizations lead to Bacon's authoritative statement about the basis of all authority in time whose dysfunction he sees in sexual metaphor: "And with regard to authority, it shows a feeble mind to grant so much to authors and yet deny time his rights, who is the author of authors, nay rather of all authority. For rightly is truth called the daughter of time, not of authority. It is no wonder therefore if those enchantments of antiquity and authority and consent have so bound up men's powers that they have been made impotent (like persons bewitched) to accompany with the nature of things" (4:79–83).

It is little wonder, then, after continuing this catalogue of errors that show the narcissism "increased by the craft and artifices of those who have handled and transmitted sciences," the "littleness of spirit" of scientists and "the smallness and slightness of the tasks which human industry has proposed to itself," and the failures of the places of learning themselves, that Bacon turns, in Aphorism 92, to hope. He begins by marking the greatest of errors: "But by far the greatest obstacle to the progress of science and the undertaking of new tasks and provinces therein, is found in this—that men despair and think things impossible." How terrible it all is—"the obscurity of nature, the shortness of life, the deceitfulness of the senses, the weakness of the judgment, the difficulty of experiment and the like"—and then the fear that "in the revolution of time and of the ages of the world the sciences have their ebbs and flows," growing in one season and withering in another, yet always so "that when they have reached a certain point and condition they can advance no further." In the midst of such temptations to despair, says Bacon, "we must observe diligently what encouragement dawns upon us and from what quarter; and, putting aside the lighter breezes of hope, we must thoroughly sift and examine those which promise greater steadiness and constancy." We must go further: "we must take state-prudence too into our counsels, whose rule is to distrust, and to take the less favourable view of human affairs."

It is in this turning point of Aphorism 92 that Bacon makes a consciously staged gesture of turning his text around: "I am now therefore to speak touching Hope; especially as I am not a dealer in promises, and wish neither to force nor to ensnare men's judgments, but to lead them by the hand with their good will." He even points toward his second book of the *Novum Organum*: "the strongest means of inspiring hope will be to bring men to particulars" and "especially to particulars digested and arranged in my Tables of Discovery (the subject partly of the second, but much more of the fourth part of my Instauration) since this is not merely the promise of the thing but the thing itself." The greater immediate task lies, however, in just what he is doing in this first book: "nevertheless that everything may be done with gentleness, I will proceed with my plan of preparing men's minds; of which preparation to give hope is no unimportant part" for it will "induce any alacrity" and "whet their industry in making trial." Bacon's great analogy for hope lies in figuration from the Renaissance world of discovery: "And therefore it is fit that I publish and set forth those conjectures of mine which make hope in this matter reasonable; just as Columbus did, before that wonderful voyage of his across the Atlantic, when he gave the reasons for his conviction that new lands and continents might be discovered besides those which were known before; which reasons, though rejected at first, were afterward made good by experience, and were the causes and beginnings of great events" (4:90–1).

For the rest of his first book of the *Novum Organum*, Bacon will give a catalogue of the hopes possible for human beings seeking knowledge and especially for scientists, the new natural philosophers. Bacon could not be clearer about the source of the greatest hope of all: "the beginning is from God." Here Bacon quotes again (but in English) "the prophecy of Daniel" on "the last ages of the world:—'Many shall go to and fro, and knowledge shall be increased'; clearly intimating that the thorough passage of the world (which now by so many distant voyages seems to be accomplished, or in course of accomplishment), and the advancement of the sciences, are destined by fate, that is, by Divine Providence, to meet in the same age."

In Aphorism 95, Bacon finds a model for his new scientist in insect imagery—the enfolding of the simile itself enacting the revelation of another hope. "Those who have handled sciences have been either men of experiment or men of dogmas," writes Bacon, and the experimenters are like ants, who "only collect and use" and "the reasoners resemble spiders, who make cobwebs out of their own substance." If the empirical and the rational are represented here, "the true business of philosophy" is represented by the Virgilian bee, (from the *Georgics*). The bee "takes a middle course; it gathers its material from the flowers of the garden and of the field, but transforms and digests by a power of its own." So the true scientist does not rely totally on the mind or on natural history "and mechanical experiments" but "lays" discoveries not "in the memory whole, as" the mind "finds" them but "in the understanding [subjectivity] altered and digested" by the method Bacon will be developing.

As a result of these catalogues, Bacon can define the kind of scientist (and reader) he desires: "Now if any one of ripe age, unimpaired senses, and well-purged mind, apply himself anew to experience and particulars, better hopes may be entertained of that man." By no surprise, in another crucial instance of autobiography in his text, Bacon presents himself as the model: "And a like judgment I suppose may be passed on myself in future ages: that I did not great things, but simply made less account of things that were accounted great. In the meanwhile, as I have already said, there is no hope except in a new birth of science; that is, in raising it regularly up from experience and building it afresh; which no one (I think) will say has yet been done or thought of" (4:91–4). Bacon can now look ahead to the second part of his *New Organon*, using a military image: the "number and army of particulars, and that army so scattered and dispersed as to distract and confound the understanding" do not give much hope from "skirmishings and slight attacks and desultory movements of the intellect," unless these particulars are gathered into "Tables of Discovery, apt, well arranged, and as it were animate" and then "the mind be set to work upon the helps duly prepared and digested which these tables supply."

In this way, axioms lead to new particulars to new axioms, "for our road does not lie on a level, but ascends and descends; first ascending to axioms, then descending to works." Thus, the "altered" understanding needs this middle stage of "true solid and living axioms, on which depend the affairs and fortunes of men," between particulars and the most general axioms, intermediate axioms that hang the understanding "with weights, to keep it from leaping and flying," a process "never yet been done. " For this establishing of axioms, a new induction is needed, not simple enumeration, but an analysis of nature "by proper rejections and exclusions; and then, after a sufficient number of negatives, come to a conclusion on the affirmative instances." It is a method, says Bacon, followed by no one before and only adumbrated by Plato. In such induction is "our chief hope" (4:94–8).

As Bacon will affirm at the end of his first book, this induction as method cannot be compared either with earlier systems because of its distrust of generalities or with concepts of *"Acatalepsia"* because it helps the understanding. His method will not be just that of science or natural philosophy but will, "by induction, embrace everything." He will also develop "a history and tables of discovery" for emotions in an incipient psychology, and "for matters political" in an incipient political science. Induction will have uses throughout the intellectual globe (4:111–2).

Besides this chief hope of induction, and the hopes to be found in "many useful discoveries," like gunpowder, silk, and the magnet, once impossible to conceive, and the invention of the printing press, "this most beautiful discovery, which is of so much service in the propagation of knowledge," Bacon offers the example of himself. After all, he is the one who has had to read (and write and experiment) on the run as the prophet Habakkuk had described. Anyone despairing should look, Bacon declares, at the Lord Chancellor who is "of all men of my time the most busied in affairs of state, and a man of health not very strong (whereby much time is lost), and in this course altogether a pioneer, following in no man's track, nor sharing these counsels with any one, [but I] have nevertheless by resolutely entering on the true road, and submitting my mind to Things, advanced these matters, as I suppose, some little way." Anything is possible, using his method, with "men abounding in leisure," anything expected from association of labours, and from succession of ages." But even if "the breath of hope which blows on us from the New Continent" were not so strong, society should still make the "trial" of a new science and method of knowledge (4:99–102).

By Aphorism 115, Bacon is ready to "close that part of my Instauration, which is devoted to pulling down [pars destruens]," and "performed by three refutations," of *"natural human reason,"* of *"demonstrations,"* and of *"theories,* or the received systems of philosophy and doctrine." This strategy has developed through "signs and evidences of causes," a process different from the strategies of the old "rules of demonstration" and more like his ideal of induction. "It is time therefore to proceed to the art itself and rule of interpreting nature," for, "in this first book of aphorisms, I proposed to prepare men's minds as well for understanding as for receiving what is to follow." Thus, "now that I have purged and swept and levelled the floor of the mind, it remains that I place the mind in a good position and as it were in a favourable aspect toward what I have to lay before it." As with any new ideas, there is the problem not only of the past but of the future, "a false preconception or prefiguration of the new thing which is presented." To clarify this future, Bacon adds his final comments.

First, he is not like the Greeks or his contemporaries, the Italians Telesio and Patrizi and the Danish Severinus who want "to found a new sect in philosophy." Rather, his purpose "is to try whether I cannot in very fact lay more firmly the foundation, and extend more widely the limits, of the power and greatness of man." Already Bacon has results not only truer and more certain but "more fruitful" than "those now received," and he will collect these "into the fifth part of my Instauration" or Learned Experience. But Bacon has "no entire or universal theory to propound." The time is not ripe for any such theory. "Neither can I hope to live to complete the sixth part of the Instauration (which is destined for the philosophy discovered by the legitimate interpretation of nature)." It is quite enough "if in the intermediate business I bear myself soberly and profitably, sowing in the meantime for future ages the seeds of a purer truth, and performing my part towards the commencement of the great undertaking." And as Bacon does not found a school or sect, so he cannot promise particular works. In fact, "although in my tables of discovery (which compose the fourth part of the Instauration) and also in the examples of particulars (which I have adduced in the second part), and moreover in my observations on the history (which I have drawn out in the third part), any reader of even moderate sagacity and intelligence will everywhere observe indications and outlines of many noble works," there is still a major challenge.

The natural history—what Bacon will now turn to in the last five years of his life—is neither large enough nor verified enough "to serve the purposes of legitimate interpretation." But if there be any other person better in this Hunt for Pan or Nature for results out of experience, let that person use both Bacon's natural history and method and "apply them to the production of new works" that will not be "like Atalanta's balls" but wait for the "harvest in its due season." In such a natural history, however generated, *all* evidence is necessary: "for the sun enters the sewer no less than the palace, yet takes no pollution. And for myself, I am not raising a capitol or pyramid to the pride of man, but laying a foundation in the human understanding for a holy temple after the model of the world." The democratic realism that has marked the modern world now finds an originating basis in Bacon's theory of the negative: "for whatever deserves to exist deserves also to be known, for knowledge is the image of existence; and things mean and splendid exist alike" and as from putrid substances rise the "sweetest odours," so from low instances "excellent light and information." Even the subtlety of a natural history, of new collections, must not be discouraging; it can be grasped by the forelock as the seizing of time or opportunity or fortune, as in the Renaissance emblem (time has "lock in front, but is bald behind") (4:103–8).

Thus, in his self-dramatization, Bacon, "relying on the evidence and truth of things," would "reject all forms of fiction and imposture." Only the truth, no matter how ambiguous, must be sought. It does not matter "whether the new world be that island of Atlantis" the ancients knew or something utterly original. The point is that "new discoveries must be sought from the light of nature, not fetched back out of the darkness of antiquity." Bacon then repeats an earlier aphorism: his texts are "a birth of time rather than of wit." In his search for truth and "the light of nature," he would destroy no philosophy or arts "at present in use," as his *Advancement* has shown (although no progress can be expected from them either). His future can be expressed in a richer metaphor (one anticipating the imagery of the Feast of the Tirsan in the *New Atlantis*): "I pledge mankind in a liquor strained from countless grapes, from grapes ripe and fully seasoned, collected in clusters, and gathered, and then squeezed in the press, and finally purified and clarified in the vat." In this method, Bacon is "building in the human understanding a true model of the world" with "a very diligent dissection and anatomy," not as "a man's own reason would have it to be" but as it actually might be. Justification of this new world is that in it making *can* be knowing and knowing, making. In that true epistemology, "truth and utility" can be known as "the very same things (res ipissimae)." Thus "works themselves are of greater value as pledges of truth than as contributing to the comforts of life" (4:109–10).

In his penultimate aphorism in this first part of the *Novum Organum*, Bacon comments once more on "the excellency of the end in view." He now rewrites history and invents a new type, a history of technology, giving at least its theoretical basis. Quoting Lucretius and Solomon, Bacon notes that "famous discoveries" held "by far the first place among human actions" and for good reason; "benefits of discoveries may extend to the whole race of man." In this glorification of the power of human culture, Bacon moves as far as he can from his initial premise of cosmic discontinuity and still remain in his essential dialectic of history. Though it is true, he argues, that the power of the new worker-scientist cannot begin except in an act of humility, "for we cannot command nature except by obeying her," still greater and worthier than "all the fruit of inventions" is "the very beholding of light . . . the very contemplation of things, as they are, without superstition or imposture, error or confusion." Such light, the ideal intuition, is the driving force for Bacon of all seriality. For this "light," "let the human race recover that right over nature which belongs to it by divine bequest, and let power be given to it." Then, says Bacon with an optimism required for closure, "the exercise thereof will be governed by sound reason and true religion."

In Aphorism 130, the last, Bacon gives an *apologia* for the second book to which the reader will now turn. It is altogether possible that, as the closing sections of the first book of the *Novum Organum* show more haste and looseness of writing than the opening, Bacon had begun to realize he could not finish. It was, as he surmised correctly, essential that he produce a text of magnitude during his current political power and prestige if he wanted to gain more readers. But, with unfinished material, Bacon would have to focus and angle its presentation. Thus, "although I conceive that I have given true and most useful precepts, yet I do not say either that it is absolutely necessary (as if nothing could be done without it) or that it is perfect." Indeed, at this critical point in his text, Bacon appears to be saying that what lies ahead is not in any sense finished. In fact, armed with a good natural history, scientists or readers may go farther in a kind of modified *Experientia Literata* or Learned Experience: "For I am of the opinion that if men had ready at hand a just history of nature and experience, and laboured diligently thereon; and if they could bind themselves to two rules,—the first, to lay aside received opinions and notions; and the second, to refrain the mind for a time from the highest generalisations, and those next to them,—they would be able by the native and genuine force of the mind, without any other art, to fall into my form of interpretation. For interpretation is the true and natural work of the mind when freed from impediments" (4:113–5).

There is even a final aphorism within the last aphorism that will sum up this new process for the reader and future convert-scientist. Printed in special typographical arrangement of narrowing (an inverted pyramid), the last sentence of the first book visually focuses for the reader, in concise form, Bacon's final teaching. It describes the process of the New Logic in the next book. Although this aphorism appears in Latin as indirect discourse, the imperative tone of the last line—the call to conversion—is clear: "Artem inveniendi cum / Inventis adolescere posse, / statuere debemus" (we ought to establish that the art of invention advances as inventions advance) (1:223, translation mine).

Book Two

"On a given body to generate and superinduce a new nature or new natures, is the work and aim [intentio] of Human Power." If this first sentence of the first aphorism of the second book of Bacon's master text sounds like a maxim from Dr. Frankenstein, it should also be noted that the full title of this book includes, as the first, the totalizing subject of "THE KINGDOM OF MAN." All the layered analysis of this most technical of Bacon's major texts has as its direction the essentially redemptive social purposes set out in the first book of the *Novum Organum* and the *Advancement of Learning*. To the charge that all of Bacon's work is hardly more than a *pars destruens* or *pars praeparativa*, that is, the establishment of a deconstructive mindset and a social gestalt that would undermine and re-determine the rest of Western culture and little else, this second book stands as partial denial. Moreover, recent studies have shown the vitality of Bacon's scientific analyses and methods of investigation, especially studies by Pérez-Ramos, Peter Urbach, and Graham Rees.[4] As these analyses have shown, Bacon adapts consistently philosophical language (or by 1620, a quasi-jargon) that he would angle toward his particular aim of inscribing his own variation of "the maker's knowledge tradition," in Pérez-Ramos' phrase.

The second sentence of Bacon's first aphorism illustrates an almost parodic accommodation of inherited terms: "Of a given nature to discover the form, or true specific difference, or nature-engendering nature, or source of emanation (for these are the terms which come nearest to a description of the thing), is the work and aim of Human Knowledge." Further, Bacon's critical term *form* is, as he admits in his second aphorism, but one more adaptation of an older medieval and classical term and, although springing from an Idol of the Tribe, still useful: "For though in nature nothing really exists beside individual bodies, performing pure individual acts according to a fixed law, yet in philosophy this very law and the investigation, discovery, and explanation of it, is the foundation as well of knowledge as of operation. And it is this law, with its clauses that I mean when I speak of *Forms*; a name which I the rather adopt because it has grown into use and become familiar."[5]

In the same way, Bacon in his second aphorism finds that Aristotle's four causes are "not improperly distributed" into material, formal, efficient, and final. Although Aristotle's "final cause rather corrupts than advances the sciences, except such as have to do with human action" and "the discovery of the formal is despaired of," and "the efficient and the material" are only "slight and superficial," Bacon will still make, in his first aphorism, a key distinction based on these terms. If the primary work of the new scientific method is the discovery of forms, the secondary involves not only "the transformation of concrete bodies, so far as this is possible" but two discoveries described in Aristotelian and Scholastic language: the first discovery rises from "every case of generation and motion, of the *latent process* carried on from the manifest efficient and the manifest material to the form which is engendered; and in like manner"—the second—"the discovery of the *latent configuration* of bodies at rest and not in motion" (4:119–20).

This retranscribing of old terms into new, with utterly different epistemological bases, or ways of perceiving the world, is revealed even more in Bacon's formulae that describe his theory of the form. Because he believes that "the roads to human power and to human knowledge lie close together," the direction for "a true and perfect rule of operation" will be the same "with the discovery of a true Form," namely *that it be certain, free, and disposing or leading to action.*" This subtle adaptation of Thomistic and Aristotelian language appears throughout the second book of the *Novum Organum* and even in a definition of the working of Bacon's form: "For a true and perfect axiom of knowledge then the direction and precept will be, *that another nature be discovered which is convertible with the given nature, and yet is a limitation of a more general nature, as of a true and real genus*" (4:120–2). Bacon is even clearer in his parody when in Aphorism 9 he sets up what he calls "the mark [scopo] of knowledge." Having elaborated on his concepts of latent process ("perfectly continuous" and "for the most part escapes the sense") and latent configuration ("a separation and solution of bodies" made by "reasoning and true induction, with experiments to aid"), Bacon then remarks: "From the two kinds of axioms which have been spoken of, arises a just division of philosophy and the sciences; taking the received terms (which come nearest to express the thing) in a sense agreeable to my own views." Then he proceeds to make his own division: "Let the investigation of Forms, which are (in the eye of reason at least, and in their essential law) eternal and immutable, constitute *Metaphysics*"; then for

"*Physics*," he would posit "the investigation of the Efficient Cause, and of Matter, and of the Latent Process, and the Latent Configuration (all of which have reference to the common and ordinary course of nature, not to her eternal and fundamental laws)." Two "practical divisions" follow "*Mechanics*" under Physics and "*Magic*" under Metaphysics (4:124–6).

This sense of parody or staged performance of old philosophical terms with new roles may be understood as the rhetorical basis of the second book of the *Novum Organum*. Bacon's text thus represents a special kind of philosophical theater that would appeal to a literate reader in 1620. Parody helps, in fact, to focus a difficult and, for some, a tedious text. Thus, given the premise that Bacon is writing his own theater (as he has attacked the older philosophical systems as Idols of the Theatre), in the investigations and conceptualizing that follow the tenth aphorism in Book Two, it should be no surprise to the reader that rhetoric and linguistic devices, especially metaphor, define the text as much as the ideas themselves. Indeed, it is a question whether Bacon's ideas *can* be extrapolated from his curiously constructed theater of science. Mary Hesse confirms this sense of mannered performance in her conclusion to her succinct, insightful analysis not only of Bacon's ideas in the second book of the *Novum Organum* but of all his philosophy and science. In fact, it is a question whether such performance is not Bacon's distinguishing means of representing new ideas. Although Bacon made, as Hesse notes, "little first-hand contribution to science," underestimating the place of hypothesis and mathematics, and "claimed a mechanical certainty for the method which is quite unjustified" and in general "failed to see the difficulties involved in introducing hidden entities and processes into science," Bacon "*encouraged* detailed and methodical experimentation"; "*saw clearly* the need for negative instances or refuting experiments in relation to all positive or confirmatory instances"; "*visualized* a structure of scientific laws which is formally not unlike that of subsequent hypothetical-deductive systems." Furthermore, "his tables of discovery constituted a method of *systematic analogy* which assisted the development of theoretical models" and "his *influence* in introducing mechanical hypotheses into seventeenth-century science can be compared with that of Descartes and Gassendi" although "finally he did not allow the *attractions* of mechanism to *blind* him to the *difficulties* of pure atomism."[6] These aspects as discussed in Hesse's analysis may not provide theater such as the masques Bacon produced, but they certainly highlight a strategy of determined mannerism used to dramatize a text not always present in other texts of philosophy or science.

Even in C.J. Ducasse's classic analysis of Bacon's scientific method, where he finds Bacon's logic incomplete and self-contradictory, or in Morris Cohen's fervent attack on Bacon's pretense toward an original New Logic, these two scholars recognize the sense of staged language, of strong organization based on rhetoric, and of audience operating as part of Bacon's performance.[7] It is, in fact, what has first engaged such critics. Thus, context cannot be separate in Bacon from text. For this reason, Lisa Jardine stresses the logical and linguistic backgrounds from which Bacon's New Logic proceeds and also points to rhetorical contexts that involve Bacon's social and scientific goals. Peter Urbach recognizes just such larger contexts in his discussion of "Certainty and Bacon's Method," although his analysis is rigorously philosophical. As Jardine remarks, Bacon's "investigator [is] to arrive at true definitions of natural kinds, starting from basic sense-experience, by simple stages"—simplicity and social accessibility being Baconian aims (at least in his later work) for all his experiments and axioms. These "definitions" are both to form the basis for more logical deduction and then to enact "instructions for successful practical operations."[8] This reaching toward further logical deduction is hardly more than the aphoristic rule of the art of discovery that ended the first book of the *Novum Organum*. Carried to an exalted level, the less "initiative" and more "magisterial" concept of "instructions," a greater theatricality, will be implemented by specific rhetorical and metaphorical strategies.

Thus aphorism 10 of Bacon's second book organizes such "instructions" for his text. "Now my directions for the interpretation of nature embrace," says Bacon, setting up another dichotomy, "two generic divisions; the one how to educe and form axioms from experience; the other how to deduce and derive new experiments from axioms." Bacon subdivides the former into "three ministrations," of "sense, memory, and mind." First, however, there must be prepared a "sufficient and good" *Natural and Experimental History*, for "this is the foundation of all; for we are not to imagine or suppose, but to discover, what nature does or may be made to do." Now to organize something so various as a natural and experimental history, Bacon would "form *Tables and Arrangements of Instances*." So, as Jardine notes, "the major part of the discussion of the interpretation of nature in the *Novum Organum*" turns "to specific instructions [so] that the best possible use is made of the senses and memory in assembling the material for the natural history, and for tabulating its contents."[9] Even then, as Bacon notes in his signpost of Aphorism 10, the understanding is still "incompetent and unfit to form

axioms, unless it be directed and guarded" (4:127). Thus, before the cataloguing of instances to follow, Bacon will deal with the larger issue of
induction, the true and legitimate method of discovering the right
forms. Then he will turn to the instances that will help the composition
of his natural history, after 1620 the next phase of his Instauration and
the main work until his death.

The Method of Induction

In Aphorism 11, Bacon begins his discussion of the process of induction
by examining the "Form of Heat." He first lists instances of heat that he
calls "the *Table of Essence and Presence*." Immediately in Aphorism 12,
Bacon sets up his method of exclusion: the valorization of the positive by
the deviant or absent or negative—in this case, the catalogue of examples to be found in "the *Table of Deviation, or of Absence in Proximity*."
Anticipated throughout Bacon's canon, this method of analysis by
exclusion is basic to Bacon's whole methodology on every level of his
work. It was analyzed as logical device first by Robert Leslie Ellis, editor
of the philosophical works in the Spedding edition, and then Thomas
Fowler gave the first masterly analysis of it in his 1889 edition of the
Novum Organum. Negation would endure as one of Bacon's strongest
contributions to modern scientific method. As the modern-day logician
Georg Henrik von Wright has remarked, "It is the immortal merit of
Bacon to have fully appreciated the importance of this asymmetry in the
logical structure of laws."[10]

In Aphorism 13, Bacon then deals with a "*Table of Degrees or Comparison in Heat*," comparing the first two sets or tables. All three sets Bacon
calls "the Presentation of Instances to the Understanding." With them,
the real process of induction can begin. At the heart of this process is
still the method of exclusion: "To God, truly, the Giver and Architect of
Forms, and it may be to the angels and higher intelligences, it belongs
to have an affirmative knowledge of forms immediately, and from the
first contemplation. But this assuredly is more than man can do, to
whom it is granted only to proceed at first by negatives, and at last to
end in affirmatives, after exclusion has been made" (4:145).

If it can be argued that the major parts of his major texts, the
Advancement and the *Novum Organum*, work from this method of the negative or the *pars destruens* to the positive, it can also be asserted that such
a concept of the negative is basic to Bacon's epistemology at all levels.[11]
If "the first work therefore of true induction (as far as regards the discov-

ery of Forms)" is that of rejection or exclusion, it reflects the order of reality, the inherent breakdown and chaos that marks nature, as well as, for Bacon, human history and European society. To describe this process of induction as it emerges from this logical method of exclusion, Bacon gives a metaphor for the process of enlightenment and purification—the ideal intuition—that will rise out of the negative: "Then indeed after the rejection and exclusion has been duly made, there will remain at the bottom, all light opinions vanishing into smoke, a Form affirmative, solid and true and well defined"—something "quickly said" but "the way to come at it is winding and intricate." This stripped and almost mystic nakedness of reality will be analogized, in Bacon's revision of the Greek myth, in the naked body of Cupid or the Atom. Such a search for nakedness leads Bacon to his strange definition of forms. They are "nothing more than those laws and determinations of absolute actuality, which govern and constitute any simple nature, as heat, light, weight, in every kind of matter and subject that is susceptible of them" (4:145–6). Forms and laws of "absolute actuality" are the same.

When he then proceeds in Aphorism 18 to give an example of this method of exclusion by applying it to the investigation of the "Form of Heat," Bacon is careful to note that "not only each table suffices for the rejection of any nature, but even any one of the particular instances" in any table of exclusion suffices. The problem then arises: how can exclusion be used when the positive—"sound and true notions of simple natures"—is not itself sufficiently known? What exactly will exclusion exclude? This question of methodology will haunt every scientific axiom of Bacon's and his whole program to the end: "I therefore, well knowing and nowise forgetting how great a work I am about (viz. that of rendering the human understanding a match for things and nature), do not rest satisfied with the precepts I have laid down" and so now will provide a catalogue of "more power-ful aids for the use of the understanding" (4:149). If these "aids" per-form as the incipient conceptualizing of hypotheses—approaching the abstractions Bacon so dreads because of the "enchanted glass" that brings them forth—they are made less abstract by their linguistic forms. Bacon's working hypotheses rise not from mathematical formu-lae but from rhetorical devices. In fact, the representations of place-logic that signify the structure of Bacon's second book of the *Novum Organum* are determined by rhetoric and mannered language. The terms that evolve and work toward hypothesis are among Bacon's most compelling metaphors and images.

The first of these Bacon calls *"Indulgence of the Understanding,* or the *Commencement of Interpretation,* or the *First Vintage."* This metaphorical "instruction" or "direction" is as far as Bacon ever went toward the fulfillment of his scientific method. Here again Bacon is dealing with his own parodies of old terms: "When I say of Motion that it is as the genus of which heat is a species, I would be understood to mean, not that heat generates motion or that motion generates heat (though both are true in certain cases), but that Heat itself, its essence and quiddity, is Motion and nothing else" (4:150). Even in the establishment of this simple nature, a "First Vintage" of Bacon's vineyard, Bacon uses the method of exclusion by showing the specific differences of his genus of motion. After four of these exclusions, Bacon arrives at a tentative definition: *"Heat is a motion, expansive, restrained, and acting in its strife upon the smaller particles of bodies."* If expansion and particle-strife here need modification, the rule for operation follows nevertheless from this "Form or true definition of heat": *"If in any natural body you can excite a dilating or expanding motion, and can so repress this motion and turn it back upon itself, that the dilation shall not proceed equably, but have its way in one part and be counteracted in another, you will undoubtedly generate heat"* (4:154–5).

At this point in his text, Bacon abandons the actual process of his interpretation of nature and the working out of his New Logic. In his crucial Aphorism 21, to which he will return at the very close of his book, Bacon sets out the strategies he now means to follow. He promises to write nine catalogues that follow roughly the stages of his Great Instauration. Only the first will be finished: the last thirty-one aphorisms of the second book of the *Novum Organum.* The others, from "the *Supports of Induction"* to "the *Ascending and Descending Scale of Axioms,"* remain only names. They perform a rhetoric of desire rather than a language of action. As Bacon writes in the penultimate instance of the long catalogue of Prerogative Instances that closes the *Novum Organum,* "to form judicious wishes is as much a part of knowledge as judicious questions" (4:233).

Prerogative Instances

Thus the only point of valorization that Bacon now extends for his method is what he calls *"Prerogative Instances."* Even then, these "royal" instances will be not for his New Logic but for his Natural and Experimental History. Oddly, therefore, the rest of the entire text of the *Novum Organum,* except for the last aphorism, consists of Bacon's catalogue of particular phenomena to be especially observed in the setting up of a proper natural history, such as was to become the central project in Bacon's *quinquennium*. In this last catalogue, Bacon ranges from "Solitary Instances which exhibit the nature under investigation in subjects which have nothing in common with other subjects except that nature; or, again, which do not exhibit the nature under investigation in subjects which resemble other subjects in every respect except in not having that nature," to Migratory Instances "in which the nature in question is in the process of being produced when it did not previously exist, or on the other hand of disappearing when it existed before" to Striking Instances, also called Shining Instances, or Instances Freed and Predominant, to Clandestine Instances, also called Instances of the Twilight, and so forth on to the twenty-sixth of the catalogue, Polychrest Instances, or Instances of General Use, this latter offering fewer summaries of all the previous twenty-five because it is simply a catch-all for unrelated observations. By now, the whole catalogue has begun to read more and more like Bacon's natural histories and like his even more loosely organized particulars in *Sylva Sylvarum*, correctly titled *The Forest of Forests*. Here too, as in the *Essays*, energies for proof have the dynamic of less directed closure and more startling opening. In addition, Bacon's tendency to ramify or invert into more and more precise divisions appears even in these serial instances. In the twenty-fourth instance, for example, Aphorism 48, Bacon summarizes, with details obviously drawn from his own observation as well as from reading and experimentation, nineteen examples of the differing motions of bodies. In his last and twenty-seventh category of Prerogative Instances, the Instances of Magic, Bacon reveals his Prospero-like attraction to necromancy and, in that attraction, the hope of an animistic nature that "what she may do when her folds have been shaken out, and after the discovery of Forms and Processes and Configurations, time will show" (4:245).[12]

In his last aphorism, Bacon becomes somewhat apologetic and even embarrassed over the long list through which the reader has progressed. As a result, he renames the organizing rubric—"the Dignities or Prerogatives of Instances"—to emphasize its connection with that most politically powerful instrument of Tudor and Jacobean kingship, the Royal Prerogative, defying which could, of course, not only cut off ears but careers and lives. Bacon now tries to make of his long catalogue a recapitulation of his whole method. The reader should remember, he begins, "that in this Organum of mine I am handling logic, not philosophy." Further, it should be "no wonder" that this place-logic and its examples are "everywhere sprinkled and illustrated with speculations and experiments in nature" because, so Bacon asserts in a figure of auxesis, his "logic aims to teach and instruct the understanding, not that it may with the slender tendrils of the mind snatch at and lay hold of abstract notions (as the common logic does), but that it may in very truth dissect nature" and be a science that "flows not merely from the nature of the mind, but also from the nature of things." Some of these instances can be investigated in detail now, but others can wait for his promised "Tables of Presentation for the work of the Interpreter concerning some particular nature" and there the method of exclusion that Bacon has just presented will act "as a soul among the common instances of Presentation" (4:246–7).

In his closure, by no surprise, Bacon dramatizes himself: "But now I must proceed to the supports and rectifications of Induction, and then to concretes, and Latent Processes, and Latent Configurations, and the rest, as set forth in the twenty-first Aphorism; that at length (like an honest and faithful guardian) I may hand over to men their fortunes, now their understanding is emancipated and come as it were of age; whence there cannot but follow an improvement in man's estate, and an enlargement of his power over nature." If the losses of the Fall can be repaired at last, this restitution can only come, so Bacon closes his book, by the sweat of the human face, the labor that identifies all life outside of the Garden of Eden. In a contemporary hermeneutical tradition deriving from Luther (and borrowed by both Bacon and Luther from Virgil),[13] the Lord Chancellor ends his book. The allusion to the curse of Genesis 3:19 is as crucial here as the last printed aphorism of the first book of the *Novum Organum* forming its inverted pyramid of Latin. By "virtue of that charter [diplomatis]," writes Bacon, giving the Vulgate line that Luther had used, "*In sudore vultus comedes panem tuum*" (in the sweat of thy face shalt thou eat bread)—the divine premise of labor in the discontinuity of fallen time—the human being [creatura] "is now by various labours (not certainly by disputations or idle magical ceremonies) at length and in some part to be subdued to supplying bread for human society, that is, to the uses of human life" (4:247–8). A new *philanthropia*, new charity, has emerged in time. It begins in making, in sweat and labor.

Chapter Seven
The *New Atlantis:* A Conclusion

Toward the end of his life, around 1624, Bacon wrote his own version of a Greek myth and transformed the shape of English narrative. Bacon's utopia in his native language had implicit epic proportions because written into the mythic text—what Bacon's chaplain Rawley calls "a fable"—is the symbolic transfer of one civilization into another, as though medieval and Renaissance Europe were being written into late twentieth-century Los Angeles. Bacon's narrative provides a new model of civilization for the planet or, in Bacon's term, the globe. Cultural breakdown is transformed in this conversion-narrative into collective action by special human beings (a transfiguration of society possible only through the conversion of individual subjectivity, as Bacon knew). The purpose of the conversion is, as Bacon's utopia reveals, to redeem the broken history Bacon sees operating at the heart of time. As in his revisions and recasting in *De Sapientia Veterum*, this "fable" appearing in 1626 would build on Bacon's special reading of the wisdom of the ancients. Only he would, as in his transformation of the Greek myths, rewrite this wisdom, and this time, as the future.

The Method of the Fable

Both in the *New Atlantis* and his immensely popular revisions of Greek myths in his 1609 *De Sapientia Veterum* and elsewhere, Bacon worked on a primitivist principle of time: in the deep past, with the true ancients, can be found the modern, the future as Bacon envisions and represents it. Such representation will take the highest form of poetry (at least the most acceptable) as Bacon describes it in his *Advancement*: "Allusive or Parabolical" or "a narration applied only to express some special purpose or conceit" (3:344). In his 1609 dedication of his book of Greek myths to Cambridge University (his "nursing mother"), Bacon touches on this method of representation: as the form of his myth-making, the "parable" is "a kind of ark, in which the most precious portions of the sciences were deposited" and the myths have so remained, despite the river of time in which the planks and flotsam rise to the top. In fact, as

Bacon's preface notes, "the most ancient times (except what is preserved of them in the scriptures) are buried in oblivion and silence; to that silence succeeded the fables of the poets; to those fables the written records which have come down to us." Such a view of history affects literary strategy. Thus, if such fables or parables, in Bacon's terms, "serve to disguise and veil the meaning" as well as "to clear and throw light on it"—the dual method of allegory—then the second usage of light and clarity can give a new myth-maker "the employment of parables as a method of teaching." In this way, "inventions that are new and abstruse and remote from vulgar opinions may find an easier passage to the understanding." Bacon is frank in his use of another varrant of the "initiative" method of knowledge. He is even bold in his historicizing. Thus, in Bacon's version of time, in ancient history, "when the inventions and conclusions of human reason (even those that are now trite and vulgar) were as yet new and strange, the world was full of all kinds of fables, and enigmas, and parables, and similitudes." Indeed, "as hieroglyphics came before the letters, so parables came before arguments" and "even now if any one [would] wish to let new light on any subjects into men's minds, and that without offence or harshness, he must still go the same way and call in the aid of similitudes." Earlier attempts to explain these myths have not understood "their true force, their genuine propriety, or their deeper reach" because, "though the subjects be old, yet the matter is new." In fact, "when transplanted into active life" such myths "acquire some new grace and vigour, and having more matter to feed them, strike their roots perhaps deeper, or at least grow taller and fuller leaved." Although his "nursing mother" should not "expect from a man of business anything exquisite; any miracles or prerogatives of leisure . . . among the thorns of business," in his 1609 book Bacon will "be throwing light either upon antiquity or upon nature itself." He and his readers will be "leaving behind us the open and level parts" and bending "our way towards the nobler heights that rise beyond" (6:691;695–9).

As with the *Essays* or the aphorisms of the *Novum Organum*, the 1609 sequence of brief annotations of Greek myths (as Bacon had received them) were each discontinuous for the reader, forming another series of "dispersed meditacions." The method for each "meditacion" was simple: narrative and commentary. In his myth on Pan "Or Nature," for instance, Bacon describes the allegorical body of Pan, immediately after his genealogy, and narrates his adventures as though they were dramatic episodes needing explanation like a painting. Their content becomes the basis for the hermeneutical act: "a noble fable this, if there be any such; and big almost to bursting with the secrets and mysteries of Nature." Similarly, the myth of Orpheus "Or Philosophy" offers radical transference through the outlines of a narrative in which the old identification of Orpheus with poetry is subverted into an identification not only with natural philosophy or science but the new technology. In its deconstruction and then reconstitution of the figure of the scientist, the poet becomes the technologist: "For as the works of wisdom surpass in dignity and power the works of strength, so the labours of Orpheus surpass the labours of Hercules." In the social-political aspect of these myths, the method of personification and theater continues: the Cyclops represent "Ministers of Terror"; the Styx, "Treaties"; Diomedes, "Zeal"; and Perseus, "War." A third perspective develops from the concerns of the *Essays* and is more personal, so that Narcissus depicts "Self-Love"; Endymion, "the Favourite"; Dionysus, "Desire"; the Sirens, "Pleasure"; and Tithonus, "Satiety."

In 1622, at about the same time Bacon was writing the *New Atlantis*, he took three of these original 1609 fables and revised them once more for *De Augmentis Scientiarum*. They represent specimens of what was yet to be done. Similarly, in the next year, he wrote a fragment based on his earlier Cupid myth, *De Principiis atque Originibus secundum Fabulas Cupidinis et Coeli, sive Parmeniis, et Telesii et praecipue Democriti philosophia tractata in fabula Cupidine*. As the foundation of a more elaborate theorizing on the nature of physical reality, the Cupid myth provided a frame for a profound discussion of the philosophies of the Pre-Socratics and of Bacon's contemporary Telesio. The work as parable represents, as Ellis points out, "the principles of heterogeneity and exclusion" (3:70). Bacon's Cupid or Eros is born without parents, from "the egg of Night," and represents the true nature of the atom, the central particle of the universe. Written near the end of Bacon's life, this bolder explication of the ancient Eros myth demonstrates Bacon's scientific method through metaphor and myth and is, for Paolo Rossi, equal in scientific explanation to the heat experiments in the *Novum Organum*. In fact, as Rossi comments: "the *De sapientia veterum* and the *De principiis atque originibus*—both allegorical, mythological works—contain the most coherent and complete renderings of Bacon's thought in its materialistic phase."[1]

In such analysis, Bacon is not only writing a new cultural anthropology for his readers but preparing the ground for his final utopian text, the *New Atlantis*. Whether Bacon is completely disingenuous in his

Greek myths and using them to camouflage his crass propagandistic motives (another instance of ancient text manipulated for contemporary ideology) or whether Bacon did actually believe such "deeper" frames of meaning existed is debatable. As with Freud's use of Greek myth, so with Bacon's: the relationship of his analysis and intention is not easily discerned. As in all his life, whether familial, courtly, or sexual, Bacon was used to disguise. Without doubt Bacon is attracted to the animism of the myths, and that attraction may have led to structures of seeming belief in his hermeneutics. It may even be, as Charles Lemmi has suggested with his analysis of Bacon's Italian sources,[2] that Francis Bacon lived in a context of communal belief lost to modern commentators, a systematic structuring of reality according to transcendent categories meaningless in the centuries that followed. In any case, by an irony, this disparity between what the myth actually says—certainly what its reception had previously been in Western culture—and what Bacon intends for the myth to say is part of its attraction. Thus, the artificiality and even theatricality of Bacon's interpretations draw readers, as a postmodern text might. Bacon's subjectivity transforms each myth into such a new and even outrageous reading that his passionate revisionism and lack of objectivity (in the midst of pretending otherwise) make the text quite entertaining. Finally, because the unspoken cultural imperatives in the later Renaissance could not but posit structures of belief, Bacon could fit his deconstruction of the old myths into his text but only for a "higher" purpose, the revelation of the world as it might become.

The Location of Utopia

Nothing could be higher in purpose than the sixth stage of Bacon's Great Instauration. Its apotheosis would represent authenticity for all the other days or stages of the new creation. It would authorize, therefore, the whole series. As the embodiment of the "ideal intuition" (yet still within the contingency of time), the representation of this final stage could not but locate itself in the genre of the Renaissance utopia invented only a hundred years before by another Lord Chancellor, Thomas More. In Bacon's narrative and in the crucial closing catalogue of the activities of the society of Bensalem, Bacon would project his intuition of the world as it might be at its most complete. The form of the fable fitted this projection.

In an obvious imitation of More, Bacon's utopia, the island of *New Atlantis*, exists in the world as it actually is. It has a contemporary setting in an undiscovered part of the globe in the South Pacific (the equivalent for Bacon of outer space). Bacon's then would be one more fiction in the series of science fictions the Renaissance had spawned, following the same pattern More had established: in a world of discontinuity and contingency, the ideal intuition exists. In fact, as Harvey Wheeler has remarked, Bacon's island in its ordering and location and "governing structure"[3] resembles modern-day Japan (and the contemporary reports of Jesuit and Franciscan enterprises there must have reached Bacon by 1624). Bacon had seen, as had the saintly More, not only the skull beneath the skin but the intuition at the heart of the series. For both, however, the process of the location of utopic text had moved, as More had radicalized the genre (differing it from Plato, for example), into the realm of the probable (as opposed to the absolute), into the discontinuity of history, and, in More's *Utopia*, into debate. This process meant, therefore, probability and inference could only be actualized by language and metaphor, and the basis of their narrative function expressed in a series of analogies. As a result of this narrative drive toward realism through analogy (and not allegory), Bacon's fictional text would become as reified as the novel form it adumbrated (as in Defoe's *Robinson Crusoe*, for example, where the traditional voyage narrative would also take philosophical direction). Thus, in its dialectical strategy of rendering realism through metaphor, Bacon's discourse could be demonstrated as solid as systematic information and matter but still remain, by its literary form, probable fiction. What is crucial to Bacon's final text and totally unanticipated in his work is that Bacon transformed the more cognitive but no less analogical and probable structures of the *Advancement of Learning* and the *Novum Organum* into a final metaphorical text. The *New Atlantis* completes the whole of his work as much as any epitome could.

Because this narrative text recapitulates so many of the themes and motifs in all of Bacon's work, realizing them in visible episodes, analysis of the work concludes appropriately this brief and general study of Francis Bacon. The *New Atlantis* metonymizes in extended metaphor or fiction the philosophical and scientific (and legal) theories adumbrated and systematized elsewhere in his canon. Events here do the work of ideas, but both are carried by Bacon's same fascination with the life and animism of nature. If Bacon can be identified with the Father of Salomon's House and the reader with the convert eagerly asking questions of this new and strangely attractive world, the first-person narrator is also Bacon's master figuration of subjectivity. He represents also both Bacon and the reader as epic questers. This text performs, therefore, that marriage Bacon had called for in his preface and plan for the Great Instauration, "a true and lawful marriage between the empirical and the rational faculty," the objective world and the observing self where the "rational" is a code-name for subjectivity. Out of this marriage of the self and the universe, there would spring the "hope (and be this the prayer of the bridal song)" of "a line and race of inventions that may in some degree subdue and overcome the necessities and miseries of humanity" (4:19;27). In the *New Atlantis*, the reader as narrator-convert is the self making this marriage of self to the true forms of objectivity as revealed in the secrets of a radically new physical and social universe located in a sea as yet unexplored. The ever-questing Bacon as well as the observing "I"-reader desires this physical contact and control in the marriage of the living world with the self as ritualized in Bacon's new narrative method.

Desire thus locates Bacon's utopia. Probability and the hope it brings to the self sets Bacon's last work as a social text to be lived as well as a "fable" to be read. Subjectivity can fully enter time through Bacon's science-fiction that contains a hortatory communal agenda for contact and control. With this double function in the text—realizing the place of control and realizing the language that controls—the *New Atlantis* confronts the problematics of all genuine utopias. They "betray a complicated apparatus," as Frederic Jameson comments, that will deconstruct their own time in terms of a special narrative history, enforcing "the topical allusion" of the author's society that engenders the text only to juxtapose a language of probability that subsumes it.[4] In other words, Bacon's utopic text shows his Caroline reader (and all other readers for which Bacon's scientific projections have not been realized) an ongoing narrative or series of episodes that exist in a time yet to come but which rise from Stuart England as much as from Bacon's own desire. In fact, as Rawley notes in his 1626 "To the Reader": "This fable my Lord devised, to the end that he might exhibit therein a model or description of a college instituted for the interpreting of nature and the producing of great and marvelous works for the benefit of men, under the name of Salomon's House, or the College of the Six Days' Works." Rawley also confronts the problematic of the "model" or probable text, with its language of the world as it might be, and actuality, with its language of the world as Bacon is confronting it: "Certainly the model is more vast and high than can possibly be imitated in all things; notwithstanding most things therein are within men's power to effect" (3:127).

The training for the task of finding that "model" or probable time (not future time in the narrative but contemporary—"within men's power to effect"), will be the experience of the text of the *New Atlantis*. It will be an experience that not only recapitulates the culture of Stuart England but reinvents its fundamental ideology, turning an old religion—Christianity—and its latest variant, the Protestant—into an even newer religion of science and technology. Thus, the Creation-week will be replayed throughout the narrative as the form of a probable completed history. Bacon's unfinished history, with its incomplete languages and metaphors, can only adumbrate this complete history—the ideal or "model" Salomon's House existing in the world side by side with Europe 1626 but not in England or Europe. For the reader, it is, after all, a society perceived only by the "I," who is an outsider becoming an insider. The reader has only Bacon's figuration of a European turning alien, choosing (as in science-fiction) to be transfigured into another realm. In this respect of side-by-side realities, it is no accident in Bacon's strategy that the state encapsulated in the Hebraic puns of "Bensalem" (and the Christian "New Jerusalem") should relate its oddly skewered Christianity to the religion of Jacobean and Caroline England. Tightly held in 1627 precisely because it was on the edge of revolution and collapse, Christianity in England epitomized the cultural crisis of Europe in which old forms met new history. Thus Bacon intends through the experience of his text, by his analogizing of English religion to the text's ideology, (in which science represents holiness) to prepare the reader—now become alien to his old European world—for his own new task. He could be "elect" in a new world to come. To be ready for this new visitation or Great Instauration of the truly ancient in the new society, the narrator-"I" must be trained as any convert for a greater religion.

It will be this training for the new task of historicizing or making that will determine the structure of Bacon's narrative. A new *Faber Fortunae*, one plural as well as singular, faces this new universe in the text, "a land unknown," in the last spoken words of the narrative. The fortune the convert will make will be directly in proportion to his act of historicizing it. All must change. The problem of European displacement appears here as after the startling Columbus-narrative of the new world: old space, old geography, must make way for the new geography of an ideology of science. As Denise Albanese remarks, in the *New Atlantis*, "religious, civil, and, ultimately, monarchial power are occluded and displaced by the inquisitional, by the power to probe nature."

Conversion-Narrative

Bacon's utopia takes the form of a confessional narrative. Its fiction actualizes a catechetical series of events-qua-teaching (classically the best method of instruction) that also includes a cataloguing device that doubly reifies the process of the probable. In the experience of this catechizing text, "seeing is more than believing," as Albanese notes. Ideology becomes reified, and seeing as knowledge "co-extensive with the act of reading and generated by it, brings the Baconian ideal into the arena of potentiality."[5] In this systematized agenda, Bacon's utopia thus differs from that of his political and intellectual predecessor. In More's *Utopia*, the reader is offered options for continuing in society as it is, including the potential for change, and at the end of this earlier utopia, these are still only options. Hytholoday may offer a world as it might be, but he will not accept the world as it is; Morus, the other voice in the dialectic, sees the probable as better but not as possible in the world of Henry VIII. The dialectic has not been resolved. On the contrary, Bacon's reader is being taught to enter a specific history and become a communicant of a society that forms a collective *Faber Fortunae*, a model of a new Christian church and new mystical Body. The dialectic has been officially resolved. At least, however unfinished, Bacon's text does not leave the question or dialectic open. His is a "model" of a higher reality that is being presented as truth, not a choice of options. The direction of the narrative is clear. Before such technological magnificence and epic magnanimity, the narrator could only choose to be saved.

Bacon's utopia structures this direction of conversion from the beginning, and such directing is typical of confessional narratives in the Augustinian mode, not the Platonic dialogue form as in More's *Utopia*. Its starting point is, not surprisingly, negation. Bacon's plot begins with social breakdown in which the narrator-"I" (eye) is literally in stasis. "We sailed from Peru," says the unnamed figure who is telling the story, and after a year of wandering and no winds, the situation has become hopeless: "so that finding ourselves in the midst of the greatest wilderness of waters in the world, without victual, we gave ourselves for lost men, and prepared for death" (3:129). The narrative begins then in breakdown. In fact, the narrative dynamic of the text is only possible because of the initial fact of disaster. It does not generate from any outside scheme of total salvation or grand progress, either actual or potential. Whatever the pressure of the conversion-dynamic, nothing can happen outside the fiction of the text (confessions may also be fictions). In fact, disaster is the source of the fictional drive of the text; the revealed splendors are nothing if not in dialectic with the "lost" condition of the narrator and the stasis in the "wilderness of waters" that is always possible outside the island of Bensalem. Destruction always surrounds the ideal intuition. Thus the episodes of the narrative partake of the allegorical mode and the older ideologies in order to prepare the new convert for his more heroic tasks in an utterly altered world, where such language is subsumed. Recapitulating the Genesis Creation history, the language of the narrator postulates, at the start, "thick clouds" on the horizon that promise "dry land." In another example of reversed ideology, this text will draw its basic figuration out of the Old Testament and the ritualizing of the ancient Jews (it would be thirty years before the return of Jews to England would occur, and a probable text like Bacon's may certainly have set the context for this actuality). Bacon's popular text is thus immediately emblematic of the older myths, one structure dialectically reproducing another in the Temple-like appearance of the city, the forbiddance of entrance, and the scroll "in ancient Hebrew, and in ancient Greek, and in good Latin of the School, and in Spanish" (and therefore official by humanist standards). The stamp on the scroll is both authoritative and ideological and, in a narrative "jump-start," comforting. The lost human beings have found a sign of deliverance recapitulated from their own Bible-oriented world, a familiar belief-structure: on the stamp are recognized marks of the angelic, "cherubins' wings, not spread but hanging downwards, and by them a cross" (3:130–1).

Bacon's daring confrontation with religion in his utopia was itself dichotomous: on the one hand, a slip here could cost him readers and bring censorship but, on the other hand, Christianity could reinforce the ideological power of the new science, the shift in epistemology, Bacon's new marriage of subjectivity and the universe. The strength of Europe's fundamental ideology could be his own through a shift in metaphor. Bacon thus performs his sleight-of-hand by rewriting myth, contemporary politics, and current events, all with a new hermeneutics. The dress of the figure of authority who first greets the seamen on their ship is suitably exotic. With his turban, he not only recalls contemporary Turks but that Other Christianity that was older, at least for some English Protestants, than the enemy Catholicism, that is, Byzantium (where Greeks wore turbans). This strong Christian identification and the legalistic requirements such as purification from bloodshedding and the shibboleth-oath, "by the name of Jesus and his merits" (3:132)—all parodies of living religions—are necessary. Bacon's largely Protestant audience comprised the emerging middle class who could fund projects such as those he would describe, and so, for them, Bacon devises a carefully composed strategy. Without the originating moment of Christianity in the *New Atlantis*, there could be no proleptic or teleological moment when fiction and science in a supreme probability could lead, however strange and startling the text, to the European conversion of subjectivity into action. For this reason, the originating moment of Christianity in Bensalem occupies an important moment in the time-space of the narrative.

On a visit from the governor of the House of Strangers, who "by vocation" is "a Christian priest," the lost seamen learn the story of the birth of Christianity in Bensalem. As the governor sits among them, speaking "familiarly," the seamen, who are being slowly indoctrinated to the meaning of the island, learn that "about twenty years after the ascension of our Saviour" suddenly during a night "cloudy and calm" there appeared "a great pillar of light; not sharp, but in the form of a column or cylinder, rising from the sea a great way up towards heaven: and on the top of it was seen a large cross of light" even brighter "and more resplendent." Borrowing from the Genesis and Exodus narratives, Bacon designs his scene like a masque: the boats of the perplexed natives surround the light but only "one of the wise men of the society of Salomon's House" can unravel the mystery of the phallic pillar of light. This wise man first observes, "having awhile attentively and devoutly viewed and contemplated this pillar and cross"—supreme images of both Old and New Testaments respectively. Then, after observing, he falls down in worship before the natural phenomenon. True distortions of nature as in miracles are rare, he says in his prayer that follows, but what "we now see before our eyes is thy Finger and a true Miracle." Following this recognition of divine interception in time and prayer, the boat is freed and can be "with silence rowed towards the pillar." Then the erect cylinder of light disappears; all that is left is "a small ark or chest of cedar, dry, and not wet at all with water, though it swam" and out of it "grew a small green branch of palm." The ark carries a book and letter, both crucial inscriptions of Bacon's new version of Christianity. The book "contained all the canonical books of the Old and New Testament" as well as "the Apocalypse itself, and some other books of the New Testament which were not at that time written." The letter here is a bold invention, for it is written by no one less than the Apostle Bartholomew (a favorite among Protestants), who had been "warned by an angel" to "commit this ark to the floods of the seas." "Therefore I do testify," the letter reads, "and declare unto that people where God shall ordain this ark to come to land, that in the same day is come unto them salvation and peace and goodwill, from the Father, and from the Lord Jesus." Bacon then adds another master parody. Immediately all who are present including "Hebrews, Persians, and Indians," as at the Feast of Pentecost, the birth-moment of the Christian Church, understand the book and letter in their own languages. This divine authorization extends to the entire kingdom and its history and not least to Bacon's own text narrating this event through its explicit analogizing of old myths and new events: "And thus was this land saved from infidelity (as the remain of the old world was from water) by an ark, through the apostolical and miraculous evangelism of St. Bartholomew" (3:135–9). Bacon's text is its own kind of "ark."

What follows is the narrator's slow immersion into the life of this perfect land theatrically blessed by God. The seaman is invited to learn about the history of the land of the new Atlantis. Especially he is told of the originating exploits of its king "Solamona," who, in a direct quotation from the Bible about Solomon, "had a *large heart*, inscrutable for good" and "whose memory of all others, we most adore; not superstitiously, but as a divine instrument, though a mortal man." This king who had lived "about" 1900 years ago (before James I, the new Solomon) recharged, as did More's King Utopus, the cultural dynamic of history. Besides introducing customs that Bacon analogizes specifically to those of modern China, including the reception of strangers like the narrator (so that most never leave), one act of this king, among many, "hath the pre-eminence." Bacon now comes to the heart of his text: "It was the erection and institution of an Order or Society which we call *Salomon's House*; the noblest foundation (as we think) that ever was upon the earth; and the lanthorn [lantern] of this kingdom. It is dedicated to the study of the Works and Creatures of God" (3:144–5). Bacon is careful to point out—or rather his Governor-character does—that the title of the order derives from the Jewish King Solomon and not the founder of the new state of Bensalem. It thus fits into the Jewish dispensation given by God to His chosen people: "I find in ancient records this Order or Society is sometimes called Salomon's House and sometimes the College of the Six Days Works." So, "instituting that House for the finding out of the true nature of all things (whereby God might have the more glory in the workmanship of them, and men the more fruit in the use of them)," the archetype-king gave this new society its Biblical name.

After learning of the extraordinary functioning of this society of celibate scientists, the narrator learns more of the nature of this island through two encounters with actual citizens. If these two episodes appear tangential in the *New Atlantis*, as with the *Essays* and other texts indirection is direction. The two contacts provide, in fact, social and cultural framing for the center of the kingdom, the scientists of Solomon's House. Both are essential to Bacon's thesis of the transfer of mythologies and ideologies. The first episode focuses once more on the social authorization of the family as the anthropological nucleus out of which celibate scientists as well as the whole society arise. The seamen are invited to "a Feast of the Family, as they call it" and "a most natural, pious, reverend custom it is, shewing that nation to be compounded of all goodness." This festal honor "is granted to any man that shall live to see thirty persons descended of his body alive together, and all above three years old, to make this feast" subsidized by the state. The elaborate masque-like imagery that follows develops Bacon's thesis of generation and special calling—indeed the "Father of the Family," who is so honored and is called "the *Tirsan*," which means, spelled backwards, "nasrite" or Nazarite or consecrated one in ancient Jewish culture. Sexual imagery dominates this description of the family-authorization; it climaxes, in fact, the sexual and generative imagery that runs as a major metaphor-motif throughout Bacon's canon. It is a "Feast" carefully watched by the fascinated "I" of the narrative.

The second contact reinforces the Biblical allusions. The strange episode of the Jew Joabin that intervenes before the last episode of the Father of Salomon's House enacts a familiar strategy of the *Essays*. An experience, especially if exalted, is deconstructed by the realism of another. Here ambiguity rises from a series of sexual allusions that play against the purity of the Feast of the Family and, by indirection, the purity of the feast to be revealed by the Father of Salomon's House. "You shall understand," says Joabin to the narrator, "that there is not under the heavens so chaste a nation as this of Bensalem; nor so free from all pollution or foulness. It is the virgin of the world." Here "there are not stews [brothels], no dissolute houses, no courtesans, nor anything of that kind" and the citizens "wonder (with detestation) at you in Europe" because such institutions as brothels "put marriage out of office," for in Europe there are "infinite men that marry not, but chuse rather a libertine and impure single life" or marry late. Coming from these temptations and bargaining over marriage, such Europeans do not "greatly esteem children" as Bensalem's "chaste men do." Also, such acts (implied as European) as "*Lot's offer*, who to save his guests from abusing, offered his daughters" are not really practical, "for that the same vices and appetites do still remain and abound; unlawful lust being like a furnace, that if you stop the flames altogether, it will quench; but if you give it any vent, it will rage." Joabin's sexual survey is sweeping: "as for masculine love, they have no touch of it" (the Latin is clearer: "istos ne fando quidem norunt") and yet they have stronger male friendships, "faithful and inviolate," than anywhere in the world. Joabin ends his discourse by naming marriage customs and laws in Bensalem that support the family unit, preserve monogamy, and even make the custom of More's Utopia—specifically named—more civil by examining, before marriage, the mate's body in "*Adam and Eve's pools*," friends of either "to see" the male or female "bathe naked" (3:151–4).

If the episode of Joabin is curious and almost pornographic in its latent purience, the key to understanding it exists not so much in its sexualizing of the whole text—this the negative after the positive generation of the Feast of the Family—as in its preparation for Bacon's finale to his epic of cultural transference. Joabin acts as a necessary negative force to the all-powerful positive force that concludes the text. The positive force that follows is the sexless world that generates not children but inventions, the offspring of the marriage of subjectivity and the world beyond self. As Bacon had said in his essay "Of Parents and Children," the reader can "see the noblest works and foundations have proceeded from childless men; which have sought to express the images of their mind" with the irony that "the care of posterity is most in them that have no posterity" (6:390). The offspring of celibate scientists who are now becoming, in this text, the new priests of European or New World culture is nothing less than technology—works in a religion that has progressed beyond Protestant Christianity to become another stage in the redeemed history of the world.

The Father of Salomon's House

In fact, Joabin, in the text the symbol of cultural discontinuity who describes subjective disorientation (through unregenerative sexuality), introduces the leader of the new priests of this world as it might be: "One of the Fathers of Salomon's House will be here this day sevennight: we have seen none of them this dozen years." Although he will come with a grand procession, "the cause of his coming is secret." As the text slowly reveals, the cause is none other than a confrontation with the narrator himself at the final stage of his conversion. "The day being come," the "I" of the text first notes the body and dress of the Father before he witnesses the elaborate procession surrounding him. The Father is "middle stature and age, comely of person, and had an aspect as if he pitied men." His clothes are the epitome of Renaissance magnificence, as though out of a Stuart masque or a Van Dyke portrait. Before an exceptionally ordered crowd, the Father makes a simple gesture as he passes by, holding up "his bare hand as he went, as blessing the people, but in silence."

After three days, continues the "I"-narrator, "the Jew came to me again, and said; 'Ye are happy men; for the Father of Salomon's House taketh knowledge of your being here, and commanded me to tell you that he will admit all your company to his presence.'" Furthermore, and this is the climactic episode of Bacon's utopia, the Father "'will have private conference with one of you that ye shall choose'" and the event is particularized: "'the next day after tomorrow'" and because it will include "'his blessing, he hath appointed it in the forenoon.'" The narrative appropriately fast-forwards. Duly arriving and having chosen the "I" of the narrative "for the private access," the Father stands up and stretches "his hand ungloved, and in posture of blessing." Each of the lost men stoops and kisses the hem of his tippet or stole. Dismissing all but the narrator, the Father speaks to him in Spanish and begins his long catalogue of the secrets of this utopia. He begins first with a generalized definition of his task and then gives his *partitio*, in appropriate oratorical form: "God bless thee, my son; I will give thee the greatest jewel I have. For I will impart unto thee, for the love of God and men, a relation of the true state of Salomon's House." The Father will have a specific order: "First, I will set forth unto you the end of our foundation. Secondly, the preparations and instruments we have for our works. Thirdly, the several employments and functions whereto our fellows are assigned. And fourthly, the ordinances and rites which we observe." The "end" marks the apotheosis of Bacon's divine week of creation: "The End of our Foundation is the knowledge of Causes, and secret motions of things; and the enlarging of the bounds of Human Empire, to the effecting of all things possible" (3:154–6).

If, for Bacon, the universe is at heart motion and progression, the "preparations and instruments" that the Father divulges reflect a continual activity that reveals the animism of this technological world that imitates so perfectly nature herself. The Father therefore delights in his catalogue, as did the Tirsan in *his* children. Immensely large and deep caves serve, for example, for experiments of "coagulations, indurations, refrigerations, and conservations of bodies." Imitation mines serve as well for the curing of disease and prolongation of life (hermits may dwell there), and burials of material such as cement in different types of earth (like the Chinese with porcelain) also are made. Enormous towers, one about half a mile high, provide for experiments in "insolation, refrigeration, conservation" for viewing meteors, winds, rain, snow, and hail, and for dwellings for observant hermits. Great lakes, both salt and fresh, support experiments with fish and fowl and the exchange of salt water into fresh, and vice-versa. Artificial wells and fountains offer opportunities for experiments with chemicals, and their Water of Paradise is "made very sovereign for health, and prolongation of life." Large houses set up artificial environmental conditions, including Chambers of Health, where control of air can cure disease, and special baths not only cure but restore "man's body from arefaction" and confirm it "in strength of sinews, vital parts, and the very juice and substance of the body." In the orchards and gardens, experiments with soil, grafting, and inoculating transform the landscape, as do the parks, pools, and enclosures for all kinds of beasts and birds, the whole range of flora and fauna. Special "brew-houses, bake-houses, and kitchens" experiment with new foods and drinks, as new pharmacies develop new drugs; certain mechanical arts, unknown in Europe, produce new materials. Furnaces "of great diversities" with differing temperatures generate new powers, including instruments that can "generate heat only by motion" (3:161), recalling the experiments in the *Novum Organum*. The Father also reveals "perspective-houses, where we make demonstrations of all lights and radiations" and colors. Precious stones can also be reproduced artificially. In sound houses, the Father describes instruments that are future telephones: "we have also means to convey sounds in trunks and pipes, in strange lines and distances." In "engine-houses" all kinds of instruments are prepared for speed and power, including war weapons, and also for flying in the air or for sailing under water. The final items are "houses of deceits of the senses" and their negative effect helps to uncover all fallacies, for "we do hate all impostures and lies." The Father concludes this section: "These are (my son) the riches of Salomon's House" (3:156–64).

For the third section, "the several employments and offices of our fellows," the Father gives a catalogue of workers that encapsulates, in fact, Bacon's scientific method as outlined in his Great Instauration. The gradation of labor recapitualizes in actuality the steps in Bacon's pyramid of knowledge, and, as Ducasse has shown,[6] demonstrates how Bacon did

conceive of methods resembling hypothesis and conjecture. The person-
alized metaphors Bacon chooses here for the stages and gradual progression of his method help to materialize through human type his new scientific logic. First, the twelve scientists that sail secretly to foreign
countries and "bring us the books, and abstracts, and patterns of experiments of all other parts" Bacon calls "Merchants of Light." Those who
collect experiments out of books are called "Depredators." The three
groups who collect experiments from mechanical arts, liberal sciences
and "practices" not yet made into a science are called "Mystery-men" or
in the Latin, "Venatores" (hunters, as in the Hunt for Pan). Then those
who make early new experiments are called "Pioners or Miners" (3:164).
In the stage following the gathering of experiments, there are three,
"Compilers," who "draw" them "into titles and tables, to give the better
light for the drawing of observations and axioms out of them." Then,
actualizing the fourth and fifth stages of his Great Instauration,
"Dowry-men or Benefactors" look into the ongoing experimentation to
see if there are any useful works for human society. "Lamps" also perform in this way by drawing from the collections and early experiments
in order "to direct new experiments, of a higher light, more penetrating
into nature than the former." Then those who "execute the experiments
so directed, and report them" are called "Inoculators." Finally, "we have
three that raise the former discoveries by experiments into greater observations, axioms, and aphorisms. These we call Interpreters of Nature"
(3:164–5).

   If later readers tend to be in awe before the plenitude of this reification and the materializing of the reader's imagination that such cataloguing can give, the lonely narrator is overwhelmed by the multiplica-
tion. Science and technology are now seen as his real human family.
Although a way out of historical discontinuity and cultural loneliness
may also provide the same justification for Bacon's endless reifying in his
Advancement and his natural histories, there is a key difference in this
text. Here the narrative leads to immediate conversion, not of nature to
self but of self to nature. Reification cannot be reduced to the human
dimension. The life that is being catalogued will keep its alien distance,
like nature itself. It is Bacon's narrator and the reader who must be converted. The modern post-romantic subjectivity must rethink Bacon's
historicity here. There is nothing personal in the world ahead; the narrator must enter a historical world ruled by the new dialectic of the essentially alien. In a textualized paradox, Bacon's European reader must now
become an alien in order to find true humanity. As in the ironies of

More's *Utopia*, the West cannot colonize this new world. The superior island held by the highest laws of secrecy is, in fact, a *New* Atlantis, and Bacon has taken Montaigne's "noble savage" considerably further than either the French ironist or the paradoxical More.

Not even the effect of the parodies and the completion of European history in this new world can displace the "absolute actuality" of the alien that the convert must now confront and become. In fact, the disclosure of the "ordinances and rites" of the new civilization of science shows the difference he must enter, especially in the two long galleries that display, in a special metonymy, the honor of the kingdom not in religious pictures or portraits of kings and noblemen but in the exhibition of actual inventions, the physical instruments themselves, and then of the statues of heroes of discovery, from Columbus to the inventor of ships in ancient times, to the monk, Roger Bacon, who invented ordnance and gunpowder. Furthermore, the oddly deistic Christianity practiced in Bensalem does not correspond to the theocentric world of the large and once active medieval St. Alban's abbey near Francis Bacon's Gorhambury nor to the salvation-centered world of his mother's radical Protestantism: "We have certain hymns and services, which we say daily, of lauds and thanks to God for his marvellous works: and forms of prayers, imploring his aid and blessing for the illumination of our labours, and the turning of them into good and holy uses" (3:166).

If these "rites" are flat, the final scene of Bacon's utopia is appropriately theatrical. The lost and nameless male sailor is alone with the Father-master of reality, the shaman who loves him: "And when he had said this, he stood up; and I, as I had been taught, kneeled down; and he laid his right hand upon my head." In this final gesture the act of conversion appears complete: "God bless thee, my son, and God bless this relation which I have made." Not surprisingly, the Father reinforces "this relation" with money, the ready cash Bacon always lacked, but that science and technology could promise and its political system of capitalism provide. "And so he left me," says the narrator at the end, "having assigned a value of about two thousand ducats, for a bounty to me and my fellows." The new science works, the reader-convert has learned; ready cash promises a consumer society with all its technical freedoms and liberation of self into fascinating technology. The culminating line of Bacon's utopia reiterates this promise: "For they give great largesses where they come upon all occasions." Subjectivity can profit from its new contact with and control of the objective world, but it is still a new and even alien world. It requires the labor of conversion.

The more appropriate closure—and the better one to conclude this general study of Francis Bacon—appears in the final words of the Father to the new convert. This is the moment of the narrator's virtual ordination, his taking on of the role of missionary for the new revelation. In that moment, the Father reminds his new "son" of the mystery of existence both Father and the convert-narrator survive in: "I give thee leave to publish it [the catalogue and, in effect, the whole first-person narrative] for the good of other nations; for we here are in God's bosom, a land unknown." If it is appropriate and indeed necessary that this text of "a land unknown" be unfinished, it is also appropriate in Bacon's totalizing strategy, in his relentless dialectic of time, that the ending be equivocal. It must be incomplete, to be perceived and read on the run (at least in the prophet Habakkuk's terms). Otherwise, it lies about reality and the truth of time and history. The new audience can only read on the run. In fact, the final word of the *New Atlantis* is "occasions," the dialectical subject of the *Essays*. This dialectic of time, then, with its constant threat of breakdown, will not go away. Continuing text must be written by continuing audiences in an ever-new labor of time for each generation. In that relentless dialectic, where leisure is rare, in Bacon's concept of ambiguous history, the work of the *New Atlantis*—in effect, Bacon's entire work—is still going on. It continues with all its dangers and all its promises.

Notes and References

Preface

1. The Latin text of George Herbert's ode can be found in *The Works of George Herbert*, ed. F. E. Hutchinson (Oxford: Clarendon Press, 1945), 436–37. For my translation and a study of the relationship between Bacon and Herbert, see William A. Sessions, "Bacon and Herbert and an Image of Chalk" in *"Too Riche to Clothe the Sun": Essays on George Herbert* (Pittsburgh: University of Pittsburgh Press, 1980), 165–78.

Chapter One

1. *The Works of Francis Bacon, Baron of Verulam, Viscount St. Alban, and Lord High Chancellor of England*, ed. James Spedding, Robert Leslie Ellis, and Douglas Denon Heath, Fourteen Volumes, the first five volumes *Philosophical Works*, the next two volumes *Literary and Professional Works*, and the last seven *The Letters and Life*, ed. Spedding alone (1858; rpt. Stuttgart–Bad Cannstatt: Friedrich Frommann Verlag, 1963) 8:109, hereafter cited in the text. All translations are Spedding's, unless otherwise specified. All italics are Spedding's, unless otherwise designated.

2. The premises assumed here develop from the conclusions of Antonio Pérez-Ramos in his study of Bacon's theories of knowledge and science in *Francis Bacon's Idea of Science and the Maker's Knowledge Tradition* (Oxford: Clarendon Press, 1988).

3. C. S. Lewis, *English Literature in the Sixteenth Century Excluding Drama* (Oxford: Clarendon Press, 1954), 307.

4. F. J. Levy, "Francis Bacon and the Style of Politics" in *Renaissance Historicism: Selections from English Literary Renaissance*, ed. Arthur F. Kinney and Dan S. Collins (Amherst: University of Massachusetts Press, 1987), 156.

5. Arthur B. Ferguson, *Clio Unbound: Perception of the Social and Cultural Past in Renaissance England* (Durham: Duke University Press, 1979).

6. Catherine Drinker Bowen, *Francis Bacon: The Temper of a Man* (Boston: Little, Brown, and Company, 1963), 79.

7. *Aubrey's Brief Lives*, ed. Oliver Lawson Dick (Ann Arbor: University of Michigan Press, 1962), 11.

8. Aubrey 9–10.

9. *The Complete Poetry of Ben Jonson*, ed. William B. Hunter, Jr. (New York: W. W. Norton & Co., Inc., 1968), 207–8.

10. Ben Jonson, *Works*, ed. C. H. Herford and Percy Simpson (Oxford: The Clarendon Press, 1925–1963), 7:590–92; 11:241–44.

11. John Noonan, *Bribes* (New York 1984), chapter 12. See also Nieves Mathews, *Francis Bacon: The Story of a Character Assasination* (New Haven: Yale University Press, 1996).

12. John C. Briggs, *Francis Bacon and the Rhetoric of Nature* (Cambridge: Harvard University Press, 1989), 249–53.

13. Aubrey 16.

Chapter Two

1. I am using this term as post-Hegelians use dialectic, not necessarily as Aristotelians or logicians in Bacon's time use it. For a succinct definition of the term I intend, see Hans-Georg Gadamer, "The Hermeneutics of Suspicion" in *Hermeneutics: Question and Prospects*, ed. Gary Shapiro and Alan Siod (Amherst: University of Massachusetts Press, 1984), especially 59.

2. Sir Francis Bacon, *The Essayes or Counsels, Civill and Morall* ed. with introduction and commentary by Michael Kiernan (Cambridge: Harvard University Press, 1985), xx, hereafter cited in text.

3. Stanley E. Fish, "The Experience of Bacon's *Essays*" in *Self-Consuming Artifacts: The Experience of Seventeenth-Century Literature* (Berkeley and Los Angeles: University of California Press, 1972), 119, hereafter cited in text.

4. Levy, "Francis Bacon and the Style of Politics," 157. Cf. Thomas Greene, "The Flexibility of the Self in Renaissance Literature" in *The Disciplines of Criticism*, ed. Peter Demetz, Thomas Greene, and Lowry Nelson, Jr. (New Haven: Yale University Press, 1968), 241–64. The most recognized restatement of the Burckhardtian topos has been that in Stephen Greenblatt, *Renaissance Self-Fashioning* (Chicago: University of Chicago Press, 1980), 161ff.

5. Sir Roy Strong, *Henry Prince of Wales and England's Lost Renaissance* (London: Thames and Hudson, 1986), especially 212 and the other references to Bacon; Christopher Hill, *Intellectual Origins of the English Revolution* (London, 1972), 213–19.

6. See also Spedding's commentary on this dedication 11:340 and the original text in British Library Ms Additional 4259 f. 155.

7. Brian Vickers, *Francis Bacon and Renaissance Prose* (Cambridge: Cambridge University Press, 1968), 87.

8. The title relates this version to Bacon's translation of *De Augmentis Scientiarum* in this period, for the second part of the Latin title relates to a new topic—*Satira Seria, sive de Interioribus Rerum* (A Serious Satire or Concerning the Interiority of Things)—that Bacon proposes for investigation in Book Seven of the *De Augumentis*. It would be one more desideratum for future scientific study, and the section in the *De Augmentis* would be followed by the Virgilian *Georgica Animi, sive de Cultura Morum* (The Georgics of the Mind, or concerning the Cultivation of Character).

9. *Hippocrates, Volume IV; Heracleitus, On the Universe*, tr. W. H. S. Jones (Cambridge: Harvard University Press, 1967), 483.

10.   Paolo Rossi, *Francis Bacon: From Magic to Science*, tr. Sacha Rabinovitch (London: Routledge & Kegan Paul, 1968), 129; 206.

11.   Aubrey 10–11.

12.   For a more developed discussion of the biblical passages and these ideas, see William A. Sessions, "Francis Bacon and the Classics: The Discovery of Discovery" in *Francis Bacon's Legacy of Texts: "The Art of Discovery Grows with Discovery"* (New York: AMS Press, 1990), 245–47.

13.   The usage here demonstrates that parody for Bacon means, as it does in the poetry of Bacon's young friend George Herbert, not satiric use of an original but an imitation that revises the original in a totally new context, with even as in Herbert, the musical sense of a counter-melody, the new out of the old. Cf. Rosemund Tune, "Sacred 'Parody' of Love Poetry, and Herbert," *Studies in the Renaissance*, 8:249–90.

14.   F. H. Anderson, *The Philosophy of Francis Bacon* (1948; rpt., 1971: Octagon Books, 1971), 81–85.

15.   For the best source for reading this fundamental discussion of time and history in Mircea Eliade, see his *Sacred and Profane* (New York: Harper Torchbooks, 1959).

16.   The fullest analysis of theater imagery in Bacon is in Brian Vickers, "Bacon's Use of Theatrical Imagery" in *Legacy*, ed. Sessions, 171–213.

17.   *Complete Writings of William Blake,* ed. Geoffrey Keynes (London, 1966), 396–410.

18.   Vickers, *Prose* 77.

19.   Peter Stein, *Regulae Iuris: From Juristic Rules to Legal Maxims* (Edinburgh, 1966), 170–74.

20.   Such a "distemper" of learning as Bacon himself attacks here and the varieties of his own prose style limit, as Vickers has definitively shown *(Prose Style* 13–14; 106–17), the analyses of both Morris Croll and George Williamson (and their followers), who see Bacon's forms as entirely in a Senecan mode.

21.   Lisa Jardine, *Discovery and the Art of Discourse* (Cambridge: Cambridge University Press, 1974), 177; 86 and passim Chapters 10 and 11.

22.   Alvin Snider, "Francis Bacon and the Authority of Aphorism," *Prose Studies* (1988): 56–67. See the development of these ideas in his larger study, *Origin and Authority in Seventeenth-Century England: Bacon, Milton, Butler* (Toronto: University of Toronto Press, 1994).

23.   Anne Righter [Barton], "Francis Bacon" in *The English Mind*, ed. Hugh Sykes Davies and George Watson (Cambridge: Cambridge University Press, 1964); rpt. in *Essential Articles for the Study of Francis Bacon*, ed. Brian Vickers (Hamden: Archon Books, 1968), 319.

24.   See William A. Sessions, "Recent Studies in Francis Bacon," *English Literary Renaissance* 17:3 (1987): 351–71.

25.   Fish "Experience," 111; cf. 78, 94, 125–26.

26. Vickers, *Prose* 217–31. For an attack on Fish's reading of the *Essays*, see Jeffrey Barnouw, "The Experience of Bacon's Essays: Reading the Text Vs. 'Affective Stylistics,'" *Proceedings of the Ninth Congress of the International Comparative Literature Association* 2 (1979): 351–57.

27. Ronald S. Crane, "The Relation of Bacon's *Essays* to His Program for the Advancement of Learning" in *Essential Articles*, ed. Vickers, 272–92.

28. Moody E. Prior, "Bacon's Man of Science," *Journal of the History of Ideas* 15 (1954): 348–70.

29. Aubrey 11; 130.

30. Cf. 3:454–55; 7:97–99 and Charles N. Cochrane, *Christianity and Classical Culture* (1940; rpt., Oxford: Oxford University Press, 1957), 70. For the depth of Bacon's reading of Virgil, see Charles Whitney, *Francis Bacon and Modernity* (New Haven and London: Yale University Press, 1986), 170–71. For a rather complete survey in Bacon of this topos of the *Faber Fortunae*, see R. C. Cochrane, "Francis Bacon and the Architect of Fortune," *Studies in the Renaissance* 3 (1958): 176–95.

31. Jardine, *Bacon*, 234.

32. Fish, "Experience," 101–8; Jardine, *Bacon*, 238–41.

33. Jardine, *Bacon*, 228.

Chapter Three

1. George H. Nadel, "History and Psychology in Francis Bacon's Theory of History" in *History and Theory* 5:3 (1966), 275–87; rpt. in *Essential Articles*, ed. Vickers, 236–50, citation 249.

2. *The Letters of John Chamberlain*, ed. N. E. McClure (Philadelphia: The American Philosophical Society, 1939), 2:430. In fact, Chamberlain was surprisingly generous: "I have not read much of yt, but yf the rest of our historie were aunswerable to yt, I thincke we shold not need to envie any other nation in that kind." The cycle of histories would have begun with Henry VII and ended with James I; Bacon discusses his plans and his theories of history in a fragment that Speed appropriated for his 1609 history acknowledging the insertion as Bacon's (6:16–22).

3. For a good introduction to the topic of Bacon and history, see the sources cited in *The History of the Reign of King Henry the Seventh*, ed. F. J. Levy (Indianapolis and New York: Bobbs-Merrill Co., Inc., 1974). Cf. Levy's own *Tudor Historical Thought* (San Marino: Huntingdon Library, 1967); Leo Strauss, *The Political Philosophy of Hobbes* (Chicago: University of Chicago Press, 1952), 86–94; and F. Smith Fussner, *The Historical Revolution: English Historical Writing and Thought 1580–1640* (London, 1962) 254ff.

4. Edward I. Berry, "History and Rhetoric in Bacon's *Henry VII*" in *Seventeenth-Century Prose: Modern Essays in Criticism*, ed. Stanley E. Fish (New York: Oxford University Press, 1971), 290; 295. See also page 292 for Berry's comparison of passages from Henry VII's blind poet-laureate Bernard Andrè's

Latin history of his king and Bacon's, and then Berry's conclusion: "What in André is conceived of primarily as event, is in Bacon conceived of as thought."

5. Francis Bacon, *Of The Advancement and Proficiencie of Learning*, in Gilbert Wats (London, 1674), 57; otherwise, in text.

6. Benjamin Farrington, *The Philosophy of Francis Bacon* (Liverpool: Liverpool University Press, 1964), 71–72; hereafter cited in text as F.

7. Leonard F. Dean, "Sir Francis Bacon's Theory of Civil History-Writing," *English Literary History* 7 (1941): 161–83; rpt. in *Essential Articles*, ed. Vickers, 211–35, citation 228.

8. Nadel 248.

9. For a convenient place to read essays on the subject of Bacon's prose style, see the first part of Stanley Fish's *Seventeenth-Century Prose*. For the complete studies of Croll on Bacon, see *Style, Rhetoric, and Rhythm: Essays of Morris W. Croll*, ed. J. Max Patrick and Robert O. Evans (Princeton: Princeton University Press, 1966), and for further discussion of the Senecan and Tacitean styles in Bacon, see George W. Williamson, *The Senecan Amble: A Study in Prose Form From Bacon to Collier* (Chicago: University of Chicago Press, 1951), especially Chapter Six "Bacon and Stoic Rhetoric." See also Robert Adolph, *The Rise of Modern Prose Style* (Cambridge: Harvard University Press, 1968). For a strong refutation of the arguments of both Croll and Williamson, see Vickers, *Prose* 13–14; 106–17.

10. Berry 308.

11. *The Complete Works of Montaigne*, tr. Donald M. Frame (Stanford: Stanford University Press, 1957), 610–11.

12. Brother Kenneth William Cardwell, FSC, "Francis Bacon, Inquisitor" in *Francis Bacon's Legacy of Texts*, ed. Sessions, 284. See his gentle refutation of Cassirer, 285.

13. Ernst Cassirer, *The Platonic Renaissance in England*, tr. J. P. Pettegrove (Austin: University of Texas Press, 1953), 48.

14. Sir William Holdsworth, *Some Makers of English Law* (Cambridge: Cambridge University Press, 1966), 102.

15. Daniel R. Coquillette, *Francis Bacon* (Stanford: Stanford University Press, 1992), 278. See all the valuable appendices in this text.

16. Paul H. Kocher, "Francis Bacon on the Science of Jurisprudence," *Journal of the History of Ideas* 18 (1957), 3–26; rpt. in *Essential Articles*, ed. Vickers, 170; 175.

17. L. Jonathan Cohen, "Intuition, Induction, and the Middle Way," *Monist* 65 (July 1983): 297–301; see also his *The Implications of Induction* (London: Methuen & Co., 1970) and his "Some Historical Remarks on the Baconian Conception of Probability," *Journal of the History of Ideas* 4 (1980): 219–31. Cf. Peter Tillers "Mapping Inferential Domains," *Boston University Law Review* 66 (1986): 885–86.

18. Holdsworth 108.

19. Huntington Cairns, *Legal Philosophy from Plato to Hegel* (Baltimore: Johns Hopkins Press, 1949), 208.

20. Coquillette 2; 295–96; 3.

21. Bernard McCabe, "Francis Bacon and the Natural Law Tradition," *Natural Law Forum* 9 (1964): 111.

22. Cairns 225–34.

Chapter Four

1. Charles Whitney, "Francis Bacon's *Instauratio*: Dominion of and over Humanity," *Journal of the History of Ideas* 50:3 (1989): 371–90. See also the discussion of this term in his book *Francis Bacon and Modernity* (New Haven and London: Yale University Press, 1986).

2. Graham Rees, "Francis Bacon's Biological Ideas: a New Manuscript Source" in *Occult and Scientific Mentalities in the Renaissance*, ed. Brian Vickers (Cambridge: Cambridge University Press, 1984), 310.

3. *The Autobiography of Charles Darwin 1809–1882, with Original Omissions Restored*, ed. Nora Barlow (New York, 1967).

4. Anderson 43.

Chapter Five

1. Maurice B. MacNamee, S.J., "Literary Decorum in Francis Bacon," *Saint Louis University Studies* 1:3 (March 1950): 3–52.

2. Charles Williams, *Bacon* (New York: Folcroft Library Editions, 1971), 148.

3. John M. Steadman, "Beyond Hercules: Bacon and the Scientist as Hero," *Studies in the Literary Imagination*, ed. Sessions 4:1 (April 1971): 3–47.

4. Robert K. Merton, *Science, Technology & Society in Seventeenth Century England* (1938; rpt., New York: Howard Fertig, 1970) and "Singletons and Multiples in Scientific Discovery: A Chapter in the Sociology of Science," *Proceedings of the American Philosophical Society* 105:5 (October 1961): 470–86.

5. For an excellent analysis of Bacon's real attitude toward mathematics, see Graham Rees' study in *Revue Internationale de Philosophie* (1986).

6. William A. Sessions, "Bacon and Herbert and an Image of Chalk" in *"Too Riche to Clothe the Sun": Essays on George Herbert* (Pittsburgh: University of Pittsburgh Press, 1980), 165–78.

7. Wilbur Samuel Howell, *Logic and Rhetoric in England 1500–1700* (New York: Russell & Russell, 1961), 365–75.

8. Lisa Jardine, "*Experientia literata* or *Novum Organon*? The Dilemma of Bacon's Scientific Method" in *Francis Bacon's Legacy*, ed. Sessions, 47–67.

Chapter Six

1. Cf. the conclusions of Antonio Pérez-Ramos.

2. Hiram Haydn, *The Counter-Renaissance* (New York, 1950).

3. Anderson 124–31.

4.   See Peter Urbach, *Francis Bacon's Philosophy of Science: An Account and a Repraisal* (La Salle, IL: Open Court, 1987) and, among many studies by Graham Rees, "Atomism and 'Subtlety' in Francis Bacon's Philosophy," *Annals of Science* 37 (1980): 549–71; "Matter Theory: A Unifying Factor in Bacon's Natural Philosophy?" *Ambix* 24:2 (1977): 110–25; "Quantitative Reasoning in Francis Bacon's Natural Philosophy," *Nouvelles de la république des lettres* 1 (1985): 27–48. For Pérez-Ramos, see above.

5.   For a full discussion of the meaning of forms in Bacon, see Pérez-Ramos, Part II.

6.   Mary Hesse, "Francis Bacon's Philosophy of Science" in *A Critical History of Western Philosophy*, ed. D. J. O'Connor (New York: Macmillan and Co., 1964), 141–52; rpt. in *Essential Articles*, ed. Vickers, 138. Emphasis mine.

7.   C. J. Ducasse, "Francis Bacon's Philosophy of Science," *Structure, Method and Meaning*, ed. Henle et al. (New York, 1951), 115–44; and Morris Cohen, "The Myth about Bacon and the Inductive Method," *Scientific Monthly* 23 (1926): 504–8.

8.   Jardine, *Bacon*, 20, but see all of Chapters 4–7; for Urbach, see 38–49 (particularly good is "A Game Theoretic Argument" and the comparison of Bacon and Pascal).

9.   Jardine, *Bacon*, 124.

10.   *Bacon's Novum Organum*, ed. Thomas Fowler (Oxford: Clarendon Press, 1889), 60–63. Fowler's introduction still offers one of the best general analyses of Bacon's philosophical work. Georg Henrik von Wright, *A Treatise on Induction and Probability* (London: Routledge & Kegan Paul, 1951), 152.

11.   Cf. William A. Sessions, "Francis Bacon and the Negative Instance," *Renaissance Papers* (1970): 1–9.

12.   Cf. Marx's praise of Bacon in Friedrich Engels and Karl Marx, *Die Heilige Familie oder Kritik der Kritischen Kritik: gegen Bruno Bauer und Corsoten* (Berlin: Dietz, 1953), 201–2.

13.   See the discussion of Luther and Virgil's *Georgics* in William A. Sessions, "Spenser's Georgics," *English Literary Renaissance* 10:2 (Spring 1980): 222–25; 236.

Chapter Seven

1.   Rossi, *Francis Bacon: From Magic to Science* 132; for the process by which ideas in the 1623 work are subsumed into Bacon's method as a whole, see Michel Malherbe, "Bacon's Critique of Logic" in *Francis Bacon's Legacy*, ed. Sessions, 69–87 and, for recent and full analysis of the relationship of Bacon and Telesio, see Jean-Marie Pousseur, "Bacon, A Critic of Telesio" in *Francis Bacon's Legacy*, ed. Sessions, 105–17.

2.   Charles W. Lemmi, *The Classic Deities in Bacon: A Study in Mythological Symbolism* (Baltimore: Johns Hopkins Press, 1933).

3. Harvey Wheeler, "Francis Bacon's *New Atlantis*: The 'Mould' of a Lawfinding Commonwealth," in *Francis Bacon's Legacy*, ed. Sessions, 309. See also Wheeler's "The Invention of Modern Empiricism: Juridical Foundations of Francis Bacon's Philosophy of Science," *Law Library Journal* 76 (1983): 78–120.

4. Frederic Jameson, "Of Islands and Trenches: Naturalization and the Production of Utopian Discourse," *Diacritics* 7 (1977): 2–21.

5. Denise Albanese, "The *New Atlantis* and the Uses of Utopia," *English Literary History* 57 (1990): 507.

6. Ducasse 72–73.

Selected Bibliography

PRIMARY SOURCES

Francis Bacon, Baron of Verulam, Viscount St. Alban, and Lord High Chancellor of England, *Works*, ed. James Spedding, Robert Leslie Ellis, and Douglas Denon Heath, Fourteen Volumes. The first five volumes *Philosophical Works*, the next two volumes *Literary and Professional Works*, and the last seven *The Letters and Life*, ed. Spedding alone (1858; rpt. Stuttgart-Bad Cannstatt: Friedrich Frommann Verlag, 1963). There is a new edition of the canon of Francis Bacon forthcoming from Oxford University Press, under the general editorship of Lisa Jardine and Graham Rees.

Farrington, Benjamin. *The Philosophy of Francis Bacon*. Liverpool: University of Liverpool Press, 1964. New translations of *Cogitata et Visa de Interpretatione Naturae, sive de Scientia Operativa;* of *Tempus Partus Masculus, sive Instauratio Magna Imperii Humani in Argumentum,* and of *Redargutio Philosophiarum* with a perceptive introductory essay.

Kiernan, Michael, ed. *The Essayes or Counsels, Civill and Morall: Sir Francis Bacon*. Cambridge: Harvard University Press, 1985. The authoritative edition of the *Essays* and the first critical edition since the nineteenth century.

Rees, Graham. *Francis Bacon's Natural Philosophy: A New Source, a Translation of Manuscript Hardwick 72A with Translation and Commentary*, assisted by Christopher Upton. Chalfont St. Giles: BSHS Monographs Series, V, 1984. The most impressive of the various discoveries made by Rees of Bacon manuscripts.

Urbach, Peter, ed. *Novum Organum with Other Parts of the Great Instauration*. Chicago and LaSalle: Open Court, 1994. New vigorous translations that correct the Spedding texts.

SECONDARY SOURCES

Coquillette, Daniel R. *Francis Bacon*. Stanford: Stanford University Press, 1992. The definitive examination of Bacon as lawyer and judge with valuable appendices and bibliography.

du Maurier, Daphne. *Golden Lads: Sir Francis Bacon, Anthony Bacon, and Their Friends*. Garden City: Doubleday & Co., 1975.

———. *The Winding Stair: Francis Bacon, His Rise and Fall*. Garden City: Doubleday & Co., 1977. For all their eccentricities of content and style, still the best biographical settings.

Fish, Stanley E. *Self-Consuming Artifacts: The Experience of Seventeenth-Century Literature*. Berkeley and Los Angeles: University of California Press, 1972. In his second chapter, "Georgics of the Mind: The Experience of Bacon's

Essays," the author focuses in his reading of Bacon the thesis of his entire book, that is, the dialectic of indeterminacy involved in reading a text as the definition of the text.

Jardine, Lisa. *Francis Bacon: Discovery and the Art of Discourse*. Cambridge: Cambridge University Press, 1974. Sets the Renaissance context for Bacon's method for composition by analyzing the texts themselves, as they develop Bacon's twofold strategies for discovery and discourse.

Martin, Julian. *Francis Bacon, The State, and the Reform of Natural Philosophy*. Cambridge: Cambridge University Press, 1992. Combines biography, legal and political theory and reform, with the program of the *Magna Instauratio* and its reform. Especially good on use of the maxim.

Pérez-Ramos, Antonio. *Francis Bacon's Idea of Science and the Maker's Knowledge Tradition*. Oxford: Clarendon Press, 1988. The most significant book on Bacon's theory of knowledge and science in the century.

———. "Francis Bacon and Man's Two-Faced Kingdom," *The Renaissance and Seventeenth-Century Rationalism*, ed. G. H. R. Parkinson (London and New York: Routledge, 1993) 140–66. Another major study on Bacon's system of knowledge with exhaustive bibliography.

Quinton, Anthony. *Francis Bacon*. New York: Hill and Wang, 1980. A sophisticated, commanding, and witty introduction to the study of Bacon.

Rossi, Paolo. *Francis Bacon: From Magic to Science*, tr. Sacha Rabinovitch. London: Routledge & Kegan Paul, 1968. The best full study of Bacon's conceptualizing by a master Baconian.

———. "Baconianism" in *Dictionary of the History of Ideas* (1973), 1:173. An excellent introduction to Bacon's system of knowledge and science.

Sessions, William A. "Francis Bacon" *Concise Dictionary of British Literary Biography: Writers of the Middle Ages and the Renaissance before 1660*. Detroit and London: A Bruccoli Clark Layman Book, Gale Research Inc., 1992, 1:2–16. Helpful for a quick and wide-ranging introduction to the life and works of Bacon.

———. *The Essential Bacon: An Annotated Bibliography of Major Modern Studies*. Forthcoming. Includes major criticism of the twentieth century as well as the major editions and bibliographical studies.

———, ed. *Francis Bacon's Legacy of Texts: "The Art of Discovery Grows with Discovery."* New York: AMS Press, 1990. Incorporates most of the essays in the volume of *Studies in the Literary Imagination* (April 1971) with revisions and new essays.

Urbach, Peter. *Francis Bacon's Philosophy of Science: An Account and a Reappraisal*. La Salle: Open Court, 1987. An excellent presentation and defense of Bacon's theories of science written with considerable wit and linguistic force.

Vickers, Brian. *Francis Bacon and Renaissance Prose*. Cambridge: Cambridge University Press, 1968. The central text by the most comprehensive Bacon scholar of the century and a definitive study of Bacon's style.

————, ed. *Essential Articles for the Study of Francis Bacon*. Hamden, Connecticut: Archon Books, 1968. Contains crucial studies, especially by historians of science.

————, ed. *The Oxford Authors: Francis Bacon*. Oxford and New York: Oxford University Press, 1996. The basic classroom text for English works of Bacon, superbly edited and annotated, including crucial minor works and letters. Should be combined with Urbach's translations of the Latin scientific works.

Whitney, Charles. *Francis Bacon and Modernity*. New Haven and London: Yale University Press, 1986. The first book-length attempt to read Bacon in the perspective of modern literary criticism.

Index

About the Author

W. A. Sessions is Regents' Professor of English at Georgia State University. He received his undergraduate degree from the University of North Carolina at Chapel Hill, where he was the first editor of the *Carolina Quarterly*, and received his doctorate from Columbia University. He was a Fulbright Scholar at the University of Freiburg in Germany, where he studied philosophy. He was named Bacon Scholar of the Year in 1988 by the Francis Bacon Library. He has published the only book-length study of the poetry of Surrey, *Henry Howard, Earl of Surrey* (Boston, 1986). His critical and cultural biography of Surrey, *"Enough Survives": Henry Howard, the Poet Earl of Surrey*, is forthcoming. He has edited *The Legacy of Francis Bacon: "The Art of Discovery Grows with Discovery"* (New York, 1990), the first book-length collection of essays on Bacon in this century. He has also published over fifty essays, articles, and book chapters in *Milton Studies, English Literary Renaissance, History Today, Journal of English and Germanic Philology, Renaissance Quarterly, Modern Philology, MLA Profession*, and other scholarly journals. His monograph on Spenser and Virgil, *Spenser's Georgics*, has been widely acclaimed and demonstrates his particular interest in the effects of classical culture on the Renaissance. He has also written on Southern literature, and his correspondence with Flannery O'Connor has appeared in *The Habit of Being*. He has published an anthology of poetry, *The Liberating Form*, and written an introduction to *Romeo and Juliet*. His poems have appeared in the *Southern Review, California Quarterly*, and the *Georgia Review*, and three of his plays have received productions; *A Shattering of Glass* was a winner in the Festival of Southern Plays and was produced at the University of Mississippi. He is currently completing a book-length bibliography of twentieth-century studies of Francis Bacon. He has also begun writing a critical biography of Bacon.